Wine & Philosophy

For Dad —
Christmas 2004
I love you!
Andrea

To Anand, Chris, Jesse, Richard, and Tony

Please see the other books in the Epicurean Trilogy, conceived by Fritz Allhoff:

 Steven D. Hales, ed.
Beer & Philosophy:
The Unexamined Beer Isn't Worth Drinking

 Fritz Allhoff and Dave Monroe, ed.
Food & Philosophy:
Eat, Think, and Be Merry

Wine & Philosophy

A Symposium on Thinking and Drinking

Edited by Fritz Allhoff

BLACKWELL PUBLISHING
350 Main Street, Malden, MA 02148–5020, USA
9600 Garsington Road, Oxford OX4 2DQ, UK
550 Swanston Street, Carlton, Victoria 3053, Australia

First published 2008 by Blackwell Publishing Ltd
1   2008

Library of Congress Cataloging-in-Publication Data

Wine & philosophy : in vino veritas / edited by Fritz Allhoff.
   p. cm.
   Includes bibliographical references and index.
   ISBN-13: 978-1-4051-5431-4 (pbk.: alk. paper)   1. Wine and wine
making—Social aspects.   2. Drinking customs.   I. Allhoff, Fritz.   II. Title:
Wine and philosophy.
   TP548.W743 2008
   641.2′2—dc22

                                                                     2007014516

A catalogue record for this title is available from the British Library.

Set in 10.5/13pt Sabon
by Graphicraft Limited, Hong Kong
Printed and bound in the United Kingdom
by TJ International Ltd, Padstow, Cornwall

For further information on
Blackwell Publishing, visit our website:
www.blackwellpublishing.com

Contents

Contents

Figures

Foreword

Paul Draper

In considering the thought-provoking essays that comprise this volume, I discern an important theme: they concern the "real" (or *terroir*) wines that many of us, as winemakers, strive to produce.[1] Though all of us may drink "beverage" wine on a weekly or daily basis, something else is being addressed here. As Fritz Allhoff states in his introduction: "there is an important difference between wine as a social lubricant and wine *itself* as an object worthy of philosophical study."[2] To me, this is the idea of wine as the result of a natural rather than industrial process – a transformation of fresh grapes into something quite extraordinary, whose distinctive character and quality come directly from a place, from the specific *terroir* in which it is grown.

In our nomadic past, the culture of wine was a civilizing force. We settled to tend the vines. Unlike grain, which could be sowed in a new place each year and harvested at season's end, the vines held us to one place. We had to wait four or five years before they produced even a small crop. Unlike grain, they required attention throughout the year – pruning in winter; shaping, or training to a tree or stake in spring; tasting for ripeness and harvesting in autumn. Once crushed, the berries met their "death," were transformed by fermentation, and reborn as wine. Unseen yeasts worked their magic;

---

[1] Matt Kramer addresses the notion of *terroir* in more detail; see his "The Notion of *Terroir*," Chapter 15, this volume. See also Randall Grahm's essay, "The Soul of Wine: Digging for Meaning," Chapter 14, this volume.

[2] See Fritz Allhoff, "Planting the Vines: An Introduction to *Wine & Philosophy*," p. 2.

man added nothing, did nothing beyond crushing the fruit. His role was to watch and to tend, as a parent might a child. He was not the "maker," as our modern term might imply. The process inspired awe and wonder, leading the ancients to consider wine sacred. As symbol and metaphor, it became part of Christian and Jewish ritual. The culture of wine spread, and so did its role as a catalyst for community, for bringing together family and friends.

In searching for today's real wines, it is easy to assume that technological advances following World War II were responsible for separation into the categories of real and beverage wine. More likely, they have existed from the beginning. Grapes come from the earth, and depend on nature for their quality and consistency. Climate and soil determine where vines can successfully be cultivated, but each year's weather determines if the wine will be good, or else if it will need intervention. The Romans added honey and spices to improve taste as freshness faded. The Greeks added pine resin to retard spoilage – we still taste that bit of history in their retsina.

With greater knowledge and understanding came better, more consistent, longer-lived wines. But vineyard sites that consistently produce distinctive character and high quality remain a very small part of the land planted to vines. In the Old World as in the New, the producer must hold yields to moderate levels for a number of years to determine whether his might be such a site. Such an investigation demands a clear vision of what wine, in its essence, is about. This essence is, I think, celebrated in this volume and in the essays that it contains.

Ridge Vineyards
Santa Cruz Mountains
May 2007

Acknowledgments

More than any other project that I have worked on, this one really feels like the culmination of a lot: time, studies, travel, friends, and, of course, wine. Unlike many that have a deep passion for wine, I was not raised in a wine home. Rather, I really did not even start drinking wine until I got to graduate school at the University of California, Santa Barbara. Growing up in Virginia, wine just never seemed that present; or, with no offense to those passionate about norton or seyval blanc, that good. Arriving in California, though, everything changed. Not only was wine really good, but there was a wine *culture* that made an interest in and the study of wine both more respectable and more possible. In Santa Barbara, I started to take wine classes, and I would especially like to thank Patrick Coffield for outstanding instruction and wines. Also, I would like to thank David and Linda Cable at East Beach Wine for their weekly tastings.

But, by far, the most important catalyst for my interest in wine was Wine Night (on Wednesdays) with my colleagues in the philosophy department at UCSB. This tradition started in my second year of graduate school and was a veritable tradition throughout the following five years. Each week, we would pick areas of the world we wanted to explore, and there were great wine stores in Santa Barbara to support our interests. Eventually, we tried to graduate to blind tastings, though these were often met with more derision than enthusiasm (as were my attempts to pull out Karen MacNeil's *Wine Bible* to "teach" about what we were drinking)! At any rate, I will forever be grateful to this core group who, while not only sharing my interest in wine, also comprises many of my closest friends: Tony Brueckner, Chris Buford, Richard Glatz, Jesse Steinberg, and Anand Vaidya.

My family also became interested in my California situation, from which we managed to start exploring places like Napa and Sonoma. My brother, Hans, also studied philosophy and understands some of its implications for wine: at a tasting at Joseph Phelps, he traded me his Insigna for my Napa Valley Cabernet Sauvignon by citing both the utilitarian calculus and his limited wine appreciation (though he has recently found his grape in pinot noir). My parents, Francis and Jean Ann, have always supported my interest for wine, and it is something that I have been able to share with my mother.

A lot of my passion in wine developed through wine travels, and I would like to especially acknowledge some of those trips and some of the wineries that were incredibly welcoming. In the production of this book, I visited Napa Valley several times and am especially indebted to Barnett Vineyards, Spring Mountain Vineyards, and Stag's Leap Wine Cellars; Shannon Howlett was particularly kind at Stag's Leap, and I thank Matt Kramer for the encouragement to get off of the "valley floor" and to explore Spring Mountain. Internationally, I had fabulous trips to: Marlborough, New Zealand (especially Seresin and Cloudy Bay); Piedmont, Italy; Rioja, Spain; Tuscany, Italy (especially Poggio Antico and Terrabianca); and Wachau, Austria (especially Domaine Wachau) – all of these trips taught me about wine, and I thank my hosts throughout. I sometimes try to describe these trips as "research" (for the book), and can almost do it with a straight face. Almost.

This book was originally conceived during a visiting research fellowship at the Australian National University; I thank John Weckert and Seumas Miller for that opportunity. Granted, I probably spent more time enjoying Clare Valley rieslings and Barossa shirazes than I did the rains of Canberra, but ANU is a great place to be, especially for philosophers. Also, I received a research release at Western Michigan University to complete this manuscript, and I thank my department chair, Tim McGrew, and dean, Tom Kent, for making this possible. Much of the editorial work was done during an extended stay in Philipsburg, Montana, and I thank Keanah Vushon for her hospitality. Philipsburg is not much for wine, but otherwise lies in one of the most beautiful areas of the country; it was easy to find inspiration there. And, of course, there are my good friends at Blackwell, who have been extremely supportive and enthusiastic about this project: Jeff Dean, Danielle Descoteaux, and Jamie Harlan. While I appreciate all of their support, I would especially like to thank Jeff – with whom it is always a pleasure to work – for his constant interest in this project and for his copious communications during its production. Also I thank Marcus Adams for proofreading the entire manuscript.

Finally, I would like to thank all of the contributors. Many of these people I have only communicated with by phone or email (though, of course, I hope that changes!), yet they already feel like friends. I appreciate the quality of their work and, of course, their willingness to slough through my seemingly unending barrage of editorial feedback; they all did this with great attitudes. I both recognize their efforts and marvel at the quality of their finished essays. It is also worth appreciating how diverse they are: essays came in from six different countries and across a range of professions, ranging from academic philosophers to various facets of the wine industry.

Finally, of course, I thank the readers of this volume: enjoy! And drink good wine. And *think* about it.

Fritz Allhoff
Healdsburg, CA
December 2006

Planting the Vines
An Introduction

Fritz Allhoff

Socrates took his seat . . . and had his meal . . . When dinner was over, they poured a libation to the god, sang a hymn, and – in short – followed the whole ritual. Then they turned their attention to drinking. At that point, Pausanias addressed the group:
"Well gentlemen, how can we arrange to drink less tonight? To be honest, I still have a terrible hangover from yesterday, and I could really use a break. I daresay most of you could, too, since you were also part of the celebration. So let's try not to overdo it."

Plato (427–347 BCE), *Symposium* 176a2–176a1

Wine and philosophy have long had a symbiotic relationship, extending back toward the origins of both. Some of the earliest archeological evidence that we have for the existence of wine comes from the Neolithic period in modern Armenia and northern Iran; a pottery jar coated with wine residue has been dated to 5400 BCE. By 2500 BCE, wine was being cultivated on Crete, and probably on mainland Greece as well.[1] But the period of time that I want to call to attention is the fifth and fourth centuries BCE when Greek philosophers, such as Plato and Aristotle, laid the foundations of what would become Western culture. Wine undoubtedly played an important social role during this time and, by extension, has had a significant impact on our own culture and history.

---

[1] Tom Standage, *A History of the World in Six Glasses* (New York: Walker and Co., 2005), pp. 47–8.

1

Fritz Allhoff

The most overt connection between wine and philosophy lies in the *symposia* that took place in ancient Greece: these were effectively wine parties that gave rise to profound philosophical dialogue. As alluded to in the epigraph, the Greeks did not drink wine during their dinner, but rather thereafter: following dinner, they would retire to an *andron*, which was a room largely dedicated to these events and one of the central architectural features of Greek homes. The ceremonies were initiated with toasts to the gods, fallen heroes, and one's ancestors, and then the drinking could begin in earnest. Greeks mixed their wine with water in a special bowl (called a *krater*); the mixtures could be adjusted depending on how serious the drinking was to be, but water was nearly always added in at least equal parts to the wine.[2] The revelry often extended late into the night, and philosophy was undoubtedly a focal point of conversation at many of the *symposia*.

What this shows, though, is that wine and philosophy were coincident: certainly wine catalyzed philosophical dialogues, but there is an important difference between wine as a social lubricant and wine *itself* as an object worthy of philosophical study. And, while I think that a strong tradition exists in the former regard, there has certainly been little tradition in the latter. This book, of course, aims to remedy that by looking at wine, along with its social and historical contexts, through a philosophical lens. To this end, the volume is composed of nineteen essays which explore various philosophical dimensions of wine. The contributors bring diverse backgrounds to this project: they comprise academics of different fields, as well as non-academics who are either winemakers or wine writers.

But, while wine certainly warrants more philosophical attention than it has previously been afforded, let us not lose sight of the fun and excitement that wine can bring to our lives. During the creation of this book, I have given a lot of thought to my own conception of and relationship to wine, and I think the following quote, from *Sideways*, helps to keep my thinking about wine in context:

> I like to think about the life of wine, how it's a living thing. I like to think about what was going on the year the grapes were growing, how the sun was shining that summer or if it rained . . . what the weather was like. I think about all those people who tended and picked the

[2] Ibid., pp. 56–7.

grapes, and if it's an old wine, how many of them must be dead by now. I love how wine continues to evolve, how every time I open a bottle it's going to taste different than if I had opened it on any other day. Because a bottle of wine is actually alive – it's constantly evolving and gaining complexity – like your '61 [Cheval Blanc] – and begins its steady, inevitable decline. And it tastes so fucking good.[3]

In the second part of this introduction, let me offer you a tour of what is going to happen in this volume, as well as sketch some of the issues that will be covered therein. There are six units: "The Art & Culture of Wine"; "Tasting & Talking about Wine"; "Wine & Its Critics"; "The Beauty of Wine"; "Wine & Metaphysics"; and "The Politics & Economics of Wine." The first three units have been organized along the following lines: societies produce wine, then people drink it, and then people inevitably talk about it. The first unit, rather than addressing specific philosophical questions, serves to motivate the rest of the volume. The next five units, however, directly correspond to dominant and traditional areas of philosophical study: philosophy of language, philosophy of perception, aesthetics, metaphysics, and ethics/political philosophy. In each case, the essays are accessible while also covering some serious philosophical ground; in many cases, they also defend novel (and sometimes controversial) positions. While I would suggest reading the first three units in order, I think that the last three may be mostly engaged independently, and I would encourage the reader to start with the essays that generate the most interest. In the rest of the introduction, I will speak specifically to the units and their constitutive essays.

The first unit, "The Art & Culture of Wine," really does a lot of work setting up the rest of the volume. Whatever else we recognize wine to be, it is important to realize that our present wine practices are rooted in deep historical and cultural traditions. I think that, to have a good understanding of where we stand, we should think about some of the historical and cultural features that have gotten us here. So, then, we start toward the beginning, with ancient Greece. As mentioned

[3] Alexander Payne and Jim Taylor, *Sideways: The Shooting Script* (New York: Newmarket Press, 2004), pp. 76–7.

3

above, wine was an important part of ancient Greek culture, and it perhaps does not overextend the point to say that philosophy is the better off for the relationship: a lot of our philosophical tradition is indebted, at least in part, to the Greek *symposia* at which wine flowed freely. The first essay of the volume is by classicist Harold Tarrant, who talks about the culture of wine in ancient Greece as well as its manifestation in writings from the time (including those of thinkers like Homer and Plato). This is a great essay to start the volume, as it really establishes philosophical longevity and significance that should be afforded wine.

The second essay, by Jonathon Alsop, brings us through the current century: we know of the wine tradition owing to the Greeks, but could then wonder what sorts of influences wine has had on contemporary American culture.[4] Alsop notices that Americans do not drink that much wine (ranking in the 30s for per capita consumption among countries); the Italians and the French drink, per capita, over five times what Americans drink.[5] *Why* is this? Alsop starts with the passion for wine displayed by our third president, Thomas Jefferson, and then moves all the way through Prohibition and concludes with *Sideways* (2004) in trying to develop an accounting of American wine culture. Third, we have an essay by Kirsten Ditterich-Shilakes, who works with San Francisco's Asian Art Museum and Fine Art Museum. She is interested in the role that wine has played in motivating art. In her essay, she considers four wine vessels from across the globe and human history and shows how these containers go beyond mere utility to embody important cultural, philosophical, and artistic themes. Finally, the first unit concludes with an essay by Frederick Paola, a physician, who writes about the important health benefits of wine and, in particular, how empirical results can be viewed in relationship to Greek philosophies regarding virtues such as moderation. Given the near-ubiquity of claims purporting some link

---

[4]   The inclusion of this essay, by the way, is not meant to suggest that there are not interesting things to talk about regarding the relationship between wine and other countries' cultures. First, some of these will be discussed in Frederick Paola's essay (Chapter 4). And, second, America certainly has had (and, in some places, continues to have) strange attitudes toward alcohol that beg for some sort of explanation.
[5]   The Wine Institute, "Per Capita Wine Consumption in Listed Countries," www.wineinstitute.org/industry/keyfacts/per_capita_wine_consumption.php (accessed December 18, 2006).

between wine and health, Paola's essay serves an important function by both analyzing many of those claims and giving them some philosophical interpretation.

In the second unit, "Tasting & Talking about Wine," we start to explore philosophical questions pertaining to, well, just that: tasting and talking about wine. These things go together insofar as we often taste a wine, and then feel inclined to say something about what we just tasted. So, first, we might be interested in the event of tasting wine itself and, in particular, about what *kind* of experience this is. Certainly, some perceptual experiences are more cognitive than others: if you just look out the window, this might not significantly engage any sort of higher-level thinking. Alternatively, in reflecting upon some great work of art, there might be all sorts of cognitive elements that are brought into that experience. Which way does wine work? One obvious thing to say is that it can work either way, depending on what sorts of things the taster is trying to accomplish. In the first essay, though, John Dilworth argues that these sorts of cognitive (or, as he calls them, "analytical") approaches to tasting are defective insofar as they ignore important "imaginative" elements of tasting. He uses an evolutionary-based account of perceptual consciousness in order to motivate his views about wine tasting.

As I mentioned above, we frequently talk about wine after we have tasted it, and "wine language" plays an important part of this discourse. In the second essay, Kent Bach asks what *use* such language is, and wonders *why* we engage in these sorts of discourses. In particular, what are they good for? By asking this question, Bach is interested not in pragmatic consequences – such as being able to get the sommelier to suggest a wine that matches your palate – but rather in the prospects that such language has for increasing our *enjoyment* of wine. Ultimately, Bach argues that the ability to render verbal descriptions of wine does *not* contribute to our ability to sense, notice, and recognize wine's qualities; rather, he thinks that "great wines speak for themselves" and that language is not necessary to be able to appreciate them. The final essay in this unit is by Keith Lehrer and Adrienne Lehrer. Keith, a philosopher, has written about discourse and representation in painting,[6] and Adrienne, a linguist, is the author of the

---

[6] See, for example, Keith Lehrer, "Representation in Painting and Consciousness," *Philosophical Studies* 117.1–2 (2004): 1–14.

important *Wine and Conversation,*[7] which analyzes wine discourse as well as the way that it has evolved across time. In their jointly authored essay, they combine their individual perspectives to develop an account of wine discourse and, in particular, one that is informed by the work in aesthetics and communication of Arnold Isenberg.

The third unit, "Wine & Its Critics," moves into the role of the wine critic, as well as philosophical questions that arise from the purported expertise that such critics have. It is an obvious fact about our wine culture that wine critics bear a tremendous amount of influence: this is especially apparent through the 100-point rating system effected by Robert Parker, Jr. and thereafter promulgated by various media outlets, especially *Wine Spectator* magazine. These critics and publications have the power to make or break wines (or even whole vintages or regions), and there are certainly associative philosophical questions. First, *does* the wine critic have any authority? If a critic says that one wine is better than another, is this "true," or rather just the expression of some subjective opinion of the critic? (Note that, even if we were to say that it is "true," we would still have to say what that *meant.*) Second, if the critic does have such authority, *where* does it come from? Is it through special training, facility with language (e.g., for describing wines), or even for physiological reasons (e.g., sensitivity of taste)?

In the first essay of this unit, John Bender tries to help us understand what is at stake and, in particular, how to understand claims regarding the purported objectivity and subjectivity of wine criticism. Ultimately, he argues that *neither* of these modes fully captures what is going on, but rather that wine criticism is inherently both objective *and* subjective: there are objective features of wines that the critics are tracking, but each critic also brings certain subjective features into the tasting. The second essay, by Jamie Goode, covers a lot of ground. After talking about the practice of wine criticism, Goode reviews recent developments in the biology of flavor perception. From these results, he explores how we translate our tasting experience into language – as the wine critic invariably must do – and then returns to a discussion of intrasubjective differences in tasting and the debate between subjective and objective wine evaluation.

---

[7]   Adrienne Lehrer, *Wine and Conversation* (Bloomington, IN: Indiana University Press, 1983).

The fourth unit, "The Beauty of Wine," takes an important area of philosophy, aesthetics, and raises the associative questions that pertain to wine. Aesthetics is a discipline that seeks to understand concepts like 'beauty', 'art', and 'taste'. Most basically, we can ask *whether* wine should be regarded as an aesthetic object and, relatedly, whether its tasting should be regarded as an aesthetic practice (i.e., one in which we reflect upon various aesthetic properties, such as beauty, as then apply them to the object of our attention). For example, we uncontroversially regard paintings as art-objects, and we think that viewing paintings can be an aesthetic experience. However, can *wine* be such an object? For various reasons, philosophers, including Plato, have been reluctant to ascribe aesthetic status to objects that engage certain sensory modalities, such as taste. Other sorts of art, such as painting and symphony, are accessed through different sense modalities (i.e., sight and hearing) and, so various philosophical arguments have gone, are therefore entitled to aesthetic status in ways that wine (or, more traditionally, food) is not.[8] The first essay in this unit, by Douglas Burnham and Ole Martin Skilleås, disputes these arguments. The authors defend the position that wine should be afforded aesthetic consideration and that (proper) wine tasting should be understood as an aesthetic practice.

Next comes an essay by George Gale. Though a professional philosopher, Gale is both an amateur winemaker and a former wine writer. We have all heard wine people (usually those trying to sell us wine) say things like "If you like it, then it's good wine." And, of course, this follows from some sort of purely subjective conception of wine experience (though note that this was a conception against which Bender argued in the preceding unit). But is this true? Do we always, as it were, get it right? Or could we like wines that are (objectively) bad wines and dislike ones that are (objectively) good wines? In the preceding unit, the essays explored similar questions regarding the relation between wine and language, but Gale's essay uses these issues in an attempt to develop an account of wine aesthetics (as opposed to wine language).

---

[8] For more on this, see Dave Monroe, "Can Food Be Art? The Problem of Consumption," in Fritz Allhoff and Dave Monroe (eds.), *Food & Philosophy* (Oxford: Blackwell Publishing, 2008).

7

Finally, this unit concludes with an essay by Steve Charters. Charters is both a Master of Wine (an extremely prestigious professional qualification) and occupier of perhaps the best job title one could think of: Chair of Champagne Management (at the Reims Management School). In this essay, he tries to get some *empirical* data regarding wine aesthetics: while philosophers often do their work in armchairs, Charters thinks that we can profitably elucidate some philosophical questions by actually talking to people.[9] In particular, he documents the extent to which wine *is* often viewed as a proper object of aesthetic attention and to which wine tasting is viewed as an aesthetic practice. His research shows various ways in which opinions regarding wine and other art forms are coincident.

Our fifth unit, "Wine & Metaphysics," is perhaps the most philosophically heady, though that property can at least be mitigated by the accessibility of the associative essays, two of which are by non-philosophers. The first is by Kevin Sweeney, an aesthetician, who talks about the extent to which certain flavors can be properly said to be *part* of a wine. To motivate this discussion, consider some tasting note which might say that a wine "is redolent of tar and roses." What does this *mean*? Certainly nobody has put tar or roses into the wine, so we might wonder what relationship these entities bear to the perceptual states effected by the wines. Is there some meaningful sense in which these flavors are *in* the wine or not? As with Bender's earlier essay, Sweeney thinks that this is a false dichotomy, and he ends up defending a more nuanced view.

The next two essays are among my favorites in the volume. The first is by Bonny Doon winemaker Randall Grahm, who studied philosophy as an undergraduate, and the second is by Matt Kramer, who has written extensively about wine and is a regular columnist for *Wine Spectator*. Grahm talks about what can make wines meaningful and, in particular, what it means for a wine to have *soul*. He motivates this discussion with an experience that he had with an Alsatian riesling, which he found to be qualitatively different from some California wines that were also part of the tasting. In his essay, Grahm tells us what it means for wines to have the sort of special character that

---

[9] While, historically, this might not have been a popular stance to take, it is one that has gained increasing attention and adherents in recent years under the guise of "experimental philosophy."

makes them deserving of high praise as against others that are simply "there to please."

The following essay by Kramer is excerpted from his important work *Making Sense of Burgundy*.[10] Kramer tackles the elusive notion of *terroir*. While the English translation is something like "sense of place" (or, to use Kramer's more colloquial expression, "some-whereness"), it is less than clear exactly what this amounts to and whether wines can meaningfully be said to express such a thing. If, for example, *terroir* admits of things like soils, microclimates, clonal variants, and so on, it is at least possible that such *terroir might* be replicated in other locales. (One sometimes hears "*terroir* cynics" derisively saying that *terroir* can be emulated just by throwing some rocks into the aging barrel.) However, a more robust conception of *terroir* includes various social and cultural features that go into winemaking, and perhaps these are less exportable. Or perhaps the physical features will, practically, not be exportable either. Kramer tries to vindicate the notion of *terroir* by considering Burgundy, which is often taken to offer its most hallowed expression, as a motivating case.

The final unit, "The Politics & Economics of Wine," starts with another pair of outstanding essays. Both of these are related to one of the most important events in the history of American wine, the so-called "1976 Judgment of Paris." In this tasting, California cabernets and chardonnays were put up against some of the top red Bordeaux and white Burgundies, respectively, in a blind tasting. The results both shocked the world and catalyzed the California wine industry: the winners were, in the red category, the 1973 Stag's Leap Cellars S.LV. Cabernet Sauvignon and, in the white category, the 1973 Château Montelena Chardonnay. This event immediately had a tremendous worldwide impact on wine consciousness, yet it was covered by only a single reporter, George Taber (who was living in Paris as a correspondent for *Time* magazine). Taber went on to write an invaluable book about this topic, and it is a privilege to have him contribute to this volume.[11] In his essay, Taber teams up with Princeton economists Orley Ashenfelter and Richard Quandt to talk more about the competition and to analyze some of the data that

---

[10]   Matt Kramer, *Making Sense of Burgundy* (New York: William Morrow, 1990).
[11]   George Taber, *Judgment of Paris: California versus France and the Historic 1976 Paris Tasting that Revolutionized Wine* (New York: Scribner, 2005).

came out of it. In particular, they talk about the statistical methods that were used to analyze the tasting and suggest that alternative methods would have been more appropriate (though they argue that the results, at least in the red category, would have been the same). The next essay in this unit is by Warren Winiarski, the winemaker at Stag's Leap Cellars, and the same one who made the 1973 Stag's Leap Cellars S.L.V. Cabernet Sauvignon that won the competition. Winiarski writes about purported differences between Old World and New World wines. The fact that his cabernet bested the top Bordeaux châteaux has shown that American wines, at least in some cases, have achieved a stature comparable to that of European wines. He then goes on to wonder what it means to make such comparisons and, in particular, whether the differences between the different types of wine are as great as has been alleged.

The final two essays of the book are by Justin Weinberg and Drew Massey, respectively. Weinberg, a philosopher, is interested in the relationship between demand for (expensive) wines and their prices. Consider his example, the 1997 Screaming Eagle, which currently goes for about $2,500. Weinberg argues that our interest in wines like this does not merely increase as the price increases, but rather increases precisely *because* the price increases. No doubt this is a great wine – it was given 100 points by Robert Parker, Jr. and lauded as "a perfect wine"[12] – but there seems to be some sort of irrationality in play if demand increases with price. In his essay, Weinberg argues that demand for wines does behave in this way (i.e., that wines often function as Veblen goods), and then goes on to ask what implications this has for our assessment of wine culture.

The last essay is by Drew Massey, a lawyer, who writes about a topic that seemed essential for this volume: wine and the law. In particular, it seemed there should be some lucid presentation of the legal (and associative philosophical) issues that attend to interstate wine shipping and why it can be so hard for residents of one state to get wines from another state. To be sure, bans on interstate wine shipping have been falling at a fairly rapid rate over the past few years, though there are still some recalcitrant states and some other states which have very complicated legislation. Massey does an admirable

---

[12]   Robert Parker, *Wine Advocate* 126 (2000), January 1.

job explaining the history of American wine law as well as its current standing. The crux of the debate hinges upon the relationship between the dormant Commerce Clause, which seems to provide for "free and untrammeled" interstate commerce, and the 21st Amendment, which repeals Prohibition and appears to allow for local control over alcohol-related commerce. The (alleged) tension between these two parts of the Constitution has been the subject of ongoing litigation, and Massey closes the volume by helping us to understand these, and related, issues.

As I hope the introduction has made clear, this volume has a lot to offer. There is coverage of a wide range of philosophically interesting topics, and the contributors have done a wonderful job in presenting these topics clearly and accessibly. Most fundamentally, I hope that the volume comprises engaging essays that are rewarding to read, but I should also point out a secondary aspiration, which is that it helps to contribute to a rising interest in the philosophical dimensions of wine. By the time this book is published, there will have already been two substantial professional meetings on philosophy and wine, one other important volume, and at least one academic journal dedicated to wine.[13] I think that the attention paid to the relationship between wine and philosophy legitimizes some of the questions that are being asked, and makes me optimistic for greater future discussion.

But, again, the primary goal of this volume is to be engaging, and I hope that the essays herein satisfy that desideratum. The contributors – who are drawn from six different countries and myriad

---

[13] The first wine and philosophy conference, organized by Barry Smith, was held at London University in 2004. At the 2007 Pacific Division Meeting of the American Philosophical Association in San Francisco, Kent Bach (a contributor to this volume) organized a one-day symposium on wine and philosophy, at which several papers from this volume were presented. The book that I mention is Barry Smith's *Questions of Taste: The Philosophy of Wine* (London: Signal Books, 2007), which certainly warrants attention. Finally, I would suggest the *Journal of Wine Economics*, which has recently been launched. This journal has broader coverage than its name indicates and is worth a look.

11

Fritz Allhoff

academic and non-academic disciplines – do an admirable job with all of their essays, and I thank them both for their contributions and for their efforts in response to editorial feedback. I hope that you enjoy the volume, and that it fosters your interest in both wine and philosophy. Cheers!

I

The Art & Culture of Wine

1

Wine in Ancient Greece
Some Platonist Ponderings

Harold Tarrant

Delights and Dangers

Homer's Odysseus tells us of the means by which he overcame the monstrous Cyclops, Polyphemus, who, in the cave where he dwelt and tended his sheep, was then imprisoning the Greek leader along with his men. Polyphemus had a voracious appetite and consumed two of Odysseus' men at a sitting. The prisoners could therefore expect a brief and unpleasant future unless Odysseus' renowned cleverness could secure their escape. Odysseus plied the monstrous one-eyed beast with the fine wine that he carried with him until Polyphemus fell into a drunken stupor. Then his Greek "guests" were able to plunge a huge sharpened stake, pre-warmed in the fire, into the Cyclops' single eye as he slept. So he lost his sight and, after further trickery, he lost his prisoners too.

Homer's work, at the beginning of European literature, seems to presuppose a great many things about wine. To begin with, it was an *ordinary* part of life, made from a common plant, and often safer to drink than water. Next, it was part of the civilized life that the Greeks and those most like them had developed, for which reason the uncivilized Cyclops is innocent both of its effects and of the expectation that it should be mixed with water. Wine varied in quality and characteristics, but it was ordinarily dark, and its value was assessed by both its strength and its sweetness. Now sweetness could be indicated by the terms *glykys* and *hêdus*, the former being translated 'sweet' as in "sugary," and the latter 'sweet' as in "delightful." In this latter case, one might doubt whether they really meant wines of a sugary or syrupy nature. However, such descriptions as *melieidês* (honey-sweet) clearly connect the sweetness of wine with the primary sweetener available to the Greeks.[1]

Whereas few of us today would relish drinking a dark red wine that was also sweet (except perhaps port), we have to remember that terms like 'sweet' are relative, and that if we were used to cheap wine of a vinegarish nature then we might use the term 'sweet' a little more freely and as a compliment rather than a criticism. In any case, it would hardly be surprising if the Greeks had interpreted certain aesthetic experiences somewhat differently from ourselves. To take a Homeric example of the delights of a sweeter wine, one could point to Odysseus' experience of the hospitality of the Phaeacians. When he is served honey-sweet wine, the poet is inspired to mention the sweet smell arising from the mixing-bowl.[2] Its sweetness evidently increased its seductiveness. The majority of the Greeks, for whom hedonism came naturally,[3] found it difficult to dismiss anything seductive, as the tale of Helen of Troy, hated and revered in approximately equal measures, demonstrates.

While sweetness was important, one cannot forget the other quality associated with good wine: its strength. As the Cyclops had discovered, this was able to turn the wine into a potent weapon. Hence it is also clear that the dangers of wine in the hands of inexperienced drinkers were well appreciated. Dionysus, the god traditionally associated with wine and sometimes almost identified with it (or with other naturally potent juices),[4] is both the bringer of calm delights

---

[1]   In the *Iliad* the following references to wine that is 'honey-sweet' (*melieidês*) may be noted:

4.348: Odysseus and his men, slow into battle, are accused of being fastest into the feast and the honey-sweet wine;
6.258: honey-sweet wine for a libation and to rouse Hector's flagging spirits;
8.506: honey-sweet wine as a contribution to the entertainment of guests;
10.579: the soldiers relax with food and choice honey-sweet wine;
12.320: the diet of kings is said to include fat sheep and honey-sweet wine;
18.546: on the shield of Achilles a ploughman is pictured receiving a cup of honey-sweet wine.

At other times the adjective 'honey-hearted' (*meliphron*) is used of wine, as at *Iliad* 8.506, 8.546, and 24.284. Both adjectives are only used in the *Odyssey*: 'honey-sweet' at 3.46, 9.208, 14.78, and 16.52, and 'honey-hearted' at 7.182, 10.356, 13.53, and 15.148.

[2]   *Odyssey* 9.210.

[3]   As evidenced by Plato, *Republic* 502b and *Laws* 663b.

[4]   See Euripides, *Bacchae*, lines 278–83 (wine); 708–11 (milk, liquid honey).

16

and a highly dangerous god for any mortal to cross, the paradox being beautifully brought out in Euripides' disturbing tragedy, the *Bacchae*.[5] Hence wine could be the source of a variety of experiences, some of them to one's apparent advantage, some to one's undoubted detriment. Its commonness in no way lessened the need to use it wisely.

The Use of Wine

When they were confronted by natural power of any kind, the Greeks desired to harness it, eliminating from their world as far as possible all that was unpredictable and beyond human control. Like Odysseus, every adult Greek male with wine at his disposal was faced with the challenge of getting it to work for him rather than against him. To judge from Greek comedy, this would involve keeping it away from those members of his household likely to use it against his own interests, including women and slaves whom he needed to perform regular tasks in an efficient fashion. But it would also involve consciousness of its long-term effects, restricting one to whatever one's physical constitution could withstand.[6]

Like so much else around them, the Greeks saw that wine had positive or negative value in accordance with how and in what circumstances it was used. Plato's *Lysis*, when making the important distinction between what is valued for its own sake and what is valued for what follows from it, chooses the example of a father who discovers his son has drunk hemlock; the father attaches considerable value to wine insofar as he believes that wine is the cure for hemlock poisoning (219e). Ultimately the high value that he then attaches to wine is similar to the high value that he attaches to the cup by which the wine is administered, for both are esteemed at that moment only because of their role in saving his son's life. This does not mean that wine, when considered in isolation from its effects, could have no aesthetic value, only that some circumstances give it a value that overrides aesthetic considerations. If one requires wine as an antidote to poison, then one does not question whether it is a

---

[5] Ibid., 677–774, 848–61, etc.

[6] In Plato's *Symposium* the participants agree (initially) to limit their drinking because the side effects of the previous night's revelry were still being felt.

17

Sauternes or a Chablis. So, given that wine, or the drinking of wine, like any other commodity or action was not in itself one of life's goals,[7] the challenge was to use it so as to facilitate rather than hinder those goals – and the philosopher could see this more acutely than most others.

Goals, Pleasant and Otherwise

The Greeks would regularly agree that happiness (*eudaimonia*, also translated as 'well-being') was the goal of life. What was more controversial is how this goal was to be interpreted. Was it some single thing, such as honor, wealth, pleasure, or freedom from trouble by which one's happiness was to be judged? Or was happiness made up of an amalgam of several things, all necessary for the best life and desirable in themselves? The ordinary person would often have some supposed human archetype of the happy life in mind, such as the King of Persia or some Greek tyrant – somebody whose wealth and power they could envy but never actually aspire to. The place of wine in such a life would no doubt have been taken for granted, but its presence there did not necessarily mean that it was actually contributing to happiness. Others, mindful of the mutability of human fortunes and some serious impediments to the happiness of such autocrats, were keen to introduce a very different set of paradigms, and so it was in the case of Herodotus' account of Solon's choices for the happiest persons of his time.[8] Often they would want to avoid pronouncing anybody happy until their entire life from beginning to end could be assessed, and a high premium would be placed upon leaving heirs behind one and achieving high honor in the eyes of one's community. The place of wine in such a life was less assured. And, for illustrating the happy life, Greek intellectuals were considerably more likely to select this alternative paradigm of the quiet achiever of honors, blessed with surviving heirs – if not one that seemed even more counter-intuitive to the artisan or goatherd.

One notable feature of Greek ethics is that it was never inherently altruistic, for it was one's own happiness at which one was expected

---

[7] See Plato, *Lysis* 219b–220b; *Euthydemus* 278e–282d; *Gorgias* 467c–468c.
[8] *Histories* 1.30–3.

to aim, and the happiness of one's friends mattered to one primarily insofar as they constituted an extension of oneself. One did of course have duties to them that one wished to fulfill – duties whose non-fulfillment would make one seriously unhappy – but the parting advice given by Plato's Socrates to his friend Crito was that his ability to be of assistance to others depended crucially on his ability to look after his own inner person (*Phaedo* 115b–c). Other characters in Plato and elsewhere tended to condemn the individual who, by neglecting his own interests, was powerless to help his friends. Therefore the primary question to be considered in the case of wine was "Can it make *me* happier?" while a secondary question might nevertheless ask "Can wine contribute to the happiness of my friends?" Most of us probably think we know the answer to both questions, but any Socrates look-alike would surely try to persuade us that we do not.

A major topic of Greek ethics was pleasure, and particularly whether or not pleasure was to be regarded as the highest goal. And if it was, then one naturally had to ask what kind of pleasure was an appropriate aim, for few were prepared to affirm that pleasures associated with the basest of acts were ever worthy of pursuit.[9] One might expect that the place of wine in the hedonist's ideal life was more likely to be assumed than in that of the anti-hedonist, since most would count either the taste of the wine or the resultant intoxication as in some sense a pleasure. In fact, the Greeks would more readily have assumed that good wine is pleasurable than we should, since one word that we have encountered for 'sweet' (of taste), *hêdys*, regularly applied to attractive wines, was also applied more generally to what was pleasurable. So it was natural to think of drinking wine, or good wine at least, as pleasurable. Therefore it ought naturally to fit into the hedonistic life, unless perhaps its pleasures were outweighed by painful consequences that would counterbalance the pleasures of the moment in the eyes of most people.[10]

---

[9] The hardened hedonist Callicles in the *Gorgias* (494–9) clearly drifts into this category, when he resists the idea that there is intrinsic merit in the pleasures of the *kinaidoi* – those who sought out the passive role in homosexual relations, or the pleasures of scratching, and ultimately has to admit to qualitative variations in pleasures that affect their claim to be good.

[10] This is the upshot of the examination of the popular concept of 'being overcome by pleasure' in Plato's *Protagoras*, 352a–358e.

Furthermore, the pleasurable life would be assumed by the majority of Greek males to involve *symposia*, at which fine food, pleasant drink, and entertainment of a sexual nature would all be present. These social occasions, where friends gathered together, and, unlike Polyphemus, had nothing to fear from others present, were the appropriate place for exploiting the pleasures of wine while minimizing the risks. The very word '*symposium*' implied social drinking, and the drink concerned was wine: usually mixed with what was held to be the appropriate quantity of water in a large broad vessel known as a *krater*, often decorated with scenes of revelry. As we have seen, the tendency to see friends as extensions of oneself naturally led to a concern for their happiness, leading to a willingness to share those things that best made one happy – and in this context the sharing of wine at *symposia* became natural, while gifts of wine were also favored by those rich enough to be giving it.[11]

Philosophers, of course, were likely to argue against many of the ideas that pervaded society, and its beliefs about pleasure and pleasurable experiences were not exempt. For instance, Plato usually argued against a straightforward hedonism,[12] though recognizing that appropriate types of pleasure did have value. For example, in his later work the *Philebus*, which deals primarily with the relation between pleasure and the good life, he willingly includes pure or harmless pleasures low down on its list of what contributes to the good life (66c–d). The wine lover will surely note that among harmless pleasures the *Philebus* and the *Timaeus* include those of smell, which were thought to involve no antecedent or consequent pains,[13] while a considerable degree of approval was given to pleasures associated with pure colors.[14] So even the most cautious Platonists could sit and admire both the bouquet and color of a decent wine, even in circumstances

---

[11] I note that Plato or an imitator wrote in an *Epistle* (361a8): "I'm sending you also 12 *stamnia* of sweet wine and two of honey." Gifts of wine, as of food, could even consist of something of which one had already partaken, as is seen from Xenophon, *Anabasis* 1.9.25–6.

[12] Much controversy persists over the concluding pages of the *Protagoras*, where Socrates appears to endorse the popular analysis of good and bad in terms of pleasant and unpleasant, but, even if the argument is not *ad hominem* as it is often claimed to be, it is never said that we should be choosing any action with a view only to its ability to yield pleasure rather than pain.

[13] *Philebus* 51e; *Timaeus* 65a.

[14] *Philebus* 51d2; cf. *Hippias Major* 297e ff.

where they would hesitate to drink it! Perhaps Plato might respond positively to the modern activity of wine tasting, where the pleasures of taste are vigorously pursued without any commitment to the pleasures of consumption. Yet it seems that he was as innocent of non-consuming wine buffs as he was of glue sniffers and paint sniffers.

Aristotle associated pleasure with unimpeded activity of an organism in its natural state (i.e., its proper activity and proper state) thereby giving his own favored activities their own special pleasures, and associating the best of pleasures with the best of activities.[15] The Stoics were able to condemn what they called "pleasure" by defining it as a *pathos*, or irrational response to an occurrence, in this case an irrational welcoming response, but their ideal human being would nevertheless experience a rational sense of elation in appropriate things; they called this elation "joy" (*chara*).[16] Since their sage was sufficiently sound in judgment to know when it was appropriate to indulge in activities generally frowned upon,[17] one can only assume that an occasion for wine would not entirely elude him. Even the hedonistic Epicureans were acutely conscious of the likelihood that many pleasures would lead to consequent distress, and were therefore to be rejected. Therefore, the hedonists shared the caution of the non-hedonists about the consumption of food and drink.

What I want to stress here, however, is that even those who took a stand against hedonism tended to suppose that the lives they advocated were the most pleasant available. Rejecting pleasure *as one's goal* did not involve banishing it from one's life or denying it value, either as a whole or in part, for most anti-hedonists would expect to enjoy *symposia*, too. Rather, thinkers such as Plato (in the majority of his works) and Aristotle (in *Nicomachean Ethics* X.4–5) preferred to argue that their preferred lives of moral and intellectual excellence, though they were not recommended *because* they would prove pleasurable, did offer very substantial pleasures – and without the pains that often followed from the direct pursuit of the life that most persons thought pleasant. Such thinkers could not be expected to advocate the use of wine simply because it is pleasant, but they might nevertheless endorse it for what else it could offer.

---

[15] Pleasure is treated in the *Nicomachean Ethics* VII.11–14 and X.1–5, with X.4–5 doing most to explain his own distinctive theory and to relate pleasure to the happy life.

[16] *Stoicorum Veterum Fragmenta* 3.431–9.

[17] *Stoicorum Veterum Fragmenta* 3.555.

The Socratic Paradigm: Overcoming the Ill Effects

Many of those who wrote philosophical works in the fourth century BCE had a new model of the happy life to offer: the example of Socrates, often considered to have achieved an extraordinary degree of justice and excellence, but likewise known to have participated without qualms in the delights of social drinking and some of its associated pleasures. To adopt Socrates as one's paradigm, as Plato and many others did, was already to concede wine a place in the good life. The challenge was to explain its admission.

Socrates' conduct at, and contributions to, the *symposia* of Athenian society swiftly became legendary, giving rise to what might be regarded as a special sub-genre of the philosophic dialogue. Socrates will be just one of a number of characters who contribute to the partially serious conversation on topics thought suitable for a "dinner-party" atmosphere. Plato wrote a *Symposium* that has been preserved for us, and so did Xenophon at around the same time. There may have been more admirers of Socrates who did likewise, and others, like Aristotle (not old enough to have heard him in person), who wrote works of the symposiac genre in the fourth century, but their work is lost to us. However, we do possess works of that genre from the early Roman imperial period, including Plutarch.

Socrates' association with wine, like his association with erotic desire which also emerges in the *Symposia* of Plato and Xenophon, means that the enjoyment of pursuits otherwise regarded as an indulgence is somehow written into the very first chapter of Greek moral philosophy; many believed that it was Socrates who was responsible for bringing philosophy down from the skies and into human life. Even though it is wrong to regard him as the first Greek moral thinker – the Greeks had long been accustomed to debating issues of right and wrong, and moral views are expressed in all sorts of earlier literature – he was perhaps the first to pursue ethical thought in the systematic manner characteristic of philosophy. It is not that Socrates ever asks his tantalizing questions about the role of wine itself, in the same way that he asks about the accepted virtues of justice, piety, good sense, courage, and wisdom – there was no confusion in people's minds about the nature of wine in the same way as there was about the key moral terms. Rather he is seen explaining some of his most inspired views when we are aware that he is involved in drinking.

Most of the participants in Plato's *Symposium* (176a–e) are celebrating the triumph of the young tragic poet Agathon at the dramatic composition associated with the Dionysia, while still suffering from the previous evening's drinking. Therefore the character Pausanias seeks to make things easy for themselves by taking a break – not abstinence, but gentle drinking. The other participants readily agree to the proposed temporary temperance, both the hard drinkers (who are suffering the worst hangovers) and those who can never keep up anyway. However, it is said of Socrates that he is up to either course of action and will be happy whatever they do. The gentle drinking that is prescribed for them by the medical practitioner Eryximachus is virtually the same as he would always recommend, the avoidance of intoxication particularly when still suffering from yesterday's hangover, so they agree that they should drink only as far as they found it pleasant. Socrates himself has no part in this conversation, confirming his indifference to their approach to wine.

As often happens after good intentions their modest indulgence does not last. The catalyst is the arrival of a drunken Alcibiades with other revelers, asking whether they are prepared to drink with him or not (212c–213a). He soon senses that the rest of the gathering is sober, and sets about organizing some serious drinking (213e), remarking that he is not plotting on Socrates who can manage any amount without getting drunk (214a, 220a). His impermeable nature is later illustrated when Alcibiades has given a speech in praise of Socrates, more revelers invade the premises, and all semblance of orderly drinking disappears (223b). Socrates persisted in regularly lubricated conversation with Agathon and Aristophanes until dawn, whereupon those two succumb to sleep while he just sets about his daily business. Rather than succumbing to it, Socrates *controls* the drink. There is an important parallel with his sexual drives, as reported by Alcibiades in the same work. Socrates has not at all sought to avoid close contact with the young man, but he is not at any stage found to lose control (218b–219d). The *Charmides* shows us a Socrates who can be bowled over by a stunning young male, yet quickly recover his wits sufficiently to direct a philosophical conversation with the beauty concerned. Overall, Socrates had an amazing reputation both for having strong drives and for controlling them.

Implications of the Socratic Paradigm

What did this paradigm of the philosopher imply for the place of wine in philosophy? Certainly it did not mean that liberal quantities should be avoided. One could, in fact, enjoy the taste of wine just as much as one wished, for it was not its taste but the resultant loss of control that could prove harmful. It did, however, mean that one should never be enjoying the feeling of intoxication, whose very presence suggested that the wine was controlling you, instead of you controlling the wine. This has a variety of consequences. It supplied philosophers with no motive for avoiding wine, unless its consumption entailed forgetting the rules of moderation – as with those whom we recognize as alcoholics who have to forfeit alcoholic beverages completely. The story is indeed told that Polemo, fourth Head of Plato's Academy, drank just water from the age of thirty,[18] but his case is exceptional. The anecdotes depict him as leading a dissolute life when younger – until such time as he stumbled in his usual intoxicated condition into a lecture of his revered predecessor Xenocrates.[19] He was deeply moved by the lecture on temperance that he heard, and duly converted to philosophy. So he may very well have suffered from that kind of alcoholism for which abstinence is the only effective cure. But Polemo, even in his life of abstinence, still seems to have retained an affection for the forbidden substance, for he was fond, it seems, of characterizing his favorite passages of the tragic poet Sophocles with a line from the comic poet Phrynichus[20] that I like to translate somewhat freely as:

"Neither a sticky, nor a tawny, but genuine ice-wine."

This was not the line of a killjoy!

The affects of Plato's adoption of the Socratic paradigm in the *Symposium* are that he is immediately conscious of the need to warn the inexperienced about lack of control, even in a work that is otherwise more of a celebration of wine (as also of love). One example of what can happen is found in Socrates' own contribution to

18 Athenaeus 2.44e.
19 Diogenes Laertius 4.16.
20 Diogenes Laertius 4.20 (Phrynichus fr. 68PCG = 65K).

24

the speech-making rituals of the *Symposium*. He tells the myth of the birth of Eros (Love), in which the father, Plenty, gets drunk in Zeus' garden on nectar (there being as yet no wine), and Poverty takes advantage of the opportunity offered by his drunken stupor to have his child (203b). So nectar, and by implication wine too, can play the flattering seductress,[21] or at least the seductress' apprentice. Not only unwanted children (well Eros always was a pest!), but also unwanted truthfulness could be among the embarrassing consequences of drunkenness according to a saying used by Alcibiades (*Symposium* 217e).

Implications of the Socratic paradigm for political thought were immediately visible in Plato's political writings, the *Republic* and the *Laws*. We expect to see wine provided for in the *Republic*'s indulgent "City of Pigs," but it is initially mentioned in the same breath as such ordinary items as bread, cloaks, and sandals (372a), as if it is not regarded as much of a luxury item in itself. However, we also see the expected passages condemning alcohol abuse (e.g., 389e), and we shall not be surprised if there are overtones of distaste when discussing the *philoinos* ("wine lover," 475a), who welcomes *any* excuse to drink *any* kind of wine. But it is the *Laws* that both regulates and institutionalizes the use of wine. The work is particularly keen to keep the potent liquid from those who are comparatively young, and to introduce greater quantities as life goes on,[22] so that senior citizens who can best *control* its effects also receive the toughest *challenges* in their efforts to demonstrate their virtue. These older men are also seen to be in the most need of something to make them let their hair down a little, so that the state will provide occasions for them to drink!

That the nature of wine may change in relation to its users is again hinted at where its mythology is discussed later in the *Laws* at 672b–d. Here the less timid Athenian mythology is contrasted with Cretan insofar as it claims that wine has been given to us as a *pharmakon* ("drug") rather than for revenge, nicely illustrating the ambiguous nature of wine, since the term *pharmakon*, though here intended mainly to suggest a healing medicine, can also signify a poison. Though

---

[21] Plato, *Gorgias* 518c1.

[22] See 637d, 645c, 646d, 649a, 666a–b where appropriate ages for different quantities of wine are discussed.

25

seeing its uses, the *Laws* only allow wine to result in inebriation at festivals of Dionysus, the appropriate god (775b), while certain persons in a position of responsibility may not consume it at all (674b–c). Overall, wine is a gift to human beings, but, in a city organized with a view to the maximization of the virtues of its citizens, it is one to be regulated by the politician so that possible detrimental effects are avoided: by control of its consumers, its quantities, or the environment of its consumption. It may be no accident that this work was written in Plato's old age, and by one who held no office that would ban his use of it!

Plato has provided us with a rich variety of material, even if it scarcely amounts to a philosophy of wine. Once Plato had set about defining the parameters of ethical debate and instituting some key topics, others would also have to turn their attention from time to time to matters of wine. One of these was his illustrious pupil Aristotle, whose *Symposium* has unfortunately been lost, though it must have provided interesting reading. At one point a comparison was apparently drawn between wine, the traditional tipple of the Greeks, and the beer-like equivalent favored by the Egyptians. The claim is made that persons drunk on wine may fall in any direction, whereas a drunken beer drinker will always fall on his back. I have still been unable to verify this intriguing claim.[23]

Conclusion: Power and Expertise

In Plato's later years the Academy had become more involved with the politics of various Greek states, as rulers sought status by consulting intellectuals, while intellectuals were glad of the patronage, and often glad of the opportunity to have others to put their ideas into practice. Plato had a long and fluctuating relationship with the Syracusan monarchy; his nephew and successor Speusippus both became involved with the Syracusan party of Dion and was in dialogue with Philip II of Macedon; and Aristotle ultimately came to tutor Philip's son, Alexander (still called the "Great" is spite of his

---

[23] Readers may enjoy consulting the third book of the Aristotelian *Problems* (I hesitate to ascribe the work to Aristotle himself), which is a collection of similar problems concerning the effects of wine.

bizarre excesses). Aristotle also seems to have had some interesting dealings with the champions of the Greek cause in Cyprus. If these philosophers were to be taken seriously by men in power then there was little chance that they would mount any very serious attack on wine. The picture of life among the Sicilian ruling elite left to us by the Platonic *Seventh Epistle* is quite sybaritic,[24] while Alexander's penchant for seriously damaging his health by heavy drinking is well known. Those who aimed to be the friends of potentates had little option but to enjoy their wine. They might warn against over-indulgence, or condemn indiscriminate drinking, but their friends would see to it that they did not make any radical onslaught on a key source of satisfaction.

Furthermore, one should perhaps note that good wine actually resembled potentates in a very important respect. Both had strength, or, to choose a different term, potency. Modern socially aware societies very often take fright at anything with potency (e.g., nuclear power, genetic manipulation, and politicians in a hurry), because they bring with them potential dangers. Nobody can deny that alcohol has been throughout its history a potentially disruptive force, with the power to wreck seemingly worthwhile lives. The philosophy of the nanny state, however, by which we are all protected whether we like it or not from anything we could seriously abuse, was not a phenomenon that the Greeks knew much about. The dangers of their world were in any case so great, and life expectancy sufficiently low, that the risks seemed less significant. Plato at least was strongly inclined to regard power as a double-edged sword, whose potential for ill exactly matched its potential for good, for even the actions that power led to were not good or bad in themselves, only in relation to the benefit or harm they could result in (*Gorgias* 467c–8e). Consequently, while autocracy was according to the *Statesman* the recipe for the most power to achieve good, it was also the recipe for the most evil; correspondingly, whereas democratic government had the least power for evil, it also had the least power to achieve good. That message is reinforced in the *Crito* (44d), where Crito's warnings about the power of Athenian democracy to harm him are answered by Socrates' expression of regret: unfortunately their power to harm is rather slight, which means that their power for good is rather slight

---

[24] 326b–c; the work's authorship is disputed, but irrelevant here.

too. So wine's power to harm should, according to the same principles, be exactly balanced by its power for harm.

Looked at in this way, the potency of wine, whose double-edged powers were already brilliantly contrasted in Euripides' *Bacchae*, should never be something to be thrown out unthinkingly because of its dangers, but rather something to be used for the better like any other power. Using anything for the better requires expertise, both a general grasp of social ethics and a more technical expertise relating to the thing being used. Plato notes at *Protagoras* 319c how non-experts are not tolerated by the Athenian people if they try to advise on any subject permitting expertise. Wine was no different in the eyes of the majority of Greek philosophers including Plato, something to be used with both an understanding of society's needs and an expertise in the specific capabilities of the substance itself. In short, one might expect experts on wine to be required to advise the nation on all policy relating to wine. Their advice must take full account of the goals of society at large (upon which other expertise may be sought), but any teetotaler who stood up before the Assembly of ancient Athens, seeking to advise the people on matters concerning wine, would expect to be hissed and booed until he stood down. Let us not, then, allow ourselves to be advised by such persons today!

Further Reading

Translations
Many of the ancient texts referred to in this essay are available in a wide variety of translations. What matters for the purpose of following up references is that translations should adhere to standard referencing methods, usually by book and line numbers for verse texts, and by Stephanus page numbers (e.g., 345b) for Plato. The following are suggestions only.

Aristotle, *Nichomachean Ethics*, translated with introduction, notes, and glossary by Terence Irwin, Indianapolis: Hackett, 1985.

Athenaeus, *The Deipnosophists*, with an English translation by C. B. Gulick, 2 vols., Cambridge, MA: Heinemann, 1927–41.

Diogenes Laertius, *Lives of the Philosophers*, with an English translation by R. D. Hicks, 2 vols., Cambridge, MA: Heinemann, 1925.

Euripides, *The Bacchae and Other Plays*, translated by Philip Vellacott, London: Penguin, 1954.

Homer, *Iliad*, translated with an introduction by Richmond Lattimore, Chicago: University of Chicago Press, 1962.

Homer, *Odyssey*, translated with an introduction by Richmond Lattimore, New York: Harper and Row, 1967 (1999).

Plato, *Complete Works*, edited, with introduction and notes, by John M. Cooper, Indianapolis: Hackett, 1997.

Plato, *Republic*, translated by Robin Waterfield, Oxford: Oxford University Press, 1993.

Plato, *Symposium*, translated by Robin Waterfield, Oxford: Oxford University Press, 1994.

Ps.-Aristotle, *Problems*, with an English translation by W. S. Hett, 2 vols., Cambridge, MA: Heinemann, 1936.

Stoics, *see* von Arnim and Long and Sedley below.

Xenophon, *The Persian Expedition* (= *Anabasis*), translated by Rex Warner, London: Penguin, 1949.

Other useful works

H. von Arnim (ed.), *Stoicorum Veterum Fragmenta*, Leipzig: Teubner, 1905–24.

Gosling, J. C. B. and Taylor, C. W., *The Greeks on Pleasure*, Oxford: Oxford University Press, 1982.

Long, A. A. and Sedley, D. N., *The Hellenistic Philosophers*, vol. 1, Cambridge, Cambridge University Press, 1987.

Murray, Oswyn (ed.), *Sympotica: A Symposium on the Symposium*, Oxford: Oxford University Press, 1990.

2

On and Off the Wagon
Wine and the American Character

Jonathon Alsop

For a nation of 300 million people, we Americans do not really drink very much wine, just a little over two gallons per person per year. That amounts to about ten bottles a year, a bottle every five weeks, or one glass of wine a week. Because 300 million people is a lot, we are number two in the world for total wine consumption these days at about 274 million cases a year, almost in spite of ourselves.[1] Flip to the per capita chart, and we are number 30-something, neighbors with wine-loving powerhouses Azerbaijan and Slovakia. Wine consumption in France has been falling steadily for years, yet the French consume about fifteen gallons of wine per person per year, nearly eight times our national consumption. In Italy, annual per capita consumption is thirteen gallons. Only Argentina shows up for the Americas in the top ten with eight and a half gallons, still besting us by four times.[2] We could double our per capita national average – think of it: *two* glasses of wine a week! – and still be at only one-third the French consumption. No one is suggesting that Americans should drink like Luxembourgers but, if we did, our national wine industry would be eight times bigger: not today's 274 million cases,

---

[1] Jack Robertiello, "Wine Consumption on the Rise, Imports Fuel Growth," Adams Beverage Group, onthehouse.typepad.com/on_the_house/2006/09/per_capita_cons.html (accessed October 1, 2006).

[2] The Wine Institute, "Per Capita Wine Consumption in Listed Countries," www.wineinstitute.org/industry/keyfacts/per_capita_wine_consumption.php (accessed September 1, 2006).

30

but 2.2 billion cases a year. American wine culture has what is known idiomatically as a "tremendous upside," an expression basketball people use to describe players with untapped potential, or very tall players who simply have not realized it yet.

Instead, our wine history begins and almost ends with America's first failed celebrity winemaker, patriot and president Thomas Jefferson. Hard as it is to believe, there is a straight line connecting the author of the Declaration of Independence to the Smothers Brothers (also celebrity winemakers, also political), Pat Paulsen (comedian, owned a winery, ran for president a few times), and Raymond Burr, the actor who played super-lawyer Perry Mason on television (vineyard owner and winemaker, once brandished the Declaration of Independence in court, if I remember right).

Jefferson was a huge wine lover, especially of red Bordeaux, which puts him about a half-century ahead of his time: Bordeaux would not experience its famous classification until 1857, by which time Jefferson had been dead more than thirty years. It is no surprise to find him ahead of the power curve on this – all wine lovers want to be tasting the next great wine – but Jefferson went further and decided to *make* the next great wine. In 1807, he embarked on an ambitious planting at Monticello of almost 300 vines from 24 different European grapevine cuttings that he selected and imported. He imagined that, like so many other crops, grapes were going to flourish in fertile, verdant Virginia. Not only did he anticipate that his vineyards would be at least as successful as anything else, he actually thought he has going to get super grapes and make super wine to first equal, then surpass Europe.

Jefferson's vineyard experiment failed spectacularly, the first time and each of the six times it was subsequently replanted. He was discovering that as counter-intuitive as it seems, wine grapes do not automatically flourish in rich soils. Virginia piedmont soils are rich in other things too, like bugs and bacteria, molds and mildews that grapes are highly susceptible to. Jefferson never learned what was killing his vines – technically, it was something called black rot and a root louse named phylloxera – but the irony was not lost on him. Native North American grapes that did grow made freakishly bad wine; any grapes worth drinking would not even take root. Luckily, he was wealthy and well connected enough to own a couple of extensive wine cellars and import all the red Bordeaux he wanted – a

31

bottle of 1787 Château Lafite from his cellar went for $160,000 at auction in 1985 – and that may have helped take the edge off his disappointment in the short term. Overall, it was a disheartening, bad first attempt at growing European wine grapes in the New World, and it was difficult not to take the vines' emphatic reaction as a rejection of the whole idea. Jefferson's transformative vision of making great wine in America would persist, but it would take centuries to realize.

In the Bible, an angry, vengeful God punishes the evil by giving them "water of gall to drink,"[3] something anti-alcohol activists have been trying to do practically since the country was founded. Wine's commercial place in American life today as a specially controlled, locally regulated, highly taxed product goes back to Prohibition, when an honest-to-goodness constitutional amendment made wine (and all other alcohol) illegal in 1920. Movement toward national Prohibition started much earlier, of course. President Andrew Jackson's drunken shenanigans during his presidency (1829–37) first galvanized public anti-alcohol sentiment by giving it a big easy target. The Reverend Howard Hyde Russell founded the Anti-Saloon League of Ohio in 1893 and the Anti-Saloon League of America followed in 1895. Twenty-five years later, the axe had fallen, and America's relationship to wine and food was altered forever.

Prohibition's most potent and enduring symbol was a pinched, violent, disagreeable woman named Carry A. Nation who was famous for attacking saloons armed only with a hatchet and her firm belief (insane notion?) that she was striking out at what Jesus "doesn't like" (her words, not mine). Nation's mother had actual verifiable psychotic delusions and believed long and actively that she was Queen Victoria. Nation may never have thought she was a member of the royal family, but she did believe her name was an assignment from God and that it was appropriate to attack people and property in the name of temperance with a hatchet, still awfully delusional in my book.

She and her followers chopped up a lot of bars and barrels and broke a lot of bottles with their hatchets of righteousness – these attacks were called "hatchetations" at the time – but better even than all that, she got tons of publicity doing it. After one flamboyant arrest

---

[3] Jeremiah 9:15.

in Wichita, Kansas, the photograph of Nation kneeling and praying in her jail cell looks like a well-styled studio shot: her face is softly illuminated from above (by the light of what: sobriety, morality, bail?) and the backlighting of the prison bars is almost Oscar-worthy. You cannot buy publicity like that, but you can sell official Carry A. Nation brand saloon-busting hatchets, which is exactly what she did, in addition to hiring a manager and traveling the country on a speaking tour as "The Famous And Original Bar Room Smasher." Her name was a registered trademark in the state of Kansas.

A book deal in 1905 brought us *The Use and Need of the Life of Carry A. Nation*,[4] an autobiography in which she spelled out her quaint views on family, morality, race relations, food, alcohol, pseudoscience, and, strangely, Masons. Nation believed there was an underground cabal of Euro-centric Masons encouraging wine and alcohol consumption in the US to further their unspecified but nefarious goals. "I believe the masons were a great curse to Dr. Gloyd,"[5] she wrote, referring to her first husband who died a raging alcoholic. Nation made no distinction between her diverse enemies. Beer, wine, whiskey, and Masons were not just equal in her eyes, but equally bad. She rarely limited her enforced self-improvement to one vice. Nation opposed cigarettes and she railed against foreign foods of all kinds, wine being a special target, both foreign and alcohol.

She devoted substantial space in her only book to debunking the myth that wine is food, one of the core principles of great European cuisine. The science behind her assertion is an almost medieval vision of two "classes" of food: "flesh formers" and "body warmers,"[6] a rhyming distinction we find both creepy and vague these days. By her frontier science, alcohol is neither a flesh former nor a body warmer (according to whom? the Flesh Forming and Body Warming Foods Association?) so it is not a food, and if it is not a food, it is a toxin. Simple as pie, which of course is a food.

---

[4] Carry A. Nation, *The Use and Need of the Life of Carry A. Nation* (Topeka: F. M. Steves & Sons, 1905).

[5] Nation, Chapter 4, www.gutenberg.org/dirs/etext98/crntn10.txt (accessed September 1, 2006).

[6] Nation, Chapter 28, www.gutenberg.org/dirs/etext98/crntn10.txt (accessed September 1, 2006).

Nation did not live to see national prohibition. By the time she died in 1911, Maine had enacted state prohibition long before in 1851, Kansas in 1880, and five more states in the twentieth century. Her epitaph – "She Hath Done What She Could" – captures the prunish personality she must have had. It leaves me feeling that ultimately we made Carry Nation give up on us; she set a very low bar and we still could not manage to get over it.

Thirteen years and yet another constitutional amendment after Prohibition was enacted, wine was legal again. The compromise that made repeal possible was that alcoholic beverage control would devolve to the lowest municipality, which is why today, decades later, we still have dry counties and dry towns scattered across the country. On a larger level, state governments clutched to their bosoms the right to regulate and tax alcohol sales within and across their borders. Individual states are still run almost like independent nations in regards to wine. For instance, to sell your Washington state wine in Rhode Island today, by law you must contract with a distributor – essentially an importer between states – and your wine has to enter the destination state through that relationship, financially and physically. Industry-wide prices are set and published, quantities and discounts are delimited, and the result is our still-sluggish wine world where everyone has more or less the same licensed wine as everyone else for about the same price.

After more than a decade of legal banishment, America's vineyards and wineries were devastated. Before Prohibition, the wine industry in Ohio was bigger than the wine industry in California today. After Prohibition, the predictable profitability of soybeans, corn, and wheat never gave an inch, and wine grapes never reemerged as a viable crop even in formerly wine-rich states. There were 256 wineries in Sonoma in 1920, only 58 by 1969, and 254 in 2005 – close, but still not even where we were 85 years ago.[7]

Thanks in large part to the apparent cultural imperative to make wine everywhere they go (the ancient Romans planted both France and Spain thick with wine grapes), Italian families in California kept

[7] Sonoma County Grape Growers Association, "Sonoma County's Wine History," www.sonomagrapevine.org/pages/vineyardviews/vvhistory.html (accessed September 1, 2006).

winemaking alive during Prohibition. Today's top tier of California winemakers is testament to this persistence: Mondavi, Sebastiani, Martini, Trentadue, Simi, Gallo, Indelicato, Parducci, Seghesio, Foppiano, the list of Prohibition survivors could go on and on. The Pedroncelli family survived in Sonoma and even profited by selling something called "wine brick," a compacted brick of dried grapes. Since it would have been a little too shameless to put directions for home-made wine right on the label, the package instead featured a famous warning: never dissolve in cool water, add yeast, nor allow to ferment two weeks. The final unspoken step in the process: do not put in mouth.

She Hath Done What She Could, not wipe out wine completely perhaps, but the next best thing: make it difficult commercially to get and drink wine, sever the ancient bond between wine and food, and shatter American wine life into so many broken, unworkable, governmentally controlled parts that it would take wine lovers a hundred years to glue it all back together.

Freedom From Wine

Artists, as the would-be creators of emotion, also find themselves sometimes on the receiving end, eliciting it as well. In the case of Norman Rockwell, American sentimentalist painter from the mid-twentieth century, these reactions range from derision in the Rockwell book *The Underside of Innocence*,[8] where author Richard Halpern discerns dirty psycho-sexual motivations in his paintings, exactly the kind of thing a person could also discern in a book with the words 'innocence' and 'underside' in its title, to authentic respect and the occasional sincere teardrop.

Rockwell was an iconist, a painter of American life scenes that were at first pungently familiar to one great semi-midwestern Anglophile swath of the public and eventually grew to represent quintessential hometown America to everyone else who gazed upon them, the 321 *Saturday Evening Post* covers especially. Rockwell explored slightly

---

[8] Richard Halpern, *Norman Rockwell: The Underside of Innocence* (Chicago: University of Chicago Press, 2006).

too intimate private moments in *Crackers In Bed*. Watershed events were a favorite theme: *Prom Dress* and *Breaking Home Ties* capture authentic lives at turning points. The good-natured aw-shucks civil disobedience of *Happy Birthday Miss Jones* is leavened considerably by the realization that the well-behaved third graders who scrawled "Happy Birthday Jonesy" on the blackboard in 1956 were Summer of Love hippies-in-waiting, at least some of them.

President Franklin D. Roosevelt wrapped up his state of the union address in January 1941 with a powerful rhetorical flourish, a passionate expression of his vision of a world organized around freedom of speech, freedom of worship, freedom from want, and freedom from fear. Although we were not technically fighting World War II yet, this freedom quatrain was used within the year to explain why we fought, once we were in it. In 1943, Rockwell published a series of paintings called *The Four Freedoms*, his most focused, affecting, and thoughtful work yet.

I am no art critic, but I have a problem with painting number three, *Freedom From Want*. Rockwell rendered a Thanksgiving archetype so powerful that to this day, people who cannot cook a chicken leg take it upon themselves to roast an entire turkey. Yet there is not a single glass of wine within a hundred miles of his Thanksgiving table. Instead, everyone's glass is full of fresh, clear, clean American water, probably tap water. There are eight of them: exactly what you are supposed to drink every day. Crazy Uncle Nut in the lower right corner, staring right into the camera as it were, looks like he might have been into something a little stronger before the dinner bell rang. Little Sister on the left flashes an impish grin down the table as if to ask, "Wonder what Granny left in the turkey this year?" Besides the mammoth bird, you can see pickles, a plate of celery, a Jell-O mold, even a bunch of grapes tauntingly in the foreground, but the family is otherwise wine free and apparently loving it.

Imagine, pointlessly, what Rockwell would have done for Thanksgiving – and wine – if *Freedom From Want* had pictured two water glasses and five glasses of wine, two white and three red (Uncle Nut's tequila shot glass optional). Thanksgiving is our national ceremonial meal, after all, and wine would benefit immensely if even part of the energy and enthusiasm that people put into special ordering and deep-frying turkeys also went into special ordering Thanksgiving wine. Rockwell's art is still a substantial commercial business today (*Homecoming Soldier* sold for $9.2 million in 2006) so maybe it would be worthwhile to insert wine digitally into the image.

One of my persistent complaints concerning the image of wine – both literally and figuratively – is how wine and wine lovers are portrayed in the media. Most of the time they are completely ignored, and elaborate cinematic meals that call for a special wine end up served with nothing. On the other end of the spectrum, in the 1995 Sandra Bullock vehicle *While You Were Sleeping*, a hard-working bottle of Sterling Cabernet Sauvignon turns up in scene after scene: first in his apartment, then hers, then at dinner at the parents' house. Each time, the bottle is angled ever-so-slightly away from the camera so the audience cannot see the label head-on. But if you are a wine lover, you want to see what other people are drinking, and in this cinematic world, they are all unrealistically drinking the same wine.

Sideways, the 2004 Oscar-winning buddy film starring Paul Giamatti as the Wine Guy and Thomas Haden Church as the Ladies' Man, fleshes out the two sides of our stereotypic ambivalence about wine with real accuracy, affection, and frivolity. On the one hand, the intellectual Miles is simultaneously immersed yet removed, tasting wine from a fourth dimension no one else inhabits, something you see at wine tastings a lot. His buddy just wants to know when he can drink the wine. They spend the rest of the movie trying to bridge this gap while they drink a lot of fantastic wine, eat a lot of excellent food, and score like Wilt Chamberlain with wine-hotties Sandra Oh and Virginia Madsen.

The boys surrender the high ground early on when they not only drink and drive, but drink *while* driving. Their first sips take place in the Winemobile as they speed away from the despicable in-laws' house. In five seconds, they break more laws than you can count. Like so many great wine experiences, this movie begins with the best of intentions but ultimately goes down the drain. Refined, civilized, appreciative tasting surrenders to gluttonous drinking and eventually ends with a naked fat man chasing our protagonists down the street. By this time, the movie's no longer about wine but about how far astray people's appetites can lead them. Women who love wine come out of the film looking best of all. Madsen and Oh portray their characters as smart, funny, and sensual, an irresistible combination. Of

37

the two guys, however, one is worse than the other. At one point, Giamatti fails to kiss Madsen after she takes his hand, so maybe they were both just really drunk. My favorite thing about *Sideways* – and the bit of writing that literally won best screenplay Oscar – is the beautiful soliloquy Madsen delivers as she explains why she loves wine.[9] My least favorite thing was how many times the pompous Wine Guy reminded me of myself.

Pinot noir sales in the US – already rising and at record levels – were up almost 16 percent in the year after *Sideways* came out. The film has created a frenzy for pinot noir as if the grape itself had won an award at Sundance. Even more compelling is the increase in repeat buyers of pinot by 40 percent, which is the sign of a new generation of pinot noir lovers being born in the film's aftermath. In comparison, repeat buyers of Miles' least favorite wine merlot decreased 3 percent nationally, suggesting there just might be such a thing as bad publicity. Overall, this boost only pushes pinot noir from 1.1 percent of the market to 1.4 percent of the market. There's a long way for pinot to go, but it is also a very big market.[10]

Jonathan Nossiter's 2004 documentary *Mondovino* looks through a wineglass darkly and sees nothing but bad behavior in the present and total ruin in the future for wine. He warns against increasing internationalization and homogenization while citing three chief villains: a winemaking technique called "micro-oxygenation," a French wine consultant named Michel Rolland (who appears to recommend and practice micro-oxygenation on a macro scale), and the Mondavi family from California. In a nutshell, micro-oxygenation and very ripe grapes are what makes Australian shiraz taste so fantastic and has helped it become a world wine phenomenon. On the international market today, wines with the Aussie shiraz flavor profile are killing everyone, especially set-in-their-ways ancient French wine producers, from whom we hear plenty in this movie. Rolland's only apparent sins are smoking like a chimney and making wines that people think taste really good. Twenty-five years ago, no one thought either of those things would ever be considered bad.

---

[9] Reprinted in the introduction to this volume; see Fritz Allhoff, "Planting the Vines: An Introduction to *Wine & Philosophy*." pp. 2–3.

[10] A. C. Nielsen, "Has 'Sideways' Put Wine Sales On An Upward Trajectory?" us.acnielsen.com/news/20050221.shtml (accessed September 1, 2006).

After *Mondovino*, the Mondavi family will never do another interview again, probably for generations, and for very good reason. The way they were portrayed visually was just repellent, and seemed to want to express overtly something, but what? At first, the Mondavi family comes off a little like the well-meaning Lennie in Steinbeck's *Of Mice and Men* as they try making wine in southern France, love it a little too much, and squeeze a little too hard for local tastes. Kicked out of bed by the French, they fall into the arms of the Italians, and Michael Mondavi is captured entertaining notions of making wine on Mars. In the end, it was just a bad interview, proving only that spooky lighting can make even the Easter bunny look demonic. During a following interview with super-critic Robert Parker, the camera wanders off, seemingly unmotivated, to give us a tight close-up of his dog's rump. Later, critic James Suckling essentially confesses (jokingly, I would say, in his defense) that he went easy reviewing his landlord's wine because of their relationship. Either way, it only confirms everything everyone thinks already: that the game is rigged and somewhere the same huge tank of wine is being used to fill up bottles of Two-Buck Chuck out of one end and $1,000 a bottle Château Petrus out of the other.

In the end, these two movies together have an almost macrobiotic effect: pinot noir is summarily elevated by *Sideways*, yet the overall good will is only a memory once *Mondovino* gets done making us feel guilty for having the bad taste to like what we like. These are two problem movies; though their problems are little ones, they show us in ways simultaneously charming, clumsy, and misguided a larger wine life than we currently live in America. Still, at the end of *Sideways*, wine does not seem to be wholly part of even the hardcore wine lover's life. The vehement merlot-hating Miles retreats to a burger joint with an extra-special bottle of wine, the legendary 1961 Château Cheval Blanc. Here he over-reaches even his own pomposity: his beloved Cheval Blanc is mainly merlot.

My Old Kentucky Wine

Americans like to say that we enjoy a distinction among industrial nations of the world in that we have never been militarily conquered nor occupied. This is not completely true: just ask anyone with deep roots in the Old South, and memories of vanquish, humiliation, and Reconstruction lie just below the surface. In spite of the fact that Washington, DC is a southern city by almost all standards, it is not its capital. The South itself stands apart from the Northeast naturally, but from the rural rest of the country too, older and richer in ghosts, newer in architecture, infrastructure, and scorched earth. After all, Boston and New York have not been occupied and sacked since at least the late eighteenth century, and there are still many Colonial buildings intact. In the south, perhaps Charleston can say the same thing. Western cities like Wichita were not even incorporated until the 1870s.

Wine began its return to the south in the early 1980s when the commonwealth of Virginia, among other things, enacted a set of laws making it administratively much easier to open and run a winery. Who knew so many aspirant winemakers were waiting in the wings for paperwork and licensing reform? Twenty years later, Virginia has 80-plus wineries, many of which equal Europe in quality, and a few even raise the bar, restoring and redeeming Jefferson's original vision after only two centuries of on-and-off trying. Wine's expansion into the South in the twenty-first century has been fueled in part by the defeat of big tobacco in court and the resulting monies from the various cases. In North Carolina, for instance, a national master settlement in the mid-1990s earmarked a delightfully multi-zeroed sum of money to help people in the tobacco industry transition into something else, and farmers specifically, to find new crops. Wine is one of the crops farmers are finding so attractive these days that the home page of the North Carolina Tobacco Trust Fund Commission has an article titled "Living with Pierce's Disease,"[11] a bacterial infection that literally slays grape vines. When I saw it, and right on page one as it were, I had to laugh: normally, an article on Pierce's disease is the kind of thing you'd see only in a technical, slightly wine-geeky vineyard industry management magazine. At first, I thought I was going to have to ferret out the subtle connection between old school

---

[11] Dave Caldwell, "Living with Pierce's Disease," North Carolina Tobacco Trust Fund Commission, www.tobaccotrustfund.org/news/PierceDiseaseAugust2006.pdf (accessed September 1, 2006).

40

tobacco and New World wine, but here it is. Caring about Pierce's disease is real love: it just screams, the problem of my friend is my problem too.

Wine grapes and tobacco share a certain affinity for well-drained soils, plenty of sun, and windy hillsides, but so do a lot of crops. The cynic inside (or is that the voice of my teetotaling southern grandmother?) cannot help but ask if all this is not just trading one sin-dustry for another as they meet on the stairway of success, one going up, the other down. Now Kentucky – a commonwealth of 120 counties, thirty of which are dry and another thirty semi-dry – has hired the first state enologist in its history to help expand beyond today's 44 wineries and 75-plus grape growers. Next on the proposed legislative agenda is gaining recognition for an official AVA (American Viticultural Area), the Bluegrass Appellation.

When NASCAR team owner Richard Childress opened a vineyard and winery five miles from his racing headquarters in Lexington, North Carolina in 2004, it marked the return of the first true celebrity wine-maker in the south since Jefferson. Wine snobs around the world shook their disbelieving heads at the realization that now *even* NASCAR was into wine (what next: Cuvée Britney Spears?). But NASCAR is more than a race: it is a market that can be sold things. Bennett Lane Winery in California has been a sponsor since 2003. Indianapolis 500 legend Mario Andretti has his own Napa winery. His neighbor in Napa and fellow racer Randy Lewis is pretty much sold out of everything but the chardonnay these days. And according to a press release I received in 2006, driver Jeff Gordon is now selling a $50 Carneros chardonnay to his fans.

Childress Vineyards is a large anchor destination that benefits some if not all of the other 37 wineries in North Carolina, a state lots of people would be surprised to discover had even one winery in it. Thirty years from now, Childress will be like Mondavi, famous for what he himself did, but important for what he did for the wineries around him. NASCAR has its roots in apocryphal high-speed moonshining adventures from Prohibition days, so Childress Vineyards can also represent a certain closing of the book, if you want it to. In the end, it looks like my people – on the crazy-driving southern moonshiner side of my family, that is – won in the form of a North Carolina claret.

My grandmother, a brittle, indomitable southern woman of Faulknerian proportions and vocabulary, was anything but a moonshiner. One main lightning rod for her relentless moral inflexibility was alcohol, and she opposed it in all its forms with her version of constructive nonviolence, church-going methods that more than once led her and others' husbands to put down the bottle (for a while at least) and fill up a pew. They were never reformed completely of course. Opposing liquor from the very heart of Kentucky, Virginia, and Tennessee bourbon country must have appealed to my grandmother's essentially contrarian nature, but she was swimming against two or three centuries of traditional sourmash making and drinking, a too-swift current that in her opinion was sweeping everyone else off to a drunken hell.

When I was about two years old, my mother – barely twenty years older – left me, for the first time in my short life, with my Uncle Johnny Ray at his house while she went to a doctor's appointment. I do not remember a lot from that day, but what I do remember, and vividly, is my mother's emotional arrival back on the scene after her appointment to discover me, my uncle, and my uncle's friend – a police officer, in uniform – in the attached garage bottling up a mess of homemade beer. I was right in the middle of topping up another Squirt bottle with home brew from a small hose when my mother walked in, her face a suspended-in-time stereotypic silent scream. She did not understand the police officer was a partner in the home brew, not making an arrest, until I said, "Look Mommy, I'm helping."

My mother bolted with me. Had my grandmother found out where I had been and what I had done, her volcanic wrath would have reduced everything around it to cinders. That was the first and last time my mother left me with my uncle or anyone else for a good long while. To me, the message was clear: to be among the women of my family was to move in sobriety, safety, and organization; among the men was an unpredictable world of tobacco and alcohol, cars, appetites, and freedom. It was the first of many encounters over the years with my family's widely ambivalent, flagrantly contradictory teetotaling, hard-drinking, homebrew-making, Prohibitionist ways. Like the other men in my family, I quickly found myself hooked on the dichotomy. Two decades of wine writing have brought me only slightly closer to understanding this tension, but the historical root of it is widespread and particularly American. This pathological ambivalence – secretly attracted, on paper abstaining, yet in reality consuming enthusiastically – extends to our whole culture. It illuminates a facet of our conflicted national character in which America in the twenty-first century is still more famous for Prohibition than for its most famous wines.

3

Muse in a Stem Glass
Art, Wine, and Philosophy

Kirsten Ditterich-Shilakes

It is an evening art opening at San Francisco's de Young Museum. Friends gather in the Wilsey Court; the chatter of voices echoes, women's heels click across the floor. A butler circles among the guests, offering California chardonnay in glasses perilously balanced on a silver tray. Museum-goers catch sight of a monumental 30′ × 30′ black-and-white Gerhard Richter artwork dominating the wall and move toward it. In front of them looms Richter's massive *Strontium*, made of 130 C-print photographs of the atomic structure of strontium titanate, the same reflective crystal substance used in the production of video screens, screams with a fuzzy energy setting the onlookers off balance. The guests sip the wine from their stem glasses, ponder their individual notions of the artwork, and invoke the "philosophical muse."

Whether at the de Young Museum today – at an axis of Silicon Valley technology and Napa Valley wine culture – or in the vineyards of Chios at the height of the Greek Classical Age, art, wine, and philosophy have long been inextricably entwined modes of connection and expression. Across time and geography, the triad of art, wine, and philosophy persists; the vessels, the wine, and the "philosophical muse" have been used as a means of communication to reach the gods or to reach other mortals. The word 'museum' is derived from *Mouseion*, an ancient Greek temple dedicated to the beguiling goddesses who inspired poetry, song, and dance. In our contemporary setting, four selected artworks within San Francisco's Fine Arts Museums and Asian Art Museum rise to the fore and embody the triad of art, wine, and philosophy: a Greek amphora from the sixth century BCE; an early nineteenth-century English painting by

44

John Singer Sargent, *Le Verre de Porto* (*A Dinner Table at Night*); a Chinese bronze wine warmer and pourer from the Shang dynasty (ca. 1300 BCE); and a contemporary Japanese Bizenware *sake* bottle by Fujiwara Yu. The representative depth of these vessels is augmented by the four beverages that once filled them: resinous grape wine, claret (or perhaps port), ancient fermented rice or millet wine, and *sake*.

All four vessels bring us to the metaphorical dining table, but not to a cocktail at the de Young Museum standing in front of Richter's *Strontium*, nor an American Thanksgiving feast of Norman Rockwell, nor even one of Guy Buffet's "cork-popping" café scenes. Rather, these vessels bring us to four classic civilizations where wine began – Greece, France, China, and Japan – each with its own unique philosophical traditions of the table. And the figurative depth of these vessels is augmented by these four distinctive beverages contained within them: resinous grape wine, claret, fermented rice or millet wine, and *sake*. The ancient Greeks celebrated the fruit of the earth through the rapture and intoxication of Dionysus, the god of wine. The same divine elixir filled Athenian vessels and fueled oratory prowess for *symposia* in the cradle of democracy. In class-conscious Victorian society, the British savored exceptional French wines, which they served in fine crystal and silver to establish their social standing. In ancient China, fermented rice or millet wine facilitated communication with ancestor spirits, who in turn cared for and protected the harmony of society. And to this day in Japan, the quiet spirit of nature threads itself through rustic *sake* vessels into the acute minds of those who appreciate the rice wine's delicate nuances.

All four iconic vessels, spanning geography, time, and types of wine, go beyond the mere utility of a container to become beautiful and philosophically purposeful works of art.

The West: Vessels of Expression

The moment resources were available to make wine and art, people did so – in the West and the East. The materials used to produce the elixirs and the way in which these products of human endeavor were viewed varied, depending upon the culture of origin. In the Western world, where differentiating oneself from the crowd and speaking one's mind are valued, wine and art also promote individual self-expression:

45

in vino veritas.[1] Among aficionados and connoisseurs pursuing taste and beauty, philosophies of individualism and materialism fuse with aesthetics. The two "iconic" wine-works that emerge from the Fine Arts Museums' Western collection are a sixth-century BCE Greek amphora and the early nineteenth-century English painting by John Singer Sargent, *Le Verre de Porto* (*A Dinner Table at Night*), which portrays a woman holding a crystal stem glass.

Divine proportions: A Greek wine amphora

According to Thucydides, the fifth-century BCE Greek historian, "The peoples of the Mediterranean began to emerge from barbarism when they learnt to cultivate the olive and the vine."[2] If this is true, then the richest material evidence of the Greeks' refined art, philosophy, and wine culture is embodied in Athenian wine vessels. Because nearly all murals and paintings from ancient Greece have been destroyed by the ravages of time, Greek wine vessels offer a unique insight into the development of Greek painting and a rare picture of contemporary wine-drinking culture. A glimpse into early Greek wine culture can be accessed through a sixth-century black-figure amphora masterpiece from the Fine Arts Museum of San Francisco (Figure 3.1).

The Grecian duality of *chaos*, or disorder, and *cosmos*, order, is rendered in this amphora. The elegant, controlled line of the amphora reveals the *cosmos*, but its painted subject matter and function hint at *chaos*. One side of the amphora presents an image from the Trojan war: a quarrel between the great heroes Odysseus and Ajax over the armor of the dead Achilles. The reverse presents Dionysus, the god of wine, theater, and fertility, as wild and erratic – an apt subject matter for a wine jar. The main figure, Dionysus, is rendered as a distinctive glossy ink-black silhouette against a background of vivid orange terracotta. Taken as such, the elegance of the amphora's shape and the wild activity it portrays represent an intriguing juxtaposition of two opposing forces in Greek cosmology: rational *cosmos* and emotional *chaos*.

---

[1] See footnote 5 below.

[2] Cited in Hugh Johnson, *The Story of Wine* (London: Octopus, 2002), p. 23.

Figure 3.1 Black-figure amphora, 510–500 BCE, Leagros Group of Painters, Athens, Greece. Terracotta. 25 3/4 × 14 3/8 in. (65.4 × 36.5 cm). Gift of M. H. de Young, 24874.1. Photograph used with the permission of the Fine Arts Museums of San Francisco.

The divine wine of Dionysus is the source of chaos, pleasure, and madness. This rare amphora, with its matching lid still intact,[3] was designed to store the mystical wine elixir. The vessel presents an image of the god in a Dionysian rite, meticulously painted by the hand of a Leagros Group workshop craftsman. The depiction echoes a scene out of Euripides' *Bacchae* in which Dionysus lured women from their domestic duties to honor his divinity through wine, music, and

---

[3] Black-figure amphora lid, 510–500 BCE, Leagros Group of Painters, Athens, Greece. Terracotta. 24874.2.

dancing. The god saunters around the belly of the vessel with his entourage of *maenads*, or "maddened female devotees," and *satyrs*, wooly creatures portrayed as half-men, half-goats. Dionysus holds his signature wine cup, the *kantharos*, celebrating the divine product of the vine. The women, *bons vivants*, and the conspicuously amorous *satyrs* are under Dionysus' influence, in a state of wine-fueled rapture invoking the divinity of the god.

The amphora was created within the complex aesthetic and philosophical framework of the time, valuing *cosmos* – a fine balance of order, rationality, and emotion. This vessel was made by a potter, not a sculptor or an architect; nonetheless, it echoes similar Greek aesthetic values. Architecture and sculpture were dictated by mathematics and its relationship to beauty. Consider that the iconic Parthenon (438–432 BCE) was constructed using Pythagorean-based symmetry. Polycleitus, the famous sculptor of the Parthenon, followed mathematical ratios: 1:2, 2:3, and 3:4, and founded the sculptor's "blueprint" for the proportionate human figure. At the same time, Greek art is remarkably sensuous and fleshy: an ageless, athletically toned, supple, taut, and naked Dionysus was carved in marble on the east pediment of the Parthenon. The Parthenon's remarkable counterbalance of emotion and sensuality on one side and rationality on the other also appears in the amphora, whose parts are commonly described as parts of the human anatomy. Lip, mouth, neck, ear (or handles), shoulder, belly, and foot, the amphora forms an elegant human line from lip to toe.

Fine Greek wine vessels such as this amphora were destined for the wine-fueled *symposium* – a hedonistic and aristocratic after-dinner party – where men garlanded with flowers lay on their left side on a bank of chaises, drank, and engaged in "table talk." One of the first detailed accounts of a Greek-enophile drinking party is found in Plato's *Symposium*, in which Plato recounts a gathering whose guests included the poet Aristophanes, the drunken Alcibiades, and the wise Socrates. In Plato's *Symposium*, all the revelers examine their beliefs about and deliver their philosophies on love. Every *symposium* offered a different topic for dialogue, challenging the intellectual prowess and wit of the guests.[4]

---

[4] Erich Segal, *The Dialogues of Plato* (New York: Bantam Books, 1986); Plato, *Symposium*, trans. Seth Benardete (New York: Bantam Books), pp. 233–86.

Wine was a nudge in the right direction on the path to finding truth in fifth-century Greece. The thought-provoking format of the *symposium* supported conversations based on the tradition of philosophical questioning. As Pliny the Elder later remarked, "In wine, there is truth."[5] The finest truth-inducing vintages of the day came from Thasos, Lesbos, and Chios, all considered superior wines. But the *premier cru* was from Chios in Eastern Greece, dubbed the "Bordeaux of ancient Greece."[6]

Dionysiac imagery on the amphora does not merely allude to the vessel's function – it begets it. Delicately painted, abstract grape vines tangle around the vessel's body and climb up the handles of the amphora. Dionysus, like the grape, revealed himself seasonally and became a metaphor for birth, fertility, and resurrection in nature. The *symposium* commenced with a toast of undiluted wine to the gods, accompanied by hymns – normally only gods drank their wine "neat." During the course of a *symposium*, three *kraters* of wine were usually consumed: the first was dedicated to the gods, the second to heroes, and the third to Zeus himself.

Vessels wrapped with mythological and wine-drinking imagery were a form of aesthetic communication. Dionysus wears his requisite ivy crown and carries a *thyrsus*, or wooden staff with a pinecone finial. Reflecting Dionysus' association with pinecones, early Greek amphorae were lined with pine resin, which imparts a distinctive tang still favored in certain Greek wines today. A *krater*, or wine-mixing bowl, might feature illustrations of drinking contests between Dionysus and Heracles. Images of the human form closely reflected the athletically perfect, strapping young men of the time who drank the wine. The *krater* was the most important decorative focal point and was always placed at the center of the room. A *kylix* or *kantharos* (chalice) might reveal an image of the wedding feast of Dionysus when the cup was emptied. An *oinochoe* (pitcher) might feature libations being poured to Dionysus. The vessels were literally doused in mythological wine imagery, constant reminders of the "gift of the god" and the divine wine they contained.

---

[5]   ". . . veritas iam attributa vino est." Pliny the Elder, *Natural History* 14.141. Latin text available online at penelope.uchicago.edu/Thayer/E/Roman/Texts/PlinytheElder.
[6]   Johnson, *Story of Wine*, p. 25.

49

The first humble earthenware amphorae debuted in the eastern Mediterranean region over 2,000 years ago as everyday transport and workhorse vessels. But it is around 600 BCE that the wine amphora moves beyond pure functionality to a highly technical and beautiful vessel when it intersects with the powerful sway of classical Greek philosophy. The Nolan-style Greek amphora, with lines very similar to the vessel shown in Figure 3.1, was identified in the early 1900s as having the same underlying mathematical proportions that are found in the Parthenon.[7] The sixth-century Greek potters seemingly reiterated the aesthetics of classical Greece by achieving near mathematical proportions as they threw, turned, burnished, and coaxed this exquisite vessel into *symmetria prisca*, pure symmetry. The result is a perfect and most civilized shape to store the wine of the gods.

Classified: John Singer Sargent's A Dinner Table at Night

The founding father of gastronomic literature, Jean Anthelme Brillat-Savarin, writes in the opening pages of his book, *The Physiology of Taste*, "Tell me what you eat and I shall tell you what you are."[8] A brief consideration of John Singer Sargent's painting *Le Verre de Porto* or *A Dinner Table at Night* (1884), from the Fine Arts Museum of San Francisco, aptly answers the question, "Tell me what you drink and I shall tell you *who* you are," through a crystal stemmed glass held by his subject (Figure 3.2).

John Singer Sargent (1856–1925) was born in Italy into an expatriate American family, which moved frequently between Switzerland, Germany, and France. He attended various art schools and salons; beginning in 1874, he trained in the classical tradition in France at the Ecole des Beaux-Arts. Sargent developed a career mainly as a society portraitist, first in Paris and then in London, where he settled permanently. Sargent painted this portrait while visiting Mr. Albert Vickers and his wife Mrs. Edith Vickers, among his earliest patrons, at their home in Sussex.

---

[7] Jay Hambidge, *Dynamic Symmetry: The Greek Vase* (New Haven, CT: Yale University Press, 1920), p. 60.

[8] Jean Anthelme Brillat-Savarin, *The Physiology of Taste: Or, Meditations on Transcendental Gastronomy* (New York: Counterpoint, 1999; translation copyright 1949), p. 3.

Figure 3.2 John Singer Sargent, *Le Verre de Porto* (*A Dinner Table at Night*), 1884. Oil on canvas, 20 1/4 × 26 1/4 in. (51.4 × 66.7 cm). Gift of the Atholl McBean Foundation, 73.12. Photograph used with the permission of the Fine Arts Museums of San Francisco.

Portraiture is an art form representing or recording people. It involves more than depicting a face and figure: in Sargent's high-society world, it was modern image-making at its finest. The British tradition of portrait painting is known for its Grand Manner style, first conceived by Flemish-born Anthony van Dyck (1599–1641) and carried on by great artists such as Joshua Reynolds (1723–92) and Thomas Gainsborough (1727–88). Grand Manner-style paintings were usually large-scale portraits, designed to accentuate the subject's wealth or aristocratic status. In this age of materialism it was necessary to draw attention to the subject's status. Artists embedded visual metaphors into paintings: a dog was a symbol of fidelity, a book suggested intelligence, and a rose signified innocence. Continuing in that tradition, in his portrait of Mr. and Mrs. Vickers, Sargent selected a glass of red wine as a metaphor to fashion his subjects.

For years, art historians have questioned whether the crystal stem glass Mrs. Vickers holds is filled with claret or port. Not just any glass of table wine could be placed in a portrait during the Victorian era (1837–1901). Sargent titled the piece *Le Verre de Porto*, which translates literally as "the glass of port." But port was distinctly second rate in the eyes of the British. Claret was the English term for wines from Bordeaux and was the most favored wine among the English, who were Bordeaux's biggest single client, especially after the Anglo-French Treaty of 1860. Little short of a French–British embargo would have prevented a discerning hostess from pulling a bottle of claret from the cellar for a portrait. It certainly appears that Mrs. Vickers is holding a glass of claret, but it is possible that when Sargent titled the painting he may have been indulging in a bit of British one-upmanship.[9]

Mid-nineteenth-century gastronomic literature introduced to Victorians new tools to discern, judge, and classify what they ate and drank. Wine and food were now elevated to the status of fine arts. In 1846, Charles Cocks published what was widely dubbed the "Bordeaux Bible," *Bordeaux, Its Wines and the Claret Country*.[10] Then the great Bordeaux classification of 1855 carefully ranked estates, clearly distinguishing the most rarefied properties.[11] The English loved their claret, so much so that Lord Byron (1788–1824) turned claret into a verb in a letter to Thomas Moore: "We clareted and champagned till two."[12] "New French clarets" of the highest quality were among the most coveted. Among these were the first growths: Haut-Brion, Lafite, Latour, and Margaux. Now wine connoisseurs could judge and order each wine's relative position. Not surprisingly, a decanter of claret is prominently arranged front and center in the foreground of Sargent's painting. The Vickers' taste in fine wine is indisputable.

It is an after-dinner scene, in the dining room of the couple's home in Sussex, England. Mrs. Vickers is seated at the head of the table, holding a glass of claret. She is a beautiful woman, exuding the poise

9 Communications with Daniel Cornell, Curator of American Art and Director of Contemporary Art Projects at the Fine Arts Museums of San Francisco.
10 Johnson, *Story of Wine*, p. 198.
11 Personal communication with Paul Wagner, wine historian, Napa Valley College.
12 Cited in Hugh Johnson, *The Oxford Companion to Wine*, 2nd ed. (New York: Oxford University Press, 1999), p. 259.

of a cameo: dark hair, white skin, sinuous neck, red lipstick. She wears a low-cut black dress, with an opaque bodice and diaphanous long black sleeves. The carnation pink shade of the candle lamps casts a rosy glow on the entire scene. Dinner service has ended; the place settings have been cleared away. Mr. Vickers has moved from the head of the table to a guest's seat. He is seated, smoking his cigarette; his body is shown in half-profile, pushed to the margin of the painting by the artist.

Item by item, Sargent validates Mrs. Vickers as an epicurean collector. As in France's *ancien régime* or *noblesse d'épée*, such collectors in effect became, in Mennel's words, "specialists in the art of consumption, entrapped in a system of fine distinctions, status battle and competitive expenditure from which they could not escape because their whole identity depended upon it."[13] On the table covered with crisp white linen are precious wine vessels, made of finely wrought metals and crystal. Unlike the mathematical precision of a Dutch still-life painting, in this portrait Sargent offers his loose impressionist hand, adding a sense of intricacy to the objects without precise modeling. From the reflective surface of the silver wine cooler and cistern to the barely discernible water glasses, he picks up precisely the right amount of light on these most valuable objects, resulting in their illusory effects. The material world described by Mennell separates Mrs. Vickers from the sensual pleasures of eating and drinking; instead, these pleasures are masked behind the rigid decorum of the Victorian era.

The glass of wine provides the first clue to a multi-layered portrait filled with wine-bathed metaphors. Red shades of wine – garnet, burgundy, and crimson – spill throughout the canvas, evoking an emotional tone. The warm red colors of the painting, much like claret's uplifting effects, beckon love, passion, and convivial chatter. The body language is quite the opposite: Mr. Vickers looks away in complete corporate indifference. The woman gazes out across the table, looking lonely or lovelorn, certainly contemplating something much larger and less restricted. Before her are sources of material and sensual pleasure: beautiful wine vessels, the fine claret, and the "third person." The mark of a good portrait artist is the ability to

[13] As quoted in Jukka Gronov, *The Sociology of Taste* (London and New York: Routledge, 1997), p. 19.

catch what goes on behind the likeness of a subject and to convey meaning beyond what is immediately apparent. Sargent daringly paints what may be a truthful scene. The viewer of the painting assumes an uncomfortably intimate position as the third person at the dinner table, peering directly into the room and into the eyes of Mrs. Vickers.

The East: Vessels of Connection

The two "iconic" vessels that emerge from Chinese and Japanese rice wine cultures are a Chinese Shang dynasty bronze wine vessel and a Japanese Bizenware *sake* bottle. These two works are separated by over 3,000 years and they could not be more divergent, both materially and aesthetically. The common philosophical thread that brings the Chinese and the Japanese to the dining table is the search for harmony. Harmony pervades the beautiful – in the spirit world, on earth, and among humans.

The spirits are drunk: A Chinese bronze vessel

It is a natural impulse, when looking at a wine vessel, to imagine drinking from it. Shang dynasty bronze vessels, however, conjure tooth- and toe-breaking visions by their daunting scale. One of China's great masterpieces of the genre is the massive *Yayi jia* wine heater and pourer from Anyang, China, dated ca. 1300–1050 BCE, from the collection of the Asian Art Museum of San Francisco (Figure 3.3).

At thirty inches high and somewhere around thirty pounds, the sheer size of this bronze is an expression of its power. The cold, unyielding qualities of bronze were a fitting symbol for the enduring power and political authority of the Shang dynasty (1600–1050 BCE). The Shang dynasty marks the height of the Chinese Bronze Age and the shift from making pots to forging metal with extraordinary skill. Creation of these "architectonic" vessels required Chinese bronze workers to be a fusion of engineer, ceramicist, sculptor and metallurgist. The surface of the cylindrical body is densely packed with bas-relief decoration. The entire circumference is encircled by two bands of *taotie*, an abstract, dragon-like creature with gaping mouth, fangs, talons, and raised, flaring eyes. The handle is a gargoyle-like bovine devouring

54

Figure 3.3 Ritual wine vessel (*Yayi jia*), ca. 1300–1050 BCE, China, Henan Province. Shang dynasty (approx. 1600–1050 BCE). Bronze. The Avery Brundage Collection, Asian Art Museum of San Francisco, B61B11+. Photograph used with the permission of the Asian Art Museum of San Francisco.

a bird. Two umbrella-shaped pegs project from the rim, used to leverage the vessel for pouring and lifting. It sits on three splayed, blade-like legs, making it ideal for warming wine over a fire. The vessel is now the color of sea-foam green but when it was placed in a tomb over 3,000 years ago, it had the dazzle of a newly minted penny.

Few art objects can capture early Chinese collective notions of the world better than this *jia* wine heater and pourer. Elaborate wine and food offerings were essential to maintaining harmony in the kingdom and an absolute obligation to the ancestors, from whom the

Shang king derived his power. Shang royalty believed in a powerful synergy between the earthly and the heavenly realms, and they attributed natural phenomena, good or bad, to the handiwork of the spirit ancestors. Mediums, messengers, and intermediaries were vital to maintaining this precarious relationship with the spirit realm. Bronze ritual wine vessels weren't simply vessels for drinking. Ownership of ritual vessels by royalty was tantamount to the ability to access spirit ancestors and ensure the continued reign of the dynasty. Only royalty and clan leaders owned bronze vessels. The three types of objects made out of bronze in the Shang dynasty were odes to the sacred and profane: ritual vessels, chariot fittings, and weaponry. In the 2,200 years spanning the Chinese Bronze Age (twenty-first century BCE to the third century CE), it was the Shang royalty that produced the largest number and most impressive bronze vessels for wine drinking.

Together, wine and bronze vessels in ancient China were a springboard to the ancestors, and they constituted quite a combination. The wine was fermented from rice or millet. Wine styles at this early time included *chang*, *li*, and *jiu*, all various rice and millet beverages technically closer to a primitive beer. *Jiu* is the generic Chinese word for all alcoholic drinks; it is represented by a pictograph in the shape of an amphora. However, the deep ritual significance and poetic impulse associated with grain-based elixirs have resulted in the translation of the word in Chinese literature, poetry, and song as "wine." Shang wines were created with the use of a starter cake, called *qu*, which worked as a saccharification and fermenting catalyst. The cakes sometimes contained hundreds of herbs, and the result was a quite pungent (and perhaps pernicious) cocktail, infused with flower and herbal essences including chrysanthemum, mulberries, and pine resin.[14] Recent investigations into Shang dynasty wine have found quite a lethal combination of ingredients. They include traces of *Artemisia*, an ingredient similar to wormwood, which is found in absinthe, a fashionable drink among the European and American literati of the late nineteenth and early twentieth centuries. Heavy consumption of wormwood-infused beverages is speculated to have

[14] Patrick McGovern, "Fermented Beverages of Pre- and Proto-Historic China." *Proceedings of the National Academy of Sciences of the United States of America*, December 8, 2004 (www.pnas.org).

contributed to Van Gogh's madness. As if that were not sufficiently debilitating, the bronze vessels containing the wine were made of an amalgam of tin, lead, and copper: heating the wine no doubt laced the liquid with lead toxins.

An overarching belief in Chinese culture is that family encompasses the living and the dead. Metaphorically speaking, wine and food rituals brought the entire ancestral family to the dinner table. Wine and food offerings were presented in ancestral halls. During ritual ceremonies, an entire repertoire of bronze dining vessels containing wine, meat, and grain offerings was unveiled. Wine was warmed in *jia* vessels, such as the one depicted in Figure 3.3, and ladled out of a *you* wine bucket and drunk from trumpet-shaped *gu* cups. The rich, heady alcohol vapors wafted up to feed the heavens as the offerings were presented to the spirits. The wine and food would lure the spirits to earth and they would take the essence of the food and wine. The remaining food and wine were consumed in a feast. A certain degree of connoisseurship was in place during the Shang period. Sheep, pigs, and fine gifts of food and wine were sent from important people outside the family to the ruler.[15] In later Zhou dynasty rituals, family members would serve as spiritual messengers. When the ancestor spirit was pleased, the spiritual messenger spoke with the authority of the spirit: "The spirits enjoy the wine and food . . . the spirits are all drunk," as stated in the Chinese *Shijing*.[16] This symbiotic wine and food ritual with the spirit ancestors brought the dead and living together, reinforcing the social order and the well-being of the state. Gleaming bronze vessels and fine wine that satiated and pleased the ancestors were the recipe for harmony.

The art of imperfection: A Bizenware sake bottle

Rooted deeply in Japanese culture is the Shinto belief that *kami*, or spirits, live in all parts of nature: trees, rocks, and even rice. There is a fundamental reverence for the natural world that places people

---

[15] David E. Armstrong, "Drinking with the Dead: Alcohol and Altered States in Ancestor Veneration Rituals in Zhou Dynasty China and Iron Age Palestine." Dissertation. York University, Ontario, 1993, p. 51.

[16] Joseph R. Allen, *The Book of Songs (Shijing): The Ancient Chinese Classic of Poetry*, trans. Arthur Waley. *The Minor Odes, Poems 161–234* (New York: Grove Press, 1996), p. 195.

Figure 3.4 *Sake* bottle by Fujiwara Yu (1932–2001), Okayama Prefecture, Japan. Bizenware; unglazed stoneware. R2002.51.1. Asian Art Museum of San Francisco. Photograph used with the permission of the Asian Art Museum of San Francisco.

as part of nature rather than serving as a force to harness it. This same spirit is extended into the art of brewing rice wine, *nihonshu* or *sake* (a generalized term for alcoholic beverages), and the vessels designed to contain it. The Bizenware *sake* bottle by Fujiwara Yu (1932–2001), from the Asian Art Museum of San Francisco, shown in Figure 3.4, is a manifestation of the aesthetic principles embodied in Japanese philosophy.

The *sake* flask or *tokkuri* is the classic *sake* bottle shape: short, stout, with a flared neck and bulbous body. It is made of earthenware clay, fired at high temperatures for seven to ten days. It is a humble-looking bottle. The color is variegated, with constantly changing hues, from light beige and purple-red to chocolate brown. The style is highly distinctive of traditional pottery made in the Bizen

58

kiln. Bizenware was first made in the twelfth century and is from the famous "six old kilns," which include Seto, Tokoname, Shigarkai, Tamba, and Echizen. The potter, Fujiwara Yu, who potted this bottle in the 1970s–1980s, designed it in the traditional Bizen style. Yu was named a National Living Treasure, honored for his skill in preserving the traditional Bizen pottery craft.

If grape wine is Occidental, then rice wine is the wine of the Orient. China is the grandfather of rice wine; archaeological evidence identifies the Chinese as some of the first wine imbibers in the world, 9,000 years ago.[17] China's unique contribution to rice wine brewing techniques derives from use of the special fermentation cake, or *qu*, mentioned above. During the second to fourth centuries CE, this technique was shared with the Japanese, who expanded on it and developed their own version called *koji*, which is still used today.[18] The earliest mention of Japanese *sake* comes from the *Weizhi*, a Chinese text written during the third century.[19]

A Bizenware *sake* bottle is made of nothing but fire and clay; *sake* is made of nothing but fermented rice and water. To make *sake*, rice is polished, soaked, steamed, and broken down into a simple sugar by *koji*; yeast is added to promote fermentation; then it is pressed. This orchestration is performed by the *toji*, or *sake*-brewing master. The *Kinkafu* (918 CE), a collection of twenty-one Japanese songs, alludes to the revered process of rice winemaking in the song entitled *Drums to Mortars*:

> *Did they who made this wine*
> *Grind their rice*
> *In drums turned to mortars,*
> *Singing at their labor,*
> *Dancing at their labor?*
> *What a rare,*
> *A precious –*
> *A vintage wine!*[20]

[17]   McGovern, "Fermented Beverages of Pre- and Proto-Historic China."
[18]   H. T. Huang, *Science and Civilization in China*. Vol. VI: 5 (Cambridge: Cambridge University Press, 2000), p. 166.
[19]   Patricia Berger, *The Art of Wine in East Asia*. Exhibition catalogue (San Francisco: Asian Art Museum of San Francisco, 1985), p. 13.
[20]   *Festive Wine: Ancient Japanese Poems from the Kinkafu*, trans. Noah Brannen and William Elliott (New York and Tokyo: Weatherhill, 1971), song no. 20.

There is an inherently organic quality to making *sake* and pottery, which share a connection to nature and to place. Bizenware is made from rice-field clay, culled from the soil found under rice paddies. Both *sake* and pottery are geological expressions of an art form: a special humble quality is yielded by working with the earth. It is no wonder an old aphorism dating back to the Momoyama period (1573–1615) states that "Bizen *sake* flasks make *sake* better!" (*Bizen no tokkuri sake ga umai*).[21] The same variables that result in the infinite tastes and aromas of a glass of wine are as layered as the art that contains it. Both the hand that makes the art and the hand that makes the wine are inextricably connected to the place they are grown or made, the *terroir*. The art and wine are equally entwined with their philosophical *terroir*.

Bizenware is more than a *sake* container, it is a spiritual expression of the Zen Buddhist aesthetic philosophy of *wabi-sabi*. The literal translation is not clear cut. Perhaps the closest is "rustic-poverty." Leonard Koren describes *wabi-sabi* as "the beauty of things imperfect, impermanent, and incomplete."[22] Just a glance at the bottle gives visual clues about the philosophy. Its shape is irregular; its surface is grainy, cracked, and dry. Bizenware is unadorned. The only decoration comes from nature within the wood-fired kiln: red scorch marks when flame strikes the surface of the vessel; beige patches or veins where the vessel was untouched by flame; or the pebbly surface that results when kiln debris kicks up and lands on the shoulder of the vessel. What appears to be an accident was deliberately sought after by Japanese potters. The Greek aesthetic of symmetry and perfection do not apply. The British fondness for blue and white underglazed, highly ornate porcelains would have been considered to be hard, calculated, and regulated by a potter working in the Zen aesthetic. *Wabi-sabi* is a whisper; a Westerner's eyes may completely overlook or dismiss the bottle and consequently miss its soul.

Twelfth- to sixteenth-century Bizenware *sake* bottles were expressly created for the Japanese tea ceremony. The tea master Sen no Rikyu (1522–91) was instrumental in establishing the principles for the tea ceremony: harmony, respect, purity, and tranquility. These were the

[21]   Robert Yellin, Japanese Pottery Information Center. www.e-yakimono.net.

[22]   Leonard Koren, *Wabi-Sabi: For Artists, Designers, Poets and Philosophers* (Berkeley, CA: Stone Bridge Press, 1994), p. 7.

very qualities that appealed to the samurai, the professional warrior elite who became the aristocracy for nearly 700 years. The profession of war and battle is seemingly at odds with Zen Buddhism, which propounded non-violence; however, Zen's emphasis on self-discipline, austerity, and meditation appealed to the values of the samurai. With constant reminders of death on the battlefield, the samurai were keenly aware of life's impermanence.

The *kaiseki ryori* is the meal served before the tea at the end of a tea ceremony. Every element of the *kaiseki* is a communication of aesthetics: sight, sound, taste, and touch. The presentation of food, drink, and ceramics was designed to appeal to the eye as well as to the palate. Initially, the ceremony was conceived as a very austere, "one soup, two side dish" formulation designed for Buddhist monks. By the Muromachi (1333–1573) and Momoyama period, samurai arbiters of the ceremony expanded the *kaiseki* to many servings of food and *sake*. Teaware collecting rose to a near cult-like preoccupation among the samurai. This occurred to such an extent that *doboshu*, special aesthetic advisors to the samurai, counseled them on tea ware and other arts. Rosanjin, a famous epicurean potter, once said, "If clothes make the person, then dishes make the food."[23]

The samurai became patrons of the arts and arbiters of taste after the twelfth century. The best *sake* brews were destined for the samurai and wealthy merchants who hosted *kaiseki* dinners in their "mountain cottages" or "hermitages" in the inner gardens of their downtown villas.[24] *Sake* was warmed in an iron kettle, transferred to a *sake* bottle and poured into very small cups called *sakazuki*. Small cups encouraged moderate drinking and social interaction through the reciprocal tradition of pouring *sake* for others, called *oshaku*. *Sake* brewed in the Kobe area was sent up the Tokaido road along the eastern seaboard of Japan. Among the great cities of Japan, Edo (today's Tokyo) was the foremost city of *sake* connoisseurs – to such an extent that the term used for first-class *sake* (*kudari-zake*) meant "*sake* sent down" to Edo.[25]

---

[23] Ibid.
[24] Louise Allison Cort, "Japanese Ceramics and Cuisine," *Asian Art Magazine* (Winter, 1990): 12.
[25] Paula Swart, *Refreshment of the Spirit: Oriental Wine and Tea Vessels* (Montreal: Montreal Museum of Fine Arts, 1990), p. 28.

61

Over the course of Japanese history, *sake* has swung the full arc of the pendulum from the Shinto "drink of the gods" and offering to the *kami* (spirits) to a premium beverage on wine lists in top American restaurants. One factor remains constant: *sake* drinking inherently demands Zen values of acute awareness – sensitivity to sight, sound, taste, and touch. The Japanese word *kiku* is used when describing the taste of *sake*; it is also a homonym, meaning "to taste" and "to hear." The quality of fired clay is also described as *tsuchi-aji* or "flavor," which can only be discerned by years of touching and tasting from exquisite vessels. Today the *toji*'s experienced hands have coaxed *sake* to the peak of refinement in delicate tastes and aromas that can only be enjoyed when heard by the *wabi-sabi* whisper.

Conclusion

Spanning geography, time, and types of wine, four wine vessels from San Francisco's Fine Arts Museums and Asian Art Museum collections encapsulate the height of classic civilizations and artistic technical perfection in the West and the East and rise to the category of "iconic."

While the liquid elixirs have long since disappeared, the vessels in which they were served are still with us, offering intriguing insights into the reasons for their creation. All lend a curious and surprisingly close proximity to the mindscapes and winescapes from which they originated. From an archaic earthenware pot to a crystal stem glass, each and every person who drank from these vessels felt the power of the muse. This was true whether the "philosophical muse" breathed life into the making of a Bizenware *sake* bottle, evoked a sense of harmony and security through Chinese ancestor worship, exuded the aura of wealth and power for the British, or buttressed the rational thought process of a Greek aristocrat. Those beguiling muses who inspired poetry, song, and dance are ever-present in art, wine, and philosophy.

4

In Vino Sanitas

Frederick Adolf Paola

*Long ago, a gentleman was riding into town when he ran into
a most unusual sight. A young man was beating an old man!
The gentleman halted his horse in order to berate the young man.*

"How dare you hit that helpless old man!"

*The young man turned and replied, "This is my son who was
born when I was 80 years old! I told him to drink the wine but
he didn't take my advice. Now he has grown old before I have."*

*The gentleman bowed down in humility before the "young
man," asking what the miraculous drink might be.*[1]

In the above tale, the "miraculous drink" is a Korean rice wine infused
with oriental herbs. Tales referencing the salutary effects of wine, however, are not limited to rice wine.

In "The Wine Doctor," Ezio Delli Castelli, the wine doctor of Nocera
Terinese, practices the healing art of enopathy:

The author wishes to thank Michele and Gianni Rocca and the Odoardi Vineyards and
Winery (Azienda Agricola Odoardi) for their kindness during the preparation of this essay.
Odoardi is located in Nocera Terinese, a town in the province of Catanzaro, in the Calabria
region. In antiquity, Calabria was known as "Enotria," which translates roughly as "land
where vines are cultivated."

[1] www.cheersbekseju.com (accessed October 30, 2005).

A chemist who had made his living chiefly as an oenologist, a specialist in wine making, he was also a part-time oenopath, a practitioner of the unique healing art of oenopathy. Patients came to him with ailments of various sorts, and he prescribed a course of treatment with this particular wine or that. The wines he recommended depended, of course, upon the patient's diagnosis and circumstances. While he closely guarded his therapeutic secrets, it was thought that his prescriptions took into account the types of grapes that went into the wine; the composition of the soil from which the grapes had been harvested; how long they had been allowed to ferment before racking; and even the condition of the barrels in which the wine was stored.[2]

Consider, too, Nathaniel Hawthorne's tale "Dr. Heidegger's Experiment," in which the good doctor prevails upon four elderly acquaintances to quaff the "liquor of youth" in order that they might grow young again:

> While he spoke, Dr. Heidegger had been filling the four *champagne* glasses with the water of the Fountain of Youth. It was apparently impregnated with an effervescent gas, for little bubbles were continually ascending from the depths of the glasses, and bursting in silvery spray at the surface. As the *liquor* diffused a pleasant perfume, the old people doubted not that it possessed cordial and comfortable properties; and though utter skeptics as to its rejuvenescent power, they were inclined to swallow it at once . . . Assuredly there was an almost immediate improvement in the aspect of the party, not unlike what might have been produced by a glass of generous *wine*, together with a sudden glow of cheerful sunshine brightening over all their visages at once . . . Meanwhile, the three gentlemen behaved in such a manner as proved that the water of the Fountain of Youth possessed some *intoxicating* qualities . . .[3]

Were they drinking water, or something else? Certainly the references to wine are undeniable. Consider also that on the first Sunday of October, the Italian town of Marino (located near Rome in the Lazio region) celebrates the "Sagra dell'uva," or grape festival. The centerpiece of that celebration is a fountain that, at nightfall, turns from water into wine. Perhaps it was wine that flowed from Heidegger's Fountain of Youth, too?

Yet despite tales such as those above, everyone knows that, consumed in excess, alcohol in any form wreaks havoc upon the human body.

[2] Fred Paola, "The Wine Doctor," *Bellevue Literary Review* 4.2 (2004): 149–51; quotation at p. 149.
[3] www.eldrichpress.org/nh/dhe.html.

The list of ailments associated with its abuse reads like a textbook of internal medicine: Wernicke's syndrome, Korsakoff's syndrome, cerebellar degeneration, peripheral neuropathy, esophageal cancer, pancreatitis (acute and chronic), alcoholic hepatitis, cirrhosis, folic acid deficiency, hypertension, cardiomyopathy, testicular and ovarian atrophy, fetal alcohol syndrome, alcoholic myopathy, osteoporosis, and hormonal derangements.

So what precisely is the relationship between wine and health?[4]

The Doctrine of Temperance

In fact, the relationship between wine and health is best defined by the philosophical doctrine of temperance. Temperance (*sophrosyne* in Greek) refers to the practice of moderation. According to Plato, temperance was one of the four cardinal virtues, the others being justice, courage, and wisdom. For him, temperance meant subordinating the desire for pleasure to the dictates of reason. Aristotle understood each virtue as the mean between vicious extremes. Temperance, then, may be understood as the mean between the extremes of overindulgence and abstinence.

Temperance is also one of those virtues corresponding to the seven deadly sins or vices: pride, envy, wrath, sloth, avarice, gluttony, and lust. Specifically, temperance is that virtue corresponding to the sin/vice of *gluttony*, which refers to overindulgence in food, drink, or intoxicants, or excessive love of pleasure. In Dante Alighieri's *Divine Comedy*, the gluttonous are dealt with in the third circle of *Inferno* and on the sixth terrace of *Purgatorio*; and the moderate/temperate are rewarded in the seventh sphere of *Paradiso*.

Temperance is relevant, too, in Eastern philosophy. For example, it is one of the Five Precepts of Buddhism: "I will not be gluttonous or abuse intoxicants."[5] The Middle Way or Middle Path (another name for the Noble Eightfold Path or the way to the cessation of suffering)

---

[4] The reader is referred to a number of excellent reviews on the subject, including Kenneth J. Mukamal, MD, "Overview of the Risks and Benefits of Alcohol Consumption"; and Christine C. Tangney, PhD and Robert S. Rosenson, MD, "Cardiovascular Benefits and Risks of Moderate Alcohol Consumption." See www.uptodateonline.com (accessed October 30, 2005).

[5] www.gardendigest.com/zen/ten.htm (accessed September 7, 2006).

is often described as the practice of non-extremism, a path of moderation avoiding the Scylla of self-indulgence and the Charybdis of self-mortification. Likewise, followers of the ancient Chinese philosophy known as Taoism are called upon to develop the characteristics of love, moderation, and humility (the Three Jewels of the Tao).

Let me suggest at this point that the doctrine of temperance is closely related to the concept of *balance*, which refers to "a stable state characterized by the cancellation of all forces by equal opposing forces."[6] Balance is of central importance in Chinese philosophy and in the traditional Chinese medicine (acupuncture and herbology) grounded in that philosophy. The equal, opposing forces relevant here are Yin and Yang. To paraphrase Justice Potter Stewart (whose concern was with the concepts of pornography and obscenity), Yin and Yang are somewhat difficult to define, "but [we] know [them] when [we] see [them]."[7] Thus, Yin is darkness, Yang is light. Yin is rest, Yang is activity. Yin is matter, Yang is energy. Yin is water, Yang is fire. Yin is female, Yang is male. Yin and Yang are opposites, yet interdependent because they mutually consume each other (as water extinguishes a fire, yet fire can turn water to steam) and because they are capable of transforming into one another (as day changes into night). Disturbances of health arise when the balance between these two opposing forces is disrupted:

> All clinical manifestations arise from a separation of *Yin* and *Yang*. In health, *Yin* and *Yang* are harmoniously blended in a dynamic balance. When *Yin* and *Yang* are so balanced, they cannot be identified as separate entities, hence signs and symptoms do not appear. For example, if *Yin* and *Yang* ... are balanced, the face will have a normal, pink, flourishing colour and will be neither too pale nor too red, nor too dark, etc. If *Yin* and *Yang* are out of balance, they become separated; there will be either too much of one or the other, and the face will be either too pale (excess of *Yin*) or too red (excess of *Yang*). *Yin* and *Yang* therefore show themselves as they are out of balance. One can visualize the *Yin–Yang* Supreme Ultimate symbol [the *Tai Ji*] spinning very fast: in this case the white and black colour will not be visible because they cannot be separated by the eye. Similarly, when *Yin* and *Yang* are balanced and moving harmoniously, they cannot be separated, they are not visible and signs and symptoms will not arise.

---

[6] *Roget II: The New Thesaurus* (New York: Berkley Books, 1988), p. 40.
[7] *Jacobellis v. Ohio*, 378 US 184, 197 (1964).

> All symptoms and signs can be interpreted in this way, as a loss of balance of *Yin* and *Yang* . . . [If] *Yin* and *Yang* are balanced, urine will be of a normal pale-yellow colour and of normal amount. If *Yin* is in excess, it will be very pale nearly like water and profuse; if *Yang* is in excess, it will be rather dark and scanty.[8]

Consumption of wine is not *per se* provocative of imbalance, but "*excessive* consumption of alcohol," while creating "a pleasant euphoria (*Yang*) . . . is quickly followed by a hang-over (*Yin*)."[9] It is perhaps not coincidental that *conoscitori* (i.e., connoisseurs) of wine refer to the harmonious relationship between a wine's constituents (e.g., acids, sugars, tannins, alcohol) as "balance," as in the phrase, "This wine is well balanced." The very fact that the quality of a wine depends upon such balance is symbolic of the relationship between wine and health.

Temperance and the J-Shaped Curve

Just how does the philosophical doctrine of temperance define the relationship between wine and health? It does so via the J-shaped curve that describes the relationship between alcohol intake and total or "all-cause" mortality.

If one plots the risk of dying on the *y* (vertical) axis against alcohol consumption on the *x* (horizontal) axis, the curve produced is J-shaped – meaning that moderate drinkers outlive both teetotalers and heavy drinkers, and that teetotalers outlive heavy drinkers. (Were the latter not true, the curve would be U-shaped rather than J-shaped.) The lowest mortality risk occurs at the level of about one to two drinks per day.

Much of the favorable effect of moderate drinking on overall or all-cause mortality is likely due primarily to the protective effects of alcohol consumption on coronary heart disease and ischemic stroke, which are discussed below. The higher risk of death in heavy drinkers, on the other hand, is due to an increased risk of cancer (including oropharyngeal, esophageal, laryngeal, liver, and breast

---

[8]   G. Maciocia, *Foundations of Chinese Medicine* (Edinburgh: Churchill Livingstone, 1989), pp. 10–11.
[9]   Ibid., p. 14.

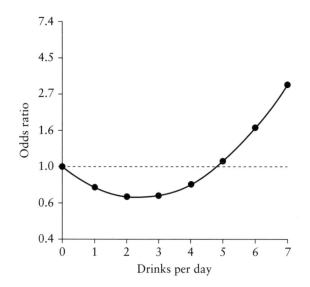

Figure 4.1 The J-shaped relationship between wine drinking and health.

cancers), liver disease, heart disease (cardiomyopathy, hypertension, and arrhythmias), hemorrhagic stroke, addiction, and accidents.

Furthermore, the benefits of moderate wine drinking vis-à-vis abstinence are reflected not only in terms of total mortality, but also in terms of lower mortality related to coronary artery disease, stroke, and cancer. Additionally, wine has been reported to decrease the incidence of kidney stones; to eradicate the bacteria responsible for food poisoning and diarrhea; to enhance insulin sensitivity; to enhance resistance to certain strains of the common cold; to be associated with a lower incidence of rheumatoid arthritis in women; and to be of benefit to cognitive function.

> "Un gotto fa bene, due non nuocciono, ti rovina un boccale."
>
> "A goblet of wine does you good, two do no harm, a jug ruins you."
> (Italian proverb)

It should be emphasized at this point that studies on the health effects of wine are confounded by a number of factors.

First, assessment of drinking status is often based on self-report; but in a 1996 Italian study, self-report was shown to be, as any clinician could have told them, unreliable. Thus, 30 percent of persons who characterized themselves as non-drinkers on a questionnaire were in fact drinkers according to dietary diaries.

Figure 4.2 An ancient Latin dictum, photographed at a winery in Sicily, which translates as: "Who never drinks wine is a lamb; who drinks it properly is a lion; who drinks too much is a pig." Photo courtesy of Alfonso Cevola.

Second, studies generally estimate average daily consumption and disregard how or when the alcohol was consumed. Yet in weighing the health pros and cons of wine drinking, the "how" and "when" may matter, a fact that, I submit, further illustrates the link between temperance and wine in health. From a health standpoint, drinking two glasses of wine a day every day is not the same as drinking fourteen glasses of wine on Saturday night and abstaining the rest of the week. Thus, in the wine-drinking cultures – which include Italy, Spain, Portugal, and France – wine consumption is higher than in the US.[10]

[10] See Jonathor Alsop, "On and Off the Wagon: Wine and the American Character," pp. 30–1 in this volume.

69

Binge and underage drinking, however, are less of a problem, possibly because of cultural considerations – including emphasis on mealtime consumption.

Third, the drinking habits of individuals, and thus their average daily consumption, change over time.

Finally, the health effects of wine must be distinguished from those of alcoholic beverages in general – which include not only wine but also beer and spirits. Studying the health benefits of wine vis-à-vis other alcoholic beverages is further complicated by the fact that wine drinkers tend to have more healthful lifestyles (diet, smoking status), to be better educated, and to enjoy a higher socioeconomic status than their beer-belting and spirit-swigging colleagues. In other words, the fact that an association exists between wine drinking and lower all-cause mortality does not prove that wine drinking is the cause of the lower all-cause mortality. It remains possible that the wine drinking is simply linked to the actual cause of the lower mortality.

The relationship between wine and health is, then, as we shall see, complex, as befits a beverage that is itself complex. Complexity is not, however, disagreeable. Indeed, "some would say that only what is somehow complex – what displays variation without being purely random – is worthy of interest."[11]

Cardiovascular Disease

Cardiovascular disease is the leading cause of death among adults in the United States. The National Institute on Alcohol Abuse and Alcoholism (NIAAA) in its 2004 Report on Moderate Drinking, found:

> In numerous studies . . . differing considerably in their adjustments for confounding risk factors, the data on [coronary heart disease]-related death are remarkably consistent: the relationship between alcohol consumption and mortality follows a J-shaped . . . curve, with one to four drinks daily significantly reducing risk and five or more drinks daily significantly increasing risk.[12]

---

[11] en.wikipedia.org/wiki/Complexity (accessed September 7, 2006).

[12] L. Gunzerath, V. Faden, S. Zakhari, and K. Warren, "National Institute on Alcohol Abuse and Alcoholism Report on Moderate Drinking," *Alcoholism: Clinical and Experimental Research* 28.6 (2004): 829–47; quotation at p. 831.

Reductions in coronary heart disease (CHD) mortality are seen in both men and women who drink moderately, with benefits first appearing when drinking exceeds about one drink a day for women and one and a half drinks a day for men, respectively. However, this cardioprotective effect is not a simple function of the *amount* of alcohol consumed. Thus, given two individuals who drink the same amount of wine on a weekly basis, the one who drinks smaller amounts more frequently will have a lower cardiac risk, all other things being equal, than the one who drinks greater amounts less frequently.

The existence of a J-shaped curve means that there are cardiovascular risks associated with heavy alcohol consumption, and that those risks exceed the "risks" associated with teetotalism. Thus, consistently heavy drinking may lead to alcoholic cardiomyopathy, an impairment of the heart muscle's pumping ability. Alcoholic cardiomyopathy typically occurs in men who have regularly consumed more than five drinks a day for more than ten years. Further, heavy episodic drinking is associated with a significantly increased risk of CHD.

> "Se bevi vino prenderai forza, ma se troppo ne berrai la perderai."
>
> "If you drink wine you will gain strength, but if you drink too much you will lose it."
>
> (Italian proverb)

How does moderate drinking protect against cardiovascular disease? A substantial portion of the protective effect has been attributed to alcohol-induced increases in HDL cholesterol ("good cholesterol"), although there is also a decrease in LDL ("bad cholesterol"). The existence of the French Paradox, however, suggests that other mechanisms are involved. Thus, between 1965 and 1988, it was noted that among twenty-one developed nations France had the second lowest CHD mortality despite having serum HDL concentrations no higher than in other countries. France did, however, boast the highest wine intake over the same period.

Thus, it has been suggested that wine might protect against CHD by interfering with blood clotting. Blood clotting is controlled by clotting factors (proteins) and platelets (cells). Alcohol alters the balance between clotting factors and anti-clotting factors, favoring the latter. Furthermore, wine appears to have antiplatelet effects that may be mediated by *polyphenols*. Polyphenols are antioxidants derived from the skins, seeds, and stems of grapes. It is said that there are approximately two hundred different types of polyphenols in each glass of wine, including trans-resveratrol, catechins, procyanidin, myricetin,

71

and quercetin. Polyphenols have been found to relax the smooth muscle in arteries, thus dilating them; to inhibit the aggregation or "stickiness" of platelets over and above the effect of alcohol itself; and to raise levels of vitamin E (an anti-oxidant) and reduce the oxidizability of LDL cholesterol, effects which might also be cardioprotective.

> "The wine had such ill effects on Noah's health that it was all he could do to live 950 years. Just nineteen years short of Methuselah. Show me a total abstainer that ever lived that long."
> Will Rogers (1879–1935)

Interestingly, ethyl alcohol (ethanol) itself, as opposed to wine, tends to *lower* blood levels of vitamin E, and has a pro-oxidant effect. These distinctions are likely clinically significant, since the phenomenon of *rebound hyperaggregability* – i.e., the ischemic strokes and sudden death sometimes seen after episodes of drunkenness – are reportedly not seen after acute wine consumption.

Cancer

Considering all cancers combined, an American Cancer Society study of middle-aged men found that mortality from cancer was significantly lower among those who consumed up to one drink a day, as compared with abstainers. The mechanism for this effect is unclear, but may have to do with wine's polyphenol content.

Carcinogenesis, or the development of cancer, can be divided into three distinct stages: *initiation*, *promotion*, and *progression* (malignant conversion). A 1997 study reported that the polyphenol resveratrol (see Figure 4.3) has anti-initiation, anti-promotion, and anti-progression activity in mice.

For example, 25 μmol of resveratrol given with a tumor promoter decreased the number of skin tumors by 98 percent and decreased

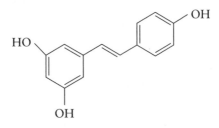

Figure 4.3 Molecular structure of the polyphenol resveratrol.

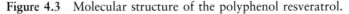

the number of mice with tumors by 88 percent. In a 1996 study, investigators fed dehydrated, dealcoholized red wine solids to mice that spontaneously develop visible tumors, then recorded the ages at which the first tumors developed. They found that the wine solid supplement delayed tumor onset.

It has been reported that drinking a glass of red wine a day may reduce a man's risk of prostate cancer by half and that the protective effect appears to be strongest against the most aggressive forms of the disease. According to a 2005 study of 753 men with newly diagnosed prostate cancer and 703 matched controls – all between forty and sixty-four years of age – the risk of developing prostate cancer decreases linearly as red wine consumption increases. Each additional glass of red wine consumed per week was associated with a 6 percent decrease in prostate cancer risk. In contrast, no statistically significant association – positive or negative – was found between prostate cancer and consumption of beer, spirits, or alcohol in general.[13]

With regard to colorectal neoplasia, a 2005 study of 2,291 patients presenting for screening colonoscopy queried them about risk factors for colorectal neoplasia and about their drinking habits. Interestingly, the study found that compared to teetotalers, study participants who habitually consumed more than eight servings of spirits or beer per week were more likely to have a "significant colorectal neoplasm" (defined for study purposes as including adenocarcinoma, high-grade dysplasia, villous tissue, adenomas 1 cm or greater and multiple (>2) adenomas of any size) discovered at colonoscopy. In contrast, those who had habitually consumed one to eight servings of wine per week were less likely than teetotalers to have a significant colorectal neoplasm discovered at colonoscopy.[14]

Even the relationship between wine and cancer, however, illustrates the importance of moderation. Thus, associations have been reported between drinking and certain head and neck cancers, as well as esophageal cancer, and the risk appears to increase directly with

[13] W. M. Schoonen, C. A. Salinas, L. A. Kiemeney, and J. L. Stanford, "Alcohol Consumption and Risk of Prostate Cancer in Middle-Aged Men," *Int. J. Cancer* 113.1 (2005): 133–40.

[14] J. C. Anderson, Z. Alpern, G. Sethi, et al., "Prevalence and Risk of Colorectal Neoplasia in Consumers of Alcohol in a Screening Population," *Am. J. Gastroenterology* 100.9 (2005): 2049.

the level of consumption. It is unfortunate for our purposes here that in most of the relevant studies, "moderate" drinking was not studied. Thus, in an Italian study from 2000, non-drinkers and moderate drinkers (less than three drinks a day) were lumped together and compared with those who drank more heavily. It would have been nice to know how the moderate drinkers fared vis-à-vis the non-drinkers. The study did find, however, that even wine-only heavy drinkers were at increased risk for developing esophageal cancer, and that the cancer risk increased as the level of consumption increased.

With regard to breast cancer, the 2004 NIAAA Report on Moderate Drinking cited above found that "alcohol may be associated with an increase in the risk of breast cancer in the population overall but that the relative effect of moderate consumption is small."[15]

The effect, if any, of moderate alcohol consumption on other types of cancer, including colorectal, pancreatic, hepatocellular, and lung cancer, is uncertain.

Cerebrovascular Accidents

Cerebrovascular accidents (i.e., strokes or CVAs) are the third leading cause of death in the United States. The relationship between drinking and stroke depends both on the type of stroke under consideration and on the level of alcohol consumption.

Ischemic strokes, which result from blood flow impairment as a result of atherosclerosis and blood clots, account for most CVAs. *Hemorrhagic* strokes (i.e., "bleeds") account for about 10 to 15 percent of all cases.

Alcohol's cerebrovascular effects are mediated in part by its tendency to raise blood pressure and its tendency to discourage blood clotting. The level of consumption likely determines which of these effects is ascendant.

Heavy drinkers (about five drinks a day) are at increased risk for both ischemic and hemorrhagic strokes compared to non-drinkers. In contrast, moderate drinking decreases the risk of ischemic stroke via a J-shaped curve. While some studies have found a J-shaped

---

[15] Gunzerath et al., "NIAAA Report on Moderate Drinking," p. 833.

relationship between moderate drinking and hemorrhagic stroke as well, this is more controversial.

Dementia

The two most common types of dementia in Western countries are Alzheimer's dementia (AD) and vascular dementia (VD). Low to moderate alcohol consumption appears to decrease the risk of VD. Whether moderate alcohol consumption decreases the risk of AD is in dispute.

Prolonged excessive alcohol intake has been associated with an increased risk of dementia.

Diabetes

The relationship between alcohol intake and the risk of developing type 2 diabetes (non-insulin-dependent diabetes mellitus, or NIDDM) is J-shaped as well. Moderate drinking reduces the risk of type 2 diabetes in both men and women, with the risk being approximately one-third lower than in teetotalers. This benefit seems to derive from the insulin-sensitizing action of alcohol. Regular moderate alcohol consumption is associated with decreased insulin resistance, though the exact mechanism for this insulin-sensitization remains unresolved.

On the other hand, heavy drinking is associated with an increased risk of diabetes. Persons who frequently drink large amounts of alcohol are at risk for the development of chronic pancreatitis, a process which can gradually destroy the pancreas. Because of the central importance of the insulin-secreting beta-cells of the endocrine pancreas in glucose homeostasis, glucose intolerance is seen not infrequently in chronic pancreatitis, with overt pancreatic diabetes usually appearing late in the course of disease.

Nephrolithiasis ("Kidney Stones")

A 1996 study of 45,000 men aged forty to seventy-five and without any history of kidney stones found that during six years of follow-up the risk of stone formation decreased by the following amounts for each 8 ounce serving consumed daily: wine, 39 percent; beer, 21 percent; tea, 14 percent; and coffee, 10 percent. In contrast, for each 8 ounce serving consumed daily, the risk of stone formation increased 35 percent for apple juice and 37 percent for grapefruit juice. A similar study done in women and reported two years later reported a 59 percent decrease in the incidence of kidney stones for each 8 ounce serving of wine consumed daily.

Cholelithiasis ("Gallstones")

Similarly, moderate alcohol intake lowers the risk of gallstones in men and women. On the other hand, the high prevalence of gallstones in patients with alcoholic cirrhosis suggests that drinking heavily enough to cause liver disease may actually increase the risk of cholelithiasis, again illustrating the importance of temperance to the relationship between wine and health.

Liver Disease

Does the J-shaped relationship between wine drinking and health hold true in the context of liver disease? In other words, is drinking wine in moderate amounts better for the liver than not drinking at all? That would seem to be asking for almost too much. After all, everyone knows that alcohol is associated with liver disease; but while chronic heavy alcohol consumption does indeed lead to the development of liver disease with its attendant morbidity and mortality, the actual level of alcohol consumption required to produce that liver disease is uncertain. There is evidence to suggest that at least five drinks a day over at least five years is needed for the development of cirrhosis; and reportedly, studies in animals show no significant effects with moderate levels of alcohol consumption.

But what about any evidence that the livers of temperate drinkers fare better than those of teetotalers? Is such evidence to be had? In fact, it has recently been reported that while heavy alcohol consumption impairs liver regeneration in rats, light alcohol consumption enhances liver regeneration by unknown mechanisms.

76

Conclusions

The relationship between wine and health, though characterized by the same complexity that characterizes wine itself, is best defined by the philosophical doctrine of temperance. Temperance may be understood as the mean between the extremes of overindulgence and abstinence. Defining temperate or moderate drinking in any particular individual, however – in other words, deciding what constitutes moderate drinking for that individual – is a fact-intensive, individualized inquiry that depends on a number of factors, including the individual's age, sex (and, if female, gestational status), size, medical condition, occupation, and family history.

Epilogue

Mention *The Days of Wine and Roses* and I suppose that most people would recall the 1962 film starring Jack Lemmon and Lee Remick as Joe and Kirsten Arneson Clay, a young couple who spiral into the abyss of alcoholism. That the film took its name from a line in Ernest Dowson's poem "Vitae Summa Brevis" might seem fitting, considering that the poet died prematurely at the age of thirty-three, allegedly of alcohol abuse.

In the context of the poem, however, the words "days of wine and roses" have an altogether different meaning:

> VITAE SUMMA BREVIS SPEM NOS VETET INCOHARE LONGAM
> They are not long, the weeping and the laughter,
> Love and desire and hate;
> I think they have no portion in us after
> We pass the gate.
> They are not long, the days of wine and roses:
> Out of a misty dream
> Our path emerges for a while, then closes
> Within a dream.
>
> Ernest Dowson (1867–1900)[16]

---

[16] www.4literature.net/Ernest_Dowson/Vitae_Summa_Brevis_Spem_Nos_Vetat_Inco/ (accessed September 7, 2006).

In Vino Sanitas

The "days of wine and roses" are the days of our lives; and if they be few in number (as they are for even the longest-lived among us), then all the more reason to cherish them in all their aspects – negative ("weeping") and positive ("laughter"), spiritual ("love" and "hate") and sensual ("wine and roses").

Cincin! E salute!

II

Tasting & Talking
about Wine

5

Mmmm . . . not Aha!
Imaginative vs. Analytical Experiences of Wines

John Dilworth

I shall argue that the highly enjoyable experiences associated with drinking good wines have been widely misunderstood. It is common to regard wine appreciation as an *analytical* or *quasi-scientific* kind of activity. Wine experts, in well-publicized comparative tasting sessions, carefully distinguish the precise sensory qualities of each wine, and then pass on their accumulated factual knowledge to less experienced wine enthusiasts. However, this analytical or purely factual model of wine appreciation is seriously defective. One good way to show its defects is to provide a better and more fundamental scientific account of what is involved in wine appreciation. In order to do so, I outline a novel, evolutionarily based theory of perceptual consciousness that explains why there must be *imaginative* as well as analytical kinds of experiences of wines. In addition, imaginative wine experiences, unlike typical imaginative artistic experiences, may be shown to involve highly individualistic, *improvisatory* elements that help to give wine drinking a unique place among the recreational arts.

What It Is Like to Consciously Experience a Wine

How could the conscious experience of the captivating sensory qualities of a great chardonnay or pinot noir be explained in broadly scientific terms? This is a wine-centric version of what is generally considered to be a central problem in the philosophy of mind, namely that of the nature of consciousness. Also, it is easy to forget

81

that the problem has not one, but two inseparably related dimensions. Not only are we conscious of particular sensory qualities of flavor, aroma and bouquet, tactile qualities, and visual appearance when drinking a wine. In addition, there is *something it is like* to experience those qualities. The nature of our own conscious enjoyment of those rewarding sensory qualities of a good wine is also part of what needs to be explained. I shall argue that this second element of personal appreciation is central to understanding why good wines are so highly prized, and that standard views of wine drinking are seriously deficient because they neglect it.

As for the issue of the nature of conscious experience, I do have a novel explanation to suggest, which works in part by breaking down the problem into manageable chunks. It is easy to forget that a wine, even one of high quality, may be consumed in a routine or habitual fashion – such as when lunching with friends, when the focus is on the conversation rather than on the wine or food. In such cases one may have little or no conscious appreciation of the qualities of the wine, nor any very definite conscious experience of what it is like to drink it. Nevertheless, it must be true that one has at least a *routine* kind of low-level or background kind of perception of the qualities of the wine in such cases. For doubtless you would instantly notice if the wine was spoiled, or if it had a different taste from its usual smooth excellence, or if it no longer went with the foods that it would otherwise complement. So the problem of explaining conscious appreciation of wines is only an *incremental* problem. It is the problem of what needs to be *added* to routine or background kinds of perception so as to explain the specifically conscious aspects of wine perception. We do not also have to explain what perception itself is – that can be taken for granted, or left to cognitive scientists.

Another manageable chunk of the problem of consciousness is implicit in the above discussion. If routine or habitual perception involves little or no conscious awareness, then presumably what makes some perceptual experiences of wine conscious is that they involve *non*-routine or *non*-habitual kinds of perception of those sensory qualities. But then we can reduce the problem of explaining the nature of conscious perceptual experience of wines to the problem of explaining what it is to perceive a wine in non-routine or non-habitual ways. In order to have a blanket term, I will describe all such cases as involving *sophisticated* rather than routine perception.

Now any scientifically respectable general account of sophisticated perception, or perceptual consciousness, would have to eventually include an explanation of its potential evolutionary advantages to creatures possessing it. By putting the emphasis on the sophisticated or non-routine aspects of conscious perception, this problem becomes more tractable. My suggestion is that sophisticated perception is typically *problem-solving* perception. Routine, non-conscious perception does not solve any problems, it just routinely collects information and uses it in routine ways. Those creatures capable, in addition, of using perception to find solutions to problems facing them would presumably have an evolutionary advantage over other creatures that lacked such perceptual problem-solving abilities.

For example, if a hungry chimpanzee can see a banana high in a tree, and see a nearby stick, and be prompted by these perceptions to knock down the banana using the stick, then the chimp would have engaged in a potentially evolutionarily advantageous form of perceptual problem solving. In such a case, the function of the chimp's perceptual processes would not just be that of routine information collection about bananas and sticks, but it would also include the function of that information *prompting the chimp to fully engage all of its problem-solving abilities* in an effort to figure out how to get the banana. My claim is that in general, perception becomes conscious when it prompts the perceiver to engage in some such sophisticated problem-solving activities, and, as illustrated, potentially there may be evolutionary support for this claim. I will call this the *self-prompting* view of consciousness, since according to it, a perception becomes conscious when it *prompts the perceiver herself to engage in sophisticated problem solving*. Of course, the possible level of sophistication depends on the general level of abilities of the species in question.

But how would this self-prompting theory apply to what apparently are purely sensory kinds of perception, such as those involved in wine drinking? It might look as if the cautious, but hopeful, experience of the first taste of an untried but well-recommended bottle of cabernet sauvignon is far removed from issues of problem solving, or of the survival of species. However, consider the evolutionary importance of tastes. Slight differences in taste of one item over another, such as in the eating of different kinds of mushroom, might make all the difference between eating a nutritious food and consuming a deadly poison. Also, as we all know, it is easy to casually swallow food items, such as cooked meats or eggs, without really paying any conscious attention to whether they taste completely fresh or not, and hence to suffer the consequences of food poisoning in some cases. As for wines, during the early history of our species all kinds of experiments with a wide variety of natural substances mixed into naturally fermenting liquids must have occurred, and taste would have been a significant indicator of potential risk versus benefit.

An analytical, fully conscious attention to tastes as such presumably involves, among other things, a very thorough cognitive search of memories of previous good versus questionable tastes, and a consideration of general principles of cautious eating and drinking, including a rough calculation of the potential benefits versus costs of consuming the particular item in question. Any such activities would involve the workings of sophisticated problem-solving abilities that are mainly unavailable to perceivers during episodes of more routine, non-conscious kinds of perception. Hence our current abilities to consciously experience the pleasantly astringent taste of a good riesling, or the extended depths of flavor of a choice syrah, have their roots in evolutionary contingencies and perceptual problem-solving abilities, even if the most salient evolutionary risk/benefit factors are no longer operative in current societies.

Nevertheless, if the current self-prompting view is correct, conscious perceptual or sensory experience of any kind always has been, and still is, a form of perceptually prompted sophisticated problem solving. So more needs to be said as to how this approach could help to explain our everyday enjoyable experiences of wines.

Evolutionary Factors in the Enjoyment of Wines

The problem of consciousness is a hard problem because it has many dimensions. So far we have made some progress in explaining what it is to be conscious of some perceptual or sensory qualities. But as of now, we have no account of what makes some special wines worthy of great enthusiasm, nor of what is involved in more common cases of enjoyment of the qualities of a good wine. As a case in point, the earlier, evolutionary argument as to how conscious experience of the flavors of wines might be a vital factor in avoiding health

84

risks – in drinking miscellaneous fermented liquids – does nothing to explain why the healthy wines might taste better than the potentially dangerous ones. The highly specific sensory pleasures associated with the drinking of a few special wines still need to be explained, even if we have potentially succeeded in explaining, in generic terms, the evolutionary origins of conscious experience of any kind.

At this point some much broader evolutionary considerations must be introduced. Human feelings of delight, attraction, and enjoyment initially earned their evolutionary keep as reinforcers of survival-enhancing behaviors such as conquering enemies, achieving success in food distribution in a tribe, and other problem-solving activities of every kind – all activities closely related to consciousness. But once the relevant cognitive and affective mechanisms were in place, they became available for reuse in entertainment, artistic activities, and play – in *recreation*, in a word. Such recreational activities also have a more indirect survival value in maintaining and enhancing mental health and cognitive abilities even when no immediate, real-world problems have to be solved. So the apparent mystery about how some wines can cause intense enjoyment, or even passion, is not as inexplicable as it might initially seem. It is not the intense feelings as such that need to be explained, because such manifestations under *some* recreative circumstances are an inevitable byproduct of the relevant evolutionary mechanisms. Creatures incapable of intense feelings under a wide variety of circumstances, and of the motivations integrally involved in them, would not survive. So the problem may be characterized as follows: why does wine in general, and then *this* wine rather than *that* wine, trigger such strong emotional reactions?

This problem too may be broken down further. Consciousness is, on the present account, a problem-solving perceptual mechanism, and given the vast range of problems needing to be solved in order to ensure survival, character traits such as wide-ranging curiosity and inquisitiveness are at a premium. (For example, Alexander Fleming would never have discovered penicillin if he had not been curious about the strange activity on one of his culture plates.) Now the early discovery of alcoholic, wine-like liquids was inevitable in human society, because their existence depends only on naturally occurring fermentation processes associated with the gathering and storage of fruits and berries. Since the consumption of food and liquids is biologically necessary for survival in any case, *some* foods and drinks

85

that are readily available in typical environments must have a potentially attractive taste that behaviorally prompts further consumption of them. Since wines are derived from nutritious fruits and berries that do have an attractive taste, it is no surprise that wines in general have tastes that are positively regarded by most consumers of them.

Also, the tastes associated with wines must have become the object of the above-mentioned widespread curiosity and investigation. Later searches for a better-tasting wine by careful choice of grape, *terroir*, and cultivation methods uses the same analytical problem-solving skills as the search for the solution to any other more central human problem. Consequently, it is no accident, or mystery, why some wines are generally agreed to taste much better than others, since those results stem from intensive investigations over many hundreds of years by thousands of highly motivated individuals, whose whole careers depend on convincing a buying public of the superior attractiveness of their products – a public which is already biologically predisposed, as discussed above, to be favorably attracted toward wines in general.

The Place of Imagination and Representation in Wine Experiences

The overall picture of how wines are able to achieve their remarkable experiential effects on wine drinkers is not yet complete. Yet another broad factor must be introduced into the discussion, which will serve to unify the other factors into a satisfying explanatory whole. To begin, recall that the sophisticated problem-solving approach to conscious experience is basically defended in terms of its contributions to evolutionary fitness. Then, as a byproduct, the experiential aspects of leisure or recreational activities such as wine drinking are explained in terms of reuse of the preexisting cognitive powers which were primarily shaped by the relevant evolutionary forces. But it yet remains to be explained exactly *how* recreational activities reuse those cognitive powers in a way relevant to wines.

Some useful analogies can be found in the arts, which constitute a whole category of recreational activities in their own right. In broad terms, artistic meaning is imaginative or representational meaning that reuses human cognitive and affective powers in a kind of trade-off.

86

Pictures, novels, music, theater pieces, dances, and so on can provide a much broader range of kinds of meaningful experience than more everyday, practical or prosaic experiences. But the cost of this increased expressive power of the arts is that the kinds of meaning achieved are only *imaginative* or *representational* rather than literal or real. The thrilling victories or bittersweet love experienced while one watches a good film are not experiences of anything real, and the tempestuous emotions felt in listening to a late Beethoven string quartet have no reality independent of the immediate experience of them by a sensitive listener.

Nevertheless, clearly it would be a serious mistake to confuse the rich experiential meaning of a passage in a Beethoven string quartet with the purely sensory configuration of heard sounds, by means of which those meanings are conveyed to a receptive listener. The listener must, in some broad sense, be attaching a representational or imaginative *meaning* to the sounds, even though there is no literal or easily describable way to specify what the sounds mean or represent independent of the listener's experience of them. I claim that an analogous distinction holds for the receptive wine drinker's experience of a great wine. In that case too it would be a serious mistake to confuse the rich experiential meaning of the flavors and aromas of a wine with the purely sensory configuration of those tastes and aromas themselves. With wine as with music, it is not the sensory qualities as such, but rather what they *represent* – in the relevant broad, non-literal sense being appealed to – that constitutes their experiential meaning.

Some cases of abstract painting, such as the works of Wassily Kandinsky, or of Pablo Picasso during his cubist period, also provide helpful analogies. A purely literal account of the visual content of a cubist picture would involve exhaustive descriptions of lines, quasi-rectangular shapes, the colors in each region of the picture, and so on. But any art critic who claimed that such a strictly literal description of a Picasso painting exhaustively described its full artistic meaning would be laughed out of the profession. Even though abstract paintings do not represent familiar objects or people, they still have a broadly non-literal meaning that cannot be identified with any literal catalogue of the sensory qualities of areas on the surface of the painting. Yet in the case of wines, exactly this kind of gross confusion of exhaustive literal descriptions of sensory qualities with experiential meaning constitutes the ruling orthodoxy in discussions of wine.

This is not to say that wine is an art form, or that individual wines are artworks (though see the succeeding sections for some related discussion). But it is to say that conscious experiences are meaningful either in analytical, ultimately survival-related ways – because of the sophisticated kinds of cognitive processing that they prompt – or in imaginative, broadly recreational ways that are dependent on sophisticated kinds of reuse of those same cognitive mechanisms.

More on Imaginative Experiences of Wines

The imaginative or representational status of meaningful experiences of wines will now be discussed further. The basic idea is that just as the surface of an abstract painting, or the sounds of musical instruments, can have an imaginative or representational role in artistic experiences of them, so also can the flavors, aromas, and colors of a wine have an imaginative role in appropriately receptive experiences of them. For example, it can be *as if* a favorite wine has transported you to a richly resonant, better place, whose presence around you, and whose desirable qualities, are reinforced by each succeeding taste of the wine. But of course, it is literally false that the wine has transported you to anywhere, since the experience is a purely imaginative one. Or, perhaps more commonly, the experience of the sensory qualities of a good wine as being *well balanced*, or as having other desirable features, involves an evaluative judgment that applies only to the wine as imaginatively experienced, rather than to a purely analytical perception of it. Similarly, a judgment that a string quartet provides a well-balanced or high-quality performance of a work pertains to the work as imaginatively experienced, not to the mere sensory qualities of the notes.

The possibility of such imaginative experiences of wines has not gone completely unrecognized traditionally. Usually such experiences have been explained as consisting in mere personal associations with, interpretations of, or reactions to a distinct sensory experience of the wine itself. So a *two-part* analysis of wine perception is assumed, according to which strictly only the first, purely sensory part is genuinely perceptual. But this traditional view seriously distorts the facts about our actual experiences of wines. We do not *first* analytically perceive the sensory qualities, and *then*, somewhat later, react to them in some subjective way. Instead, there is a single, unified imaginative experience of enjoying the flavors and aromas of the wine.

To be sure, no one denies that it is possible to taste a wine in a purely analytical way, just as no one denies that it is possible to analytically perceive the surface of a painting, or the sounds made by a string quartet. Nevertheless, the underlying view of perceptual experience assumed by the traditional two-part analysis – as involving a purely sensory component, plus a distinct non-perceptual component, such as a feeling of pleasure or approval caused by the perception – has long since been abandoned in cognitive science and the philosophy of perception.

The current imaginative account of wine perception also integrates well with the current self-prompting theory of conscious experience. The theory predicts that the only aspects of perception that are consciously experienced are those aspects that require *sophisticated processing*. Now as indicated above, the perceiver can decide whether to perceive things in an analytical or in an imaginative manner. In the analytical or survival-related mode, the sophisticated processing would include exhaustive memory searches and assessments of risks and benefits in ingesting the wine. By contrast, in the imaginative or recreational mode, the purely sensory data is only superficially or routinely perceived, and hence it is not consciously experienced as such. Instead, all of the sophisticated processing goes into the creation of the conscious imaginative experience of the wine.

Hence, to summarize, the self-prompting theory predicts that there must be a *fundamental division* of perceptual experiences into survival-related analytical kinds on the one hand, and recreational imaginative kinds on the other hand. Standard theories of perception completely neglect imaginative kinds, probably because even now – nearly one hundred and fifty years after Darwin wrote *The Origin of Species* – they fail to give any consideration to the fundamental significance of evolutionary factors in structuring human perceptual consciousness. In the case of wines, this is a disastrous mistake to make, because the perceptual experience of wines provides a paradigm case, if anything does, of an imaginative, almost purely recreational kind of perceptual experience.

John Dilworth

The Neglected Role of Alcoholic Content in Experiences of Wines

Another underappreciated factor in understanding wine experiences is as follows. It is easy to forget that wines have a significant advantage in the competition for attention and influence in human recreational activities. Wine is an *alcoholic* beverage, and alcohol is a potent drug, many of whose effects are well known. It might be thought that great wines must be valued solely for their taste, rather than for any ancillary effects of their relatively tasteless alcoholic content. But any who are tempted to believe this are invited to conduct the following experiment. Obtain a range of the best available non-alcoholic wines (there are only a few of any quality). These few claim to be carefully prepared from fine wines that have the alcohol removed only after the final stages of processing, so that the resulting tastes do resemble those of the real wines from which they are derived. Some have apparently even won competitions in taste comparisons with alcoholic wines. But I suspect that you, like me, will find that these products, though having recognizable tastes and aromas, are nevertheless *dead on arrival*. They have none of the life and animation of natural wines, and *what it is like* to drink them is completely different from what it is like to drink real wines, in spite of some similarities in sensory qualities. (Some writers describe the difference as being that alcoholic wines have more body or texture because of the alcohol, but there is much more to it than that.) This experiment is particularly salient because it shows the falsity or hollowness of standard kinds of discussions of the qualities of wines based on comparative wine-tasting sessions, which attempt to explain wine experiences exclusively in terms of the perceived sensory qualities of a wine.

But why should the presence of alcohol in wines make such a difference? My speculation is that it makes a difference, not to the sensory characteristics of the wine itself, but instead to *oneself*, while one is experiencing the wine. The alcohol turns a sober or prosaic sensory experience into a less inhibited, mildly hallucinogenic experience in which the cognitive system of the drinker has been transformed into one having more dreamlike and suggestible characteristics. Under such conditions one's critical faculties become disarmed,

90

and wider ranges of affective and cognitive exploration become possible, of which one's fully sober self would normally be incapable. (Doubtless this kind of explanation is oversimplified, but it identifies a factor that must not be ignored.) The alcoholic content of the wine provides a kind of permission, or entry ticket, into a parallel world in which – in the terminology of Immanuel Kant – a *free play of the imagination* can take place. In this manner a richness and depth of cognitive processing can be achieved that no sensory qualities – no matter how complex or refined they might be – could succeed in prompting by themselves.

Wine Drinking and Improvisatory Theater

This concluding section will attempt to further pin down the precise relations of imaginative wine experience to perceptual experiences in the arts. A basic distinction is that the purely sensory qualities of a wine, though complex in their own way, nevertheless can be experienced to the full within a period that is usually considerably less than a minute. (Which is not to deny that wines can be enjoyed over much longer periods.) But clearly plays or pieces of music involve a significantly greater range of complex factors, a full experience of which may take an hour or more. Also, the complexity of visual data derivable from the surface of a painting is many orders of magnitude greater than that of the tastes or smells associated with a wine. Even the best wine critic would be very happy to identify, say, seventeen distinct sensory components and their magnitudes in a wine, but even a tiny corner of a painting supplies much more sensory data.

I acknowledge that these distinctions are genuine and significant, but nevertheless claim that they are the *wrong comparisons* to make between wine experiences and artistic experiences. A wine is not like an artwork. Instead, what it is like is a *sensory theme*, upon which the drinker carries out *art-like improvisations*. Drinking a glass or more of a wine, I claim, involves a series of related imaginative improvisations, in which the common theme of the sensory qualities of the wine is subject to a variety of spontaneous variations, each involving a different kind or kinds of sophisticated imaginative processing of the same sensory data. On this view, drinking a wine is not like experiencing a previously finished artwork, but instead it is an

91

exploratory, spontaneous activity in which *you yourself* are the artist or creator of what you experience. In these respects it is like the fertile activity of a jazz artist as he creatively improvises on a standard jazz tune, or, more specifically, like the spontaneous, try-anything creativity of an actor in an improvisatory theater production, who decides herself what to say at any moment rather than following a preexisting script.

This is not to deny that, in the case of a familiar wine, one can have a high degree of certainty as to what one's imaginative inter-action with it will be like. I suggest that there is an initial period of adjustment with an unfamiliar wine, in which one tries out various imaginative attitudes toward it, before settling on one that seems most appropriate to its qualities, as well as most satisfying to oneself. Thereafter one expects to be able to engage in the same familiar kinds of interaction with that wine in subsequent sessions. But this definite knowledge of what to expect with a familiar wine is fully consistent with its improvisatory origins.

An advantage of this "imaginative improvisatory theater" approach to wine drinking is that it helps to explain the crucial role of the alcoholic content in experiences of wine, as discussed in the previous section. Most people are much too inhibited to think of themselves as being capable of engaging in any artistic-like activity, let alone of a kind that requires them to freely and creatively extemporize a personal performance or interpretation of something. So the reason why non-alcoholic "wines" are experienced as being "dead" or inert is because they do nothing to energize *you*, the drinker, into the kinds of personal imaginative efforts that are needed to make the drinking of the wine into a varied, lively, and personally satisfying improvisatory series of experiences revolving around the particular wine that you are drinking.

The improvisatory approach also throws light on the issue of wine quality. It is a fact, bemoaned by wine experts generally, that the majority of people seem to enjoy mass-produced fruit-forward wines more than the complex specialty wines favored by enthusiasts. Now if wines were like artworks, for which there are standards of quality independent of individual tastes, the situation would indeed be cause for concern. It would show that most people have deplorably bad taste with respect to wines. However, once it is recognized that a wine is only the raw material for a series of highly personal impro-visational experiences, the problem disappears. What works best in stimulating my spontaneous improvisations may not work best in stimulating yours, and vice versa. The differences can be explained in terms of harmless, non-judgmental differences in individual psychology, rather than as showing that some people have a better appreciation of wine quality than others. Of course, differences in knowledge and enthusiasm concerning wines will still persist, but those who harbor secret admiration for some wines that are out of favor with the critics need no longer feel guilty concerning their tastes.

As for the issue of whether wine drinking actually *is* currently a variety of improvisatory theater, or whether that is just the closest analogy to it in the art world, I favor the latter conclusion. Many activities in the art world require explicit artistic intentions in order to count as art-related. For example, someone who molds a lump of clay in various ways in order to improve her hand dexterity does not qualify as being engaged in creating a sculpture, even if all of the hand movements, and the various configurations of the clay, could have been part of deliberate artistic activity by a genuine sculptor. Since most people do not drink wines with the intention of engaging in improvisatory theater, that is a good reason for denying that they are so engaged. Nevertheless, my point remains that the perceptual and psychological processes involved in wine drinking and improvisatory theater are intimately related, apart from the purely intentional aspects. Hence if the present theory of wine drinking should catch on and become popular – so that wine enthusiasts would come to think of themselves as being engaged in a form of improvisatory theater – then nothing more would be required for them to be correct in their belief.

To conclude, here is some more evidence in favor of an improvisatory approach to wine drinking. For most art enthusiasts, the ideal experience of an artwork, such as a film or piece of music, is one in which one's attention is completely concentrated on the artwork in question, with no interruptions. (There is nothing more annoying than being distracted at a crucial point in an absorbing movie.) So if a wine were like an artwork, one would expect that total concentration would be the standard for wine experiences as well. However, clearly this is not so. Wine enthusiasts as a group are generally happy to enjoy their favorite wines while eating and conversing with others, even though art enthusiasts as a group would typically resent such interruptions and distractions.

More specifically, music is an art of sound, and it is competing *sounds* that are distracting, such as conversation, or the sound of a lawn mower. Someone who blocks your *view* of a painting or movie destroys your enjoyment of that visual art. But most wine lovers have no problem ingesting a wide range of foods and other drinks along with their favorite wines. Why is this? The difference can be explained by the improvisatory nature of wine experiences. Since these experiences are freely created by the drinker, and since there are no independent standards of an ideal or fully concentrated wine experience – as there are for experiences of artworks of various kinds – wine drinkers can be much more flexible and relaxed about the conditions under which they experience wines.

To be sure, some distractions could be significant enough so that the wine itself is no longer consciously experienced at all for a period of time. But since the drinker's improvisatory freedom in experiencing the wine has no restrictions beyond his own spontaneous current preferences, there is nothing questionable about the behavior of someone who chooses to have her wine experiences in an intermittent way. The tastes of wines, and how we choose to experience them, are indeed purely matters of personal imagination.

6

Talk about Wine?

Kent Bach

There is a problem when these people list all these flavours and aromas they think they have detected. It then gets on to the label of the bottle and what you are looking at appears to be a recipe for fruit salad.

Hugh Johnson[1]

I much prefer drinking wine to writing about it. I was prompted to write about it by an experience I often have when I offer a good wine to a novice. They will say something like, "Don't waste that on me. I don't know anything about wine," implying that they will not be able to enjoy the wine. This raises the obvious question of whether and, if so, to what extent, knowing about wine is necessary for enjoying and appreciating it. I take it as obvious that there are all sorts of practical benefits to knowing a lot about wine, even if you are not a winemaker, wine seller, sommelier, wine writer, or wine critic. Knowledge and experience help you decide which wines to try, which wines to buy, and which wines to serve with which foods, as well as to recognize tainted, oxidized, or otherwise flawed wines. But none of this knowledge, I claim, is essential to actually enjoying wine. Much of this knowledge provides pleasure of its own, thanks to the fact that there is so much to learn about wine and that so much about it is interesting, but this pleasure is mainly intellectual, not sensory.

---

[1] www.bibendum-wine.co.uk/news.asp?id=60&Archived=1.

That, in a nutshell, was how I answered the question, "What good is knowledge in enjoying wine?" in an article called "Knowledge, Wine, and Taste."[2] Now I want to ask a different but closely related question: what good is being able to talk about wine for enjoying wine? Here, I do not mean the practical value of wine talk. For example, being able to describe precisely what sort of wine you would like should enable a restaurant sommelier to suggest a wine that fits the bill – assuming he takes your description in the way you intended. Conversely, being able to decipher the tasting notes of wine critics may help you narrow down what wines to buy and drink. And being able to talk about wine has one indisputable benefit: it enables people to enjoy talking about wine! Wine lovers love to do that. But that is not the sort of enjoyment that I am talking about. Rather, I am talking about the pleasure in drinking wine.

Why ask this question? We would not ask it about fruit juices or soft drinks. Some people might ask it about coffee or single-malt scotches, about cheeses or chocolates. Professional tasters, concerned with maintaining styles or standards, have to be able to recognize and identify deviations so that they can be corrected, but only the most compulsive connoisseur seeks to find just the right words for the tastes for these things. Why should it be any different with wine? Here is a plausible answer, at least regarding wines of high quality. Not only do they taste really good to a good many experienced tasters and therefore seem worth learning and talking about, they are also very complex and diverse, right down to the chemical level. They contain hundreds of compounds to which normal tasters are responsive, and they vary considerably from one another in precisely which compounds they contain and in what concentrations. So the possibilities are virtually endless. Someone who raves that the 2003 Lafite-Rothschild is a modern-day version of the 1959 is making a very specific claim, considering the subtle ways in which even wines from the same producer and place can differ from one another.

It is not obvious that learning how to describe the different elements one smells or tastes (or, for that matter, sees or feels) in a wine makes a difference in how one experiences it or what one experiences in it.

---

[2]   That article was based on a talk given at the first-ever conference on wine and philosophy, held in London on December 10, 2004. It appears in Barry C. Smith (ed.), *Questions of Taste: The Philosophy of Wine* (Oxford: Signal Books, 2007).

It may facilitate the process of analytic tasting (i.e., methodically focusing on specific qualities) as engaged in by wine professionals and many wine lovers, but is having a rich vocabulary at one's disposal really necessary for isolating those qualities in one's experience? A great winemaker requires sensory acuity to blend a wine to his satisfaction, but it is not obvious that he needs words in order to do it. Why can't his tasting experience do the trick? And why can't ours enable us to appreciate the results?

What Comes with Experience?

Being able to talk about wine requires experience at drinking wine as well as learning a specialized vocabulary. But why isn't experience enough for just enjoying and appreciating different wines? It is clear you cannot enjoy wines to the fullest without the benefits of experience. Initially, you might be able to do little better than tell wines you like from those you do not. If they are drinkable, that is enough for you. The ones you most like are likely to be ones whose flavors are readily accessible – you will not yet be into subtleties. Your taste in wine might be no more sophisticated than most people's taste in soft drinks, pancakes, or bananas. You may have heard that wines made from different grapes and in different places taste different, but you will not yet have any idea what these differences are, much less how much they matter, never mind differences in vintages, vinification, and maturity. You have no idea what to look for in a wine, how that wine tastes against its peers, or what standards there might be for wines of that type and from that place, much less what people mean by the "sense of place" that a wine "communicates." You have no conception of the variety and subtlety of flavors that wines can display or of how they can differ in complexity, structure, balance, and elegance.

With experience at tasting fine wines from specific regions, made from particular grapes and in particular styles, you can develop a sense of the possibilities wines are capable of and come to recognize similarities and differences. Learning the names of important places and producers will help you impose a certain order on this ever-growing range of experience. Rather than fall into the trap of attaching mystical significance to the names of these places and producers, you can treat these names as helpful means for remembering what the wines are like and which ones you like. Then you can return to those wines and be better prepared to recall how they were as compared to how they are. You will be able to tell if a particular bottle is not up to snuff. Different vintages of the same wine will become meaningfully comparable, and so will different wines from the same region and vintage. You will be able to recognize wines that are atypical for their type and region. During the course of this learning process your tastes will change. These changes will generally be gradual, but every so often a particular wine will blow you away or, to put it more reverently, give you an epiphany. Taste a number of these and your excitement about wine will intensify, even as you lose interest in many wines you previously loved.

Once you have gained experience in tasting diverse wines and have developed the habits and skills enabling you to expose your senses to what a wine has to offer, it should be enough to sense a wine attentively to enjoy it to the fullest. That requires knowing-how, of course, but not knowing-that (i.e., factual knowledge). You do not have to be able to label the wine's aromas and flavors in order to discern and appreciate them. That ability is needed for discussing wines, inquiring about them, writing about them, and selling them, and it may be conducive to remembering them, but it is not essential to enjoying and appreciating them.

What about assessing a wine? Perhaps having a rich wine vocabulary is needed for that. But is there anything you have to know beyond knowing how to carefully and attentively expose it to your senses? (For the moment, I am concerned only about assessing the wine you are tasting, not applying standards for comparing it to other wines of the same type.) You look at the wine in your glass for its shade, depth, and density of color and, as you swirl it, for its viscosity. Then you sniff it to check for its intensity and cleanliness of smell, hoping not to detect any unpleasant musty or even foul odors, and notice its aroma. After that you taste the wine for its level of sweetness, acidity, bitterness, and astringency. In fact, astringency is partly tactile, since it produces drying and puckering sensations. Also tactual is the high alcohol level or "hotness" of some wines. Tactual in a different way is the wine's weight or body, which can be thought of as on the scale of wateriness to creaminess. Finally, there is the finish, the perhaps lingering aftertaste. It might be short and thin or long and rich.

Tasting a wine is a complex process, involving a series of actions that yield a multifaceted, temporally structured experience. Doing it well takes time and practice. Tasting a wine is not as easy as the novice might think, but talking about it is harder still. What does that add to the experience?

What Might Be Wine Talk Good For?

There is pleasure to be had in comparing the wine one is drinking with others one has tried; obviously that requires more than just being able to savor the wine of the moment. As we will see later, it is difficult to test people for consistency and reliability in using wine descriptors. For now let us pretend that it has been established that you, the people you talk about wine with, and the professionals you read and listen to have all been certified as consistent and reliable wine talkers. That is supposing a lot, for people who talk profusely about wine are generally not put to the test. They, like many wines, can make a good impression without being all that good. We should not rule out the possibility that we can be easily fooled into thinking that our talk about wine is far more consistent and reliable than it is. Who is going to tell us that we are wrong? Wine talkers are generally too polite to criticize each other's claims, and where there is disagreement it tends to be written off as the result of differences in sensory reactions or personal preferences rather than in our understanding of wine terms. But let us suppose that we are consistent and reliable wine talkers. The question is this: what does being able to talk, consistently and reliably, about wines add to our ability to enjoy and appreciate them?

Comparative pleasure

Wine lovers enjoy comparing different but similar wines. For example, they like to compare different wines of the same varietal, place, and vintage, and to compare different vintages of the same wine. Indeed, they like to discern how, on a particular occasion, wine from the same bottle or even in the same glassful "opens up" over a few minutes. They like to revisit a wine periodically to see how it has developed over the years. Wine lovers also like to compare how different wines go with a particular food and to compare how a particular wine goes with different foods.

Obviously, wine language is needed for talking about these things, for sharing and comparing experiences, but is it really needed for having the experiences? Suppose we had elaborate vocabularies for delineating the details of sunsets, faces, foot massages, or roller coaster rides. Would words somehow enhance our ability to experience any of these to their fullest? Probably not, but being able to describe these experiences would surely enhance our ability to compare them and obviously would be necessary for discussing them. Comparative pleasure and the ability to articulate it seems to be much more widely cultivated and highly valued in the case of wine. There is no comparable culture, so far as I know anyway, with categorizing the looks of sunsets or the feels of foot massages. In principle, they could be classified, based on some devisable taxonomy, but who would bother, other than perhaps a poet. Lacking the ability to describe sunsets and foot massages does not seem to detract from experiences of them, and it is doubtful that having it would enhance their quality or be needed for comparing them (except in conversation). So why should the case of wine be any different?

Wines change over time, even short periods of time, and there is pleasure in noticing these changes from one glass to the next. This goes beyond enjoying the distinctive character of the wine at each moment during the course of its change. It involves discerning particular ways in which the wine has changed. For example, its fruitiness and freshness may be evident only after it "opens up." Obviously, words are needed to communicate these changes, but are they needed to help one discern or remember those changes over the short term? Why can't this ability be based on purely sensory memory – a memory for flavors and aromas – without having to be supported by a rich vocabulary that purportedly puts these flavors and aromas into words?

Perhaps more is required for long-term memory, the kind needed for comparing wines tasted at different times. There is pleasure, not just aesthetic but even sensory, in being able to compare a wine with relevantly similar wines, such as previous vintages of the same wine, other wines from the same vineyard and/or vintage, and other wines that may be interestingly similar. Without being able to remember the specific wines by name and vintage, one could have only vague recollections. Part of the pleasure one has in savoring a wine is comparing it with wines that one has tasted previously, especially similar ones. That requires remembering what the other ones tasted like, and that in turn requires identifying those wines by producer, region (or even appellation or vineyard), varietal (or name), and vintage.

Recognition and novelty

Memory is also required for the pleasure of recognition. Tasting a wine you are fond of for the first time in a long time is like seeing an old friend. However, familiarity can breed contempt, or at least boredom. Drink even a great wine too often and you will eventually lose interest in it. If your wine collection consisted entirely in case after case of one spectacular wine, you would be better off not being able to remember what it tastes like. Then, instead of growing sick and tired of it, you would able to replicate the otherwise unrepeatable experience of tasting it for the first time.

Fortunately, there is no end to the variety of fine wines currently available, including ones from unheralded regions. Although we enjoy the pleasure of recognition, familiarity goes only so far. We value novelty too. Appreciating novelty (and distinctiveness) requires memory, since it is in comparison to other, particularly similar wines, that the one being tasted now can be judged as novel, that is, interestingly distinctive. But again, words are not necessary for enjoying and appreciating novelty or distinctiveness in a wine. Rather, it is lack of familiarity, experienced against a background of a wide range of wines one has previously encountered.

Applying standards

I have been pretending that all that matters when you open a bottle, pour some into a glass, and put the glass to your lips is the wine's sensory qualities. The focus has been on how a wine *does* taste, not on how it *should* taste. But wine people have ideas about that, especially about how specific wines ought to taste. For example, Champagne producers aim to maintain a particular "house style," a certain specific character year after year, especially in their non-vintage wines. Many producers of vintage wines, while adjusting to the variable effects of weather from one harvest to the next, also try to maintain a certain style, so that, for example, a Château l'Effete

101

will always recognizably be a Château l'Effete. Then there is typicity. This can be specific to a certain region, even a specific appellation. The idea is that a wine should taste the way wines from that place are supposed to taste. It follows that a wine that lacks typicity could nevertheless taste great, however misleading its label. The same point applies to varietal typicity. An atypical pinot noir might taste more like a syrah, a heavily oaked sauvignon blanc more like a chardonnay. Many wine lovers would be disappointed rather than delighted to be fooled in this way, and would judge the wine deficient for not tasting the way it is "supposed to."

Words and Experience: Questions, Questions

I have conceded that having labels for wines, consisting pretty much in the information that is on their labels, is needed for the pleasure of comparing wines, but now let us return to the main question, about the value of wine words for enjoying and appreciating a particular wine. As we have seen, it is clear that experience, learning, and memory enhance one's ability to enjoy, appreciate, and assess a wine and expand one's idea of what wines can taste like. But what does having and using a vocabulary for describing the qualities in a wine add to all this?

Being able to find words to describe the qualities you sense in a wine might seem to be a good skill to develop. Presumably it enables you to understand what other people say about wine as well as to delineate in detail what it is that you like and dislike in a given wine and to explain your preferences in general. Presumably, I say, because I can think of a range of pertinent (and impertinent) questions that might not have encouraging answers:

- Does being given an accurate and perceptive description of a wine's qualities add to our enjoyment of them?
- Can apt descriptions even enable us to detect aspects of a wine's character that we otherwise wouldn't have noticed?
- Does a wine taste different after someone singles out and aptly describes its qualities, or does the description ring true only because it captures the experience one is already having?
- Can a wine taste better just because we can describe what it tastes like?

102

- Can describing a wine's aroma and flavor detract from our experience of it?
- Can we become *too* analytical in tasting wine, too concerned about discriminating and labeling the various flavor components of a wine?
- Does having wine descriptors at our disposal enhance our memory for wines?

Just raising such questions takes something for granted that we might not be entitled to assume. Asking about the importance of being able to describe the qualities assumes that one can learn to do so consistently and reliably. Ideally, this means that on different occasions one would describe the same wine in pretty much the same way and that different people trained in the same way and with the same vocabulary would tend to agree with one another about the qualities of particular wines. All this is testable, but not easily.

Testing Tasting Talk

Addressing these questions experimentally would not be easy (never mind the cost of the wines). The chemical senses (i.e., taste and smell) are markedly different from the other senses. They are naturally hedonic, they are much slower to react, and their reactions are much slower to subside. This makes side-by-side comparisons more difficult. Relatively long time intervals between samples must be imposed because of adaptation, the tendency of taste and smell to lose their responsiveness with repeated stimulation (hence the value of "palate cleansers" in multi-course meals). The conditions of tasting – for example, the temperature of the wine, not to mention condition of the taster – have to be controlled for. How a wine is experienced and evaluated is subject to variations in conditions of tasting (e.g., wines already tasted, temperature of the wine, ambient temperature, glass, bottle variation, etc.). And, of course, wines change over time, and there can be variation in taste of the same wine from one bottle to the next. Finally, people differ in their wine-tasting experience and, indeed, in their sensitivity to different aromas and flavors, both in kind and in degree. For example, some people find red wine, coffee, and black tea almost painfully bitter.

103

Suppose all these obstacles could be overcome. What could we test for? One obvious thing to test for is whether having a rich wine vocabulary enhances one's ability to taste and recognize wines. We would have to compare two groups, people who have been trained in wine talk and people who have not been, but whose experience at tasting wine is otherwise comparable. If having a rich wine vocabulary enhances one's tasting ability, then one should be able to distinguish wines that someone lacking such a vocabulary cannot distinguish. So the way to test for this would be to find wines that the wordless taster can't discriminate but the verbal one can. Also, we could present people with a wine and then, a few minutes later, present them with the original wine along with four or five similar wines. Perhaps there would be many instances where people without a wine vocabulary could not recognize the wine they tasted previously whereas those with the words for what they previously tasted could recognize the original wine. Applying methods like these would provide evidence for whether or not having a rich wine vocabulary really enhances people's ability to discern the wine aromas and flavors and to recognize them.

Ideally, what could we hope to learn from careful scientific testing of people's abilities to taste wines and to talk about them? The most optimistic outcome would be that people can in fact be trained to use wine talk consistently and reliably, to apply much the same terms to the same wines and be able to convey to one another the aromas and flavors they detect in a given wine. Adequately trained and experienced people would demonstrably be able to match wines with descriptions and descriptions with wines. Give them a wine and they could tell which of a number of descriptions describes it. Give them a description and they could tell which of a number of wines it describes. But why should we be so optimistic?

Let us get specific. Here's a description of a particular wine:

> Fabulous purity of crushed fruit – strawberries and raspberries, with hints of fresh roses. Full-bodied, with an amazing concentration and a palate that goes on and on and on. Ultraripe tannins. Terrific balance and richness.[3]

---

[3]   *Wine Spectator*, July 31, 2004.

Obviously, this wine critic thinks very highly of this wine. But even if his description tells you what the wine is like, does it tell you enough to distinguish this wine from others, much less indicate what is so great about it? I do not think so. Now ask yourself the same questions about this description:

> Medium red with a hint of amber. Ethereal aromas of red currant, dried rose, violet, tobacco, marzipan and white truffle. A wine of great penetration and thrust, with fruit of steel and powerful structure. Wonderfully floral in the mouth and on the gripping aftertaste.[4]

This description gives more detail than the previous one, but it too does not tell you enough to distinguish this wine from others, much less to indicate what is so great about this wine. Oh, in case you are wondering, these two tasting notes describe the same wine, the 2000 Bruno Giacosa Barolo Le Rocche del Falletto Riserva. Interestingly, the aromatic of fresh roses to one critic is redolent of dried roses to the other.

A study could be made of different wine critics' tasting notes on the same wines to determine the extent to which they agree on each one's aromas and flavors. My bet is that some wines would be described in unrecognizably different ways, as the example above illustrates. There might even be instances of differently tasting wines described in the same way. In another kind of study, people trained in descriptive vocabulary could be directly tested. Tasters could be presented with a number of broadly similar wines and with a number of descriptions and asked to match wines with descriptions and descriptions with wines. No doubt there would be plenty of points of agreement, but there would undoubtedly be many other points of disagreement too. This would be especially likely if the test were set up so that some of the wines were intended not to fit any of the descriptions, and some of the descriptions were intended not to apply to any of the wines. If people were given multiple-choice questions that included "none of the above" as an option, then, for each item, they would not be forced to assume that one of the options is the "right" one. They would only choose a description that rings true of the given wine and only a wine that snugly fits the given description.

---

[4]   *Stephen Tanzer's International Wine Cellar*, Nov./Dec. 2004.

To be optimistic, suppose it turned out that people trained in the use of wine descriptors largely agreed in their descriptions of particular wines. Even then, we could still ask what the descriptors signify. Do they really describe qualities of a given wine? It is an interesting fact that tastes and smells are generally described in terms of what they are the tastes and smells of, such as asparagus, asphalt, black cherries, freshly mown lawn, jasmine, licorice, and roses. So, we might wonder, do terms tasters use genuinely describe the wine, or do they merely identify salient similarities or even just vague associations between the wine and familiar items with characteristic tastes or smells? The distinguished wine writer Hugh Johnson is skeptical: "A wine is not apply or black-currant. People don't sniff a rose and say, 'Oh yes, pineapple, cucumber'. It smells like a rose – and a bottle of wine smells like wine. Too much of this borrowing of terms to describe wines really doesn't help."[5] So, we might well ask, does a wine described as showing notes of cigar box or saddle leather really smell like a cigar box or saddle leather? (And why should we care what other things a wine smells or tastes like?)

Tastes and Words

What difference does it make to one's experience and enjoyment of a wine to be able to describe what it tastes like? In fact, that's an ambiguous question. "What it tastes like" can mean either how it tastes or what it tastes similar to. Let us discuss each in turn.

Does knowing how to describe the taste of a wine matter to what it tastes like in the sense of how it tastes? Obviously, being able to articulate how it tastes is necessary for conveying this to others, but that is another matter. Less obviously, it may facilitate remembering how the wine tastes. But does it enhance one's tasting of the wine? Does having words for the different elements and qualities in the aroma or flavor make them easier to experience, and perhaps even make some of them possible to experience? I do not see why. To the contrary, it would seem that experiencing them is necessary for describing them. Having words for the sensory qualities of the wine may enhance one's powers of recognition, but even that may be an

---

[5] www.bibendum-wine.co.uk/news.asp?id=60&Archived=1.

exaggeration. Perhaps it is enough to have nonverbal recognitional concepts of the different qualities. Why should the ability to recognize this quality or that quality require having names for them? That is not necessary for recognizing familiar places or faces.

Does being able to verbally compare the wine one is tasting with wines one has previously tasted enhance one's ability to taste the wine? If one tastes a series of wines, does being able to compare them verbally enhance one's experience of each? Obviously it enhances one's ability to talk about them. Less obviously, it enhances one's ability to structure one's knowledge of what each of them tastes like. But, and this is a big "but," it seems that one must first be able to attend to the various elements and qualities in the aroma and flavor of the wine, to be able to taste the wine in all its complexity, in order to talk about these elements and qualities.

However, and this is a big "however," someone else's words, perhaps the words of an astute taster and articulate describer, can call one's attention to qualities one may not have noticed, to describe relationships between different elements that one may have overlooked, and perhaps even to draw comparisons to the aromas and flavors of other wines or even other substances and thereby enhance one's experience of the wine itself.

Do common wine descriptors – words such as 'cherry', 'anise', 'grassy', and 'petrol' – really capture elements in the flavors of different wines? Or do they merely identify substances that some aspect of the wine bears a certain similarity to, or even just something that one associates with that aspect? Is there literally a cherry, anise, grassy, or petrol flavor or aroma in a particular wine, or just something somewhat like that? I venture to say that even a detailed description of a wine in such terms does not give a faithful account of how the wine smells and tastes. It might help distinguish a wine from most other wines, it might give one some idea if one will like the wine, but it is unlikely to give one a clear sense of how the wine would actually taste, so that one could say, upon tasting the wine, that indeed it was this wine that the description described. Such a description could just as well apply to many other wines, each distinguishable from the others. Try reading a description of a fine wine that you are about to try. Read all the descriptions you want. Then taste the wine. Do these descriptors really capture what the wine is like and convey what it is that you – and the wine writers – loved about it? I doubt it. Indeed, we should not rule out the possibility that descriptions can detract from one's experience of the wine.

Verbal Tricks

It is a platitude that your memory plays tricks on you. In the case of wine, you can think you remember what a certain wine tastes like and be wrong. You taste a wine that you have tasted before and it seems "different." That could be because it *is* different – perhaps the wine has dramatically changed since the last time you tasted it, or perhaps this bottle came from a different lot than the last one. But maybe you are just wrong about how it tasted before and now have a false expectation of what this bottle should taste like.

Words can play similar tricks and aid and abet the tricks of memory. You can take the fact that a certain descriptor, say 'cigar box', occurs to you when you taste a wine as evidence that it describes some aspect of the wine's aroma (presumably you do not chew on cigar boxes). Yes, that is some evidence, but it might be misleading. Perhaps thinking of that descriptor gives you the (false) impression that the aroma you are detecting is cigar box. This may seem unlikely, but consider how easily we are subject to suggestion, especially by so-called experts, about what we smell and taste in a wine. We defer to experts on the theory that they know more, have sensitive palates, and are merely reporting on what they taste and smell, not using their imagination. And there are many other well-known sources of suggestibility, such as the identity of the producer, the type of grape(s), the place of origin, and, most notoriously, the wine's price and the label. Even whether the wine is red or white can affect how a wine seems to taste and smell.

For an extreme example of suggestibility, though not one involving wine, consider the observation that Parmesan cheese smells like vomit. Fortunately, few people realize this (sorry I mentioned it). That is because they are rarely put in the position of detecting the smell without having some idea what it is they are smelling. As you can well imagine, whether you think it is Parmesan or vomit determines whether you find the smell attractive or repulsive.

It might seem that we ought to be able to distinguish purely descriptive words and phrases from the more evaluative or even figuratively used expressions to talk about wines. So, you might think, there's a big difference between using expressions like 'rose', 'jasmine', 'cedar', 'caramel', and 'cherry' and using ones like 'polished', 'focused', 'firm', and 'flamboyant'. Terms in the first group seem clearly descriptive, whereas those in the second group seem clearly evaluative. But does a wine literally smell like a flower or herb, much less taste like any fruit or vegetable? Well, at least it might give off a note of jasmine or contain something that is contained in cherries. In some cases, the wine might contain a compound (or combination of compounds) that is present in the stuff in question (strawberry, jasmine, or whatever) and accounts for its characteristic taste or aroma. In other cases, the compound might be different but trigger a response from the same olfactory receptors. Consider that we have hundreds of different kinds of olfactory receptors, each responsive to just a few volatile compounds. The same compound may trigger more than one receptor. So smell is not just a matter of reacting to compounds that enter one's nasal cavity. There is a lot of complex processing going on. Perceived similarities in smell may or may not be the result of the same compounds impinging on one's olfactory receptors. Different combinations of compounds can produce somewhat resembling effects. And substances containing some of the same compounds can smell very differently because of interactive effects with different other compounds in those substances, especially when those substances are as complex as wines.

Bottom Line

It sounds plausible to think that being able to describe how wines smell and taste (and look and feel) enhances one's pleasure in smelling and tasting them. Yet, as I have suggested, that remains to be shown. No doubt this ability enhances one's pleasure *while* smelling and tasting wines, but does it really enhance one's pleasure *in* smelling and tasting them? Being able to verbally identify the qualities in a wine is not really needed to be able to sense, notice, and recognize its qualities. Discriminating and recognitional capacities can be based on sensory concepts, built up out of specific taste, smell, and tactile elements. They do not have to be put into words. Verbal commentary can make mediocre wines seem more interesting than they are, but great wines do not need the help of such commentary.

Indeed, it is doubtful that words, even when employed by trained, experienced, and sensitive wine tasters, can really do justice to really great wines. Words might be useful for pinning down particular aromatic and flavor elements, but they do not seem adequate to the task of capturing what is distinctive about a distinctive wine, much less what makes a great wine great. They are just not precise and specific enough, even in combination.

Wine is a very interesting subject. Naturally, it is most interesting to people who love wine. Much of the pleasure that wine talk provides, leaving aside the obvious pleasure in showing off and perhaps being admired, is in learning and understanding and in teaching and explaining. This reflects the spirit of conviviality and generosity that wine evokes. There is much to understand and appreciate about the wines you drink, even ones you would rather not. It is fun to try to identify a wine's distinctive qualities (if it has any), it is fun to try to figure out why it has the particular qualities it has, and it is fun to compare a wine, for better or worse, with interestingly similar ones. Wine talk aids in tracking and organizing one's experience with wine and, obviously, in sharing it. But great wines speak for themselves!

7

Winespeak or Critical Communication? Why People Talk About Wine

Keith Lehrer and Adrienne Lehrer

Introduction

Wine, like objects of art, is enjoyed by the sensory experience of the object and enhanced by discourse. But exactly what is the role of discourse, of communication, about wine? There are obviously commercial implications of descriptions of wine. However, people have an avid interest in discussing wine aside from commercial interests. A description can interest a person in tasting a wine, perhaps a description such as "This cabernet sauvignon has a fruity nose, with notes of red cherry, black raspberry, and a hint of lychee, a firm, muscular, rich body, and an exquisite lingering aftertaste." Some people enjoy talking about wines in these ways. The popularity of wine courses suggests that others aspire to do so. But what do they mean by all that speech?

Research by Adrienne Lehrer showed that ordinary discourse about wine does not convey information with exact enough accuracy for one person to identify and distinguish one wine from another on the basis of such descriptions. In a series of experiments by A. Lehrer, subjects, mostly non-experts, describe wines in words that are intersubjectively incompatible.[1] Whereas some subjects describe a wine as thin and sour, others may describe the very same wine as fruity, well balanced, and of medium body. In a matching

[1] Adrienne Lehrer, *Wine and Conversation* (Bloomington: Indiana University Press, 1983).

111

experiment, where one subject has to describe three wines differently so that his or her partner can match the same wine from those descriptions, subjects do no better than chance. Experts do better, but only on wines on which they have been trained.

Moreover, the results have been robustly replicated. So the avidness that people exhibit in discussing wine, especially those with considerable wine experience, is not explained by the desire to describe a wine in a manner that could enable another person to pick it out. Yet those who engage in such discourse remain convinced that they are communicating something meaningful and which characterizes what they taste and smell. They may be interested in impressing others with their remarks, but, vain as we all are, there is something more than showing off in talking about wines. Indeed, the desire to impress others is fulfilled by communicating with them in a way that hearers or readers find intelligible and leaves them with the conviction that they have learned something about the wine.

But what do we learn from communication about wine if the discourse does not have the kind of descriptive efficacy and accuracy to enable another person to identify the described object? Our claim in this essay is that discourse about wine calls attention to features of the wine that become part of the meaning or content of the words used. For example, the label on Talus 2002 Lodi Merlot describes the wine as having "Vibrant flavors of fresh blackberries and blueberries and just a hint of oak." The winemakers are calling attention to features of the wine. However, the reader will not know exactly what a blueberry or blackberry flavor in a wine is like until they taste it. What they identify as the blackberry taste in the wine will then become part of the meaning or content of the word "blackberry flavor" used to describe a wine. Our thesis below is that discourse about wine, like discourse about other objects of aesthetic interest, those of the fine arts, acquires its meaning, in part, from experience resulting from the way our attention is directed toward these objects in critical communication.

Critical Communication

Critics, as well as the rest of us, describe works of art, paintings for example, in ways that communicate information about the artwork

112

but leave critical information to be filled in by the experience of the work of art. When someone describes a painting to you as "mysterious," the *Mona Lisa*, for example, you are aware that to know what the word means applied to the painting you need to see what the painting is like. The line of thought we wish to develop concerning the meaning of discourse about art and wine is derived from a famous article by Arnold Isenberg.[2] Discussing a critical remark made by Goldschneider about the wavelike contour of a line in a painting, *The Burial of the Count of Orgaz*, Isenberg says:

> Now the critic, besides imparting to us the idea of a wavelike contour, gives us direction for perceiving, and does this *by means* of the idea he imparts to us, which narrows down the field of possible visual orientations and guides us in discrimination of details, the organization of parts, the grouping of discrete objects into patterns. It is as if we found both an oyster and pearl when we had been looking for a seashell because we had been told it was valuable. It *is* valuable, but not because it is a seashell. (p. 137)

Isenberg then puts forth his analysis of what is achieved. He says:

> I may be stretching usage by the senses I am about to assign to certain words, but it seems that the critic's *meaning* is "filled in," "rounded out," or "completed" by the act of perception, which is performed not to judge the truth of his description but in a certain sense to *understand* it. And if *communication* is a process by which a mental content is transmitted by symbols from one person to another, then we can say that it is a function of criticism to bring about communication at the level of the senses; that is, to induce a sameness of vision, of experienced content. (pp. 137–8)

Isenberg concludes that critical communication is distinguished from ordinary communication, and he might have added scientific communication as well, by this dependence of the meaning or content of the discourse on experience. His conclusion is, "Reading criticism, otherwise than in the presence, or with direct recollection, of objects discussed is a blank and senseless employment – a fact which is concealed from us by cooperation, in our reading, of many non-critical

---

[2]   Arnold, Isenberg, "Critical Communication," in W. Elton (ed.), *Aesthetics and Language* (New York: Philosophical Library, 1954), pp. 114–30. Subsequent page references are given in the text.

purposes for which the information of the critic is material and useful" (p. 139). When the critical remarks concern a wine, one non-critical purpose is a commercial one of attempting to induce purchase of the wine.

These remarks of Isenberg seem to explain the use of metaphorical descriptors in reference to wine. Wines are described as masculine or feminine, muscular or sinewy, for example, in addition to being described as heavy or light, delicate or harsh. Moreover, specific flavors are mentioned, the taste of coffee, tobacco, as well as raspberries, blueberries, and chocolate. For example the label on Quails Gate Old Vines Foch 2001 says, "Aromas of coffee, cassis and berry are complemented by firm tannins, deep color and a full body." The label on BV Coastal Cabernet Sauvignon 2002 reads, "Cool coastal morning fog allowed the grapes extra time to ripen on the vines, yielding an exceptional wine with rich, delicious blackberry and cherry flavors. Ripe and subtle with spicey vanilla aromas and moderate tannins." The label on de Lyeth Cabernet Sauvignon 2002 reads, "This [wine] perfectly expresses the structure of the varietal, offering rich flavors of black currant, plum and chocolate."

What is accomplished by such descriptions? Some have suggested that we have the capacity to literally experience such flavors in wine, and perhaps this research will be confirmed by those scientists investigating the correlation of chemical properties with tasters' perception. However, a description can direct a taster's attention to some quality of a wine, for example a chocolate taste. The taster may notice the feature described by 'chocolate' even if the taste is no more similar to chocolate than a pearl is to a seashell. Perception follows the lead of discourse to experience of some feature made salient by the words. The words then take on their meaning or content from the experience. This creates an "I get it" response as the meaning of the remarks of the critic get filled in by the tasting experience of the listener. When you have such an experience – e.g., "Yes, I get the chocolate taste down the center of the tongue," when tasting 1997 Los Vascos Cabernet Sauvignon – there is a sense of successful communication.

In recent years there has been much insightful research on taste and smell, and great strides in the psychophysics of these areas have been made. One thing that has been established is that there are great individual differences. Linda Bartoshuk describes *supertasters*, individuals with many more tastebuds than other people who are much more sensitive to bitter and sweet tastes than others.[3] Some people have specific anosias, that is, they are insensitive to a specific chemical or class of compounds.[4] Morton Meilgaard and K. A. Syborski report, "with the exception of anosmics, most healthy persons appear to show normal sensitivity for most substances, but each person tends to show high sensitivity for certain substances and low sensitivity for a few substances. No "supertaster" who had high sensitivity to all substances was found by any of the participating laboratories, nor was any pair of tasters discovered who showed exactly the same pattern of sensitivity."[5] In view of these facts, critical communication may help those with higher thresholds, by getting them to attend to a subtle taste that they may not perceive at first but can then get with concentration.

Lawless also discusses a "tip of the nose" phenomenon. This happens when someone can perceive a familiar smell but is unable to recall the name. Critical communication can provide help when someone else provides the name. People seem to take pleasure in recognizing the name that they cannot recall.

In addition, there is an element of phatic communion, which is conversation that creates and maintains social bonds.[6] This often occurs in informal social settings when wine drinkers try to agree on a characterization of a wine they are all drinking, as Adrienne Lehrer has proposed. Discourse can lead to the sharing of the experience of sensory features, whatever intersubjective precision or lack thereof results from the experience.

We assume without further argument that Isenberg is right in his cited claims about critical communication in application to the experience about wine. The meaning of discourse about wine is filled in, rounded out, and completed by the experience of wine, as he says. This semantic phenomenology leaves us with important unanswered

---

[3] Linda M. Bartoshuk, "The Biological Basis of Food Perception and Acceptance," *Food Quality and Preference* 4 (1993): 21–32.

[4] Harry T. Lawless, "Olfactory Psychophysics," in G. K. Beauchamp and L. Bartoshuk (eds.), *Tasting and Smelling* (New York: Academic Press, 1997), pp. 125–93.

[5] M. C. D. S. Meilgaard and K. A. Syborski, "Reference Standards for a Beer Flavor Terminology System," *American Society of Brewing Chemists* 40.4 (1982): 119.

[6] Bronislaw Malinowski, "The Problem of Meaning in Primitive Language," in the supplement to C. K. Ogden and I. A. Richards, *The Meaning of Meaning* (New York: Harcourt Brace, 1953).

questions. One is the question of how experience fills in meaning. Another is whether the resulting meaning is the personal meaning of an idiolect or the social meaning of a communal language. The final question concerns how the filling in of meaning by the tasting experience is connected with value judgments.

Filling in Meaning

To answer the question of how meaning can be filled in by discourse, we need to presuppose at least the outline of features of meaning; we have offered a theory of word meaning that we shall apply here.[7] We divide word meaning into two components which we call *sense* and *reference*, as other philosophers do, but we use the words somewhat differently. The sense of a word is explicated in terms of the semantic entailment, synonymy, antonymy, association, and other relations of the word to other words in the same field. An example would be words for weight, such as 'heavy' and 'light'. These words apply conventionally to the body of wine. When they are used for bodily characteristics such as being thin, big, muscular, brawny, lean, etc., these latter words can easily be extended as metaphors for wine, keeping the same intralinguistic relationship. Therefore, a big wine is a heavy one, given the association of 'heavy' and 'big'. 'Brawny' and 'lean' will be opposites in wine, just as they are for body types. Reference is the disposition to apply the term to some objects, features or relations. We have argued that both sense and reference involve some indeterminacy. We note that there may be some conflict between the dispositions of sense and reference. For example, one may be inclined to apply the term 'heavy' to a wine and, at the same time, describe the wine as 'elegant', even though one has a disposition to infer 'not elegant' from 'heavy'. Our theory of meaning is intended to map onto usage at the expense of losing the formal advantages of a theory of meaning that unifies intralinguistic and extralinguistic features of meaning. This difference is acknowledged rather than insisted upon in the present context.

---

7 Adrienne Lehrer and Keith Lehrer, "Networks, Fields, and Vectors," in F. Plamer (ed.), *Grammar and Meaning: Essays in Honor of Sir John Lyons* (Cambridge: Cambridge University Press, 1994).

Our claim is that the theory of meaning is useful for explaining how meaning is filled in by the tasting experience. Other theories of meaning may be equally effective, and we welcome investigation of the application of alternative theories to the data acknowledging that data underdetermine theory. It is not difficult to understand how the tasting experience could influence the dispositions of a person to apply a word, such as 'chocolate', to a wine. Noticing the feature described as a "chocolate taste" may result from the discourse of another, say a wine critic, whose use of the word both directs attention to a feature of the wine and suggests, at the same time, the use of the word 'chocolate' to describe the feature.

Contrary to Kent Bach,[8] we suggest that the use of that word might lead a taster to notice the feature that he or she might have missed without hearing the description. Tasting the wine without hearing the discourse might fail to reveal the feature. This is the reason we value the remarks of wine experts, though, in fact, it is important to distinguish the skills of the expert taster from those of an expert wine communicator. It is easy enough to imagine someone, and here we agree with Bach, who has remarkable abilities to discern and discriminate wine tastes and smells while lacking the linguistic sensitivities to call the attention of another to the features he discerns and discriminates. There is more than one skill in the use of the tongue.

Successful critical communication can reset the dispositions or vectors of sense and reference. Is that an adequate account of the role of the experience of the chocolate taste in the Los Vascos Cabernet? It is clear that the experience of the taste, when remembered, may lead to the identification of further wines, and it may lead one to infer that taste down the middle of the tongue is *not lemony*. So the dispositions or vectors of sense and reference may be reset by the experience. We concede that the claim is one that is subject to experimental confirmation or disconfirmation, and so the claim remains a conjecture.

There is, however, something more to the way that the tasting experience fills in, rounds out, or completes the meaning of 'chocolate' used by the wine critic. The experience exhibits what the meaning

---

[8] Kent Bach, "Knowledge, Wine and Taste: What Good is Knowledge (in Enjoying Wine)?," in Barry C. Smith (ed.), *Questions of Taste: The Philosophy of Wine* (Oxford: Signal Books, 2007). See also Kent Bach, "Talk about Wine?" Chapter 6, this volume.

of 'chocolate' is like when used to describe the wine. How can an experience exhibit the meaning of the word when the meaning is dispositional? Dispositions are, after all, functional states that lack the immediacy of an exhibit. But tasting the chocolate taste down the middle of the tongue shows us what the taste is like and exhibits what is meant by saying that there is a chocolate taste in the wine. We suggest, following the work of Keith Lehrer, that the experience, as a sensory exemplar or particular, stands for other experiences and, therefore, shows us what experiences that are part of the reference of the word are like at the same time that it produces the disposition.[9] Put another way, there is a certain content to the experience, which we describe with 'chocolate'. The experience is an inseparable part of the content that exhibits what it is like.

The philosophical question raised by the account is: How can the content of an experience and the disposition to apply a word be inseparably connected with the experience that exhibits what it is like? After all, it would appear that the same dispositions might exist without experience, in principle, at least, if not in fact. Our answer is twofold. First of all, there is the empirical conjecture that various experiences are the basis of some dispositions that could not, in fact, arise without them. A person born without taste who suddenly acquired it would not instantly acquire the dispositions to use taste words. Rather, subsequent experience would be essential. The same may be true of wine words. Without the combination of discourse and taste, the dispositions to use the words would not exist. We learn the meaning of words from critical communication about wine.

However, there is another role for the experience in exhibiting the meaning of the word. The remembered experience shows us what our disposition is like. It represents to us the disposition that we have. We lack theoretical knowledge of what our dispositions are. Linguists and psychologists discover that. But we have some knowledge of what our disposition to apply the word 'chocolate' to wines is like from knowledge of what the taste is like. Some of our knowledge of meaning, or personal knowledge of what we mean, is exhibited to us by the taste of chocolate in the wine. The experience of the wine at the same time fills in the meaning of the word and exhibits

[9] Keith Lehrer, "Representation in Painting and Consciousness," *Philosophical Studies* 117.12 (2004): 1–14.

to us what the critic and now we mean by the word. The exhibit provides us with some information about how we are disposed to apply the word and, indirectly, what inferences we are disposed to make in the use of 'chocolate' to describe a taste of wine.

The view just described has, as we noted at the outset, similarities to the views of David Hume, Thomas Reid, and Nelson Goodman.[10] A particular taste signifies, as Hume and Reid suggest, a class of experiences. Goodman proposes that the particular taste refers to the properties or predicates that particular and other members of the class exemplify. Keith Lehrer has proposed, with Hume, that the particular taste or sensory exemplar stands for the class of tastes in a process he calls *exemplarization*.[11] We are proposing that there is a kind of interaction between the listener's attention to a taste of the wine and the use of the taste noticed to effect the meaning of the word in the listener's idiolect. The taste exhibits to the listener what the meaning is like. The common components of the theories of Hume, Reid, Goodman, and Lehrer are illustrated by the way in which, as Isenberg suggests, and we have analyzed, experience generated by critical communication fills in, rounds out, and completes the meaning of that communication.

Individual and Communal Language

In our previously mentioned essay, we considered the problem of the relationship between idiolect meaning, the personal dialect of every speaker, and language meaning, the communal meaning of speakers of the language. The problem becomes salient in discourse about wine. Recent research shows that some experts agree in their use of specific wine descriptors. There is especially great consensus in detecting and identifying defects. It seems appropriate in this case to delegate authority, as Putnam and Reid suggested, to the experts.[12]

---

[10]   David Hume, *A Treatise of Human Nature* (London: John Noon, 1739), Book I, Part I, Section VII; Thomas Reid, *Thomas Reid's Inquiry and Essays*, eds. R. E. Beanblossom and Keith Lehrer (Indianapolis: Hackett, 1983), pp. 234–43; Nelson Goodman, *Languages of Art* (Indianapolis: Bobbs-Merrill, 1968).

[11]   K. Lehrer, "Representation in Painting and Consciousness."

[12]   Hilary Putnam, "The Meaning of Meaning," in K. Gunderson (ed.), *Language, Mind and Knowledge*, Minnesota Studies in the Philosophy of Science VI (Minneapolis: University of Minnesota Press, 1975).

119

We treated this phenomenon, following Keith Lehrer and Carl Wagner, as giving greater weight to the experts in the use of such words to determine the communal language.[13] We note, however, that weights allow for indeterminacy in the communal meaning. There is a good deal more to say on this topic and to investigate. The brief consideration is that communal meaning is determined by the weights that members of the community give to experts. This delegation of authority to experts gives them the role of teaching and informing others about the use of words conveyed by critical communication. This in turn shapes the meaning of the word in idiolects of individuals as their attention is directed to features of wines by the critical discourse of the experts. So individuals shape the communal language that influences the meaning of words in the idiolects of individuals in critical communication. The personal and the interpersonal are connected causally and critically in the formation and exhibition of meaning. The question of whether the individual or society comes first in the formation and exhibition of meaning is like the problem of the chicken and egg. They fly and fry together. That is compatible with some chickens having more influence than others on the social product, however.

To elaborate on this issue in wine discourse, it is important to notice that there are several groups of experts: enologists, experts in the wine trade, writers, sommeliers, and connoisseurs. With respect to all technical and chemical terms, all the other experts defer to the wine scientists. With some of the trendy metaphorical terms like 'brawny', 'hedonistic', 'feminine', and 'aggressive' – those words created by the wine writers – sommeliers, merchants, and connoisseurs may defer to the wine writers (an empirical question). But the enologists would not use them, at least not in their scientific writing.

Evaluation

We come finally to the issue of value. It was the special contribution of Isenberg to note that critical communication was not an argument to prove the value of a work of art. Critical communication may yield

---

[13] Keith Lehrer and Carl Wagner, *Rational Consensus in Science and Society: A Philosophical and Mathematical Study* (Dordrecht: Reidel, 1981).

agreement, he suggested, by directing our attention to what the work of art is like. Once you notice what the work of art is like, once the features and content of it are exhibited and fill in the meaning of critical discourse, one might agree about the merit of the work. All this may be said about wine as well.

However, there is a further point that needs to be noted about the role of critical communication. In art and wine many of the words used to describe wine are evaluative. A thin wine has a defect, a light wine does not. Delicacy and finesse are features of wines. Consider the remark that a wine has "a delicious fruity aftertaste on the back of the palate," or "an exquisite evanescent frontal taste on the front of the tongue." As a result of such critical remarks, a person may notice the feature. Moreover, they may notice that the aftertaste is delicious or that the frontal taste is exquisite. We offer the suggestion that the meaning of 'delicious' aftertaste and 'exquisite' frontal taste may be filled in by the experience of the deliciousness of the one taste and the exquisiteness of the other. The meaning of these words may be shaped and shown by critical communication directing our attention to those tastes.

No doubt, the deliciousness of the taste is dependent on other aspects of the taste, but so, perhaps, is the chocolatiness of the taste. Investigations of the psychochemical basis of such tastes might shed light on the question of whether exquisiteness is reducible to other tastes. It is more likely, however, that the exquisiteness is the result of a complex interaction of factors that are not reducible to others. In short, we propose that lightness, elegance, and even exquisiteness and deliciousness may be features a person tastes in wine as the result of critical communication directing attention to just that feature of the wine. Value may supervene on other features as philosophers are wont to believe; or our words of evaluation, like other words used to describe wine, may take their meaning from the experience of those features in the wine. A wine critic once remarked that when you drink great Bordeaux wines, first growths in great years, you should not worry too much about whether you like them. Just taste them as carefully as you can. They are the great wines against which the greatness of wines is judged. Might he not have implied that, with care, you taste the greatness in the wine? Perhaps the experience of that taste fills in, rounds out, and completes the meaning of 'great' applied to wine.

121

III

Wine & Its Critics

8

What the Wine Critic Tells Us

John W. Bender

Why Do They Keep Saying That?

I am a philosopher and a wine taster. I have written thousands of wine notes, published articles on wine, discussed their wines with many winemakers, taught wine-tasting classes, and judged in wine competitions. I have been around. So it always surprises and irks me a bit when, even in semi-professional situations, the first comment that will be exchanged is that "it's all subjective anyway." Why are we having a *judging* here if it is all subjective? We need some clarity. "It's" not all subjective, though my ultimate evaluation of a wine is certainly subjective in the sense that it is *mine*! But, of course, that is not what is usually but foggily meant by the subjectivity claim. It is something more like this: "people's reactions to the same wine can vary and no one can say that one is right and another is wrong. It's all subjective." I do not deny that there is some truth here, but there is also confusion. We must separate the juice from the skins!

The standard wine note – whether from Robert Parker, *Wine Spectator*, or the local newspaper – is really rather complex. It contains literal and sensory description of the wine, aesthetic description (which is often evaluatively loaded and metaphorical in character), and, finally, an all-things-considered evaluation of the wine, often accompanied by a numerical score. Obviously, other elements also get folded in, such as history and facts about the vineyard or vintage, biography of the winemaker, and comparisons to other wines, but these are ancillary to the philosophical logic of the note.

Wine descriptions certainly report the wine taster's *reaction* to the wine, just as art criticism expresses the critic's reaction to the artwork, but there are at least two quite different models for these reactions: the perceptual/objective model and the phenomenological/ subjective model. Does the wine expert *perceive* more of the subtle properties of the wine than does the average wine drinker, or is the critic someone with a richer and imaginative reaction to wine, along with the verbal ability to report that purely subjective experience to others? Can a wine be stalwart, reticent or muscular because these are apt metaphors for the relations obtaining among the wine's physical properties – relations whose subtlety requires the expert's palate to discern – or do these terms mark only imaginative associations in the mind of the critic? This essay will examine the strength of the arguments supporting the two models of what the wine critic tells us.

Objective Perception, Metaphorical Description

My position is that a good wine taster is one who perceives, differentiates, and attends to the complete set of properties that a wine exemplifies, bases his or her aesthetic descriptions on those perceptions, and grounds a final evaluation of the wine on these descriptions and interpretations. This is an analytic procedure and not a simple pleasure reaction. It involves acuity, attention, sensibility, sensitivity, memory, and experience. It involves objective perception.

There is, to begin, the dimension of precision to a wine description. It is perfectly acceptable that thousands who enjoy wine are happy with a very general characterization of their wine: it is soft and fruity; it is a touch smoky, and so on. But it is possible to raise the bar in regard to detail and precision. "Soft and fruity" is not going to enable you to discriminate between the twenty-five Beaujolais in front of you!

This is most vividly illustrated in the work of Ann Noble, the UC Davis enologist who created the Wine Aroma Wheel, reproduced in Figure 8.1. The most general descriptions are those in the center of the wheel, but as you work your way to the outside perimeter, the descriptions become more precise. It seems that there *can* be an objective fact whether this Tokaj has the aroma of tea or of tobacco.

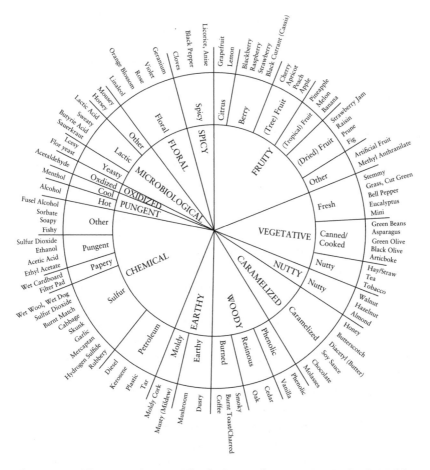

Figure 8.1 The Wine Aroma Wheel. Copyright 1990, 2002, A. C. Noble. www.winearomawheel.com.

These descriptions are grounded in veridical perception and are chemically justifiable: when you smell the fierce, honeyed aroma of a Sauternes, you are smelling botrytis; when you find your Cornas a little "barnyardy," you are detecting brettanomyces; that "corked" bottle that you sent back at the restaurant because it smelled like wet newspaper really does smell of wet newspaper because that is how 2,4,6-trichloranisole smells. You are on the mark! So precision of a wine description does not necessarily bring along with it a degree of subjectivity.

Of course, just as we can be mistaken about other sorts of object-ive facts, tasters can be mistaken about wine facts. Simple inatten-tion can explain many of these mistakes. Someone may say that this Rheingau has a lemony aroma when, in fact, its aroma is clearly more tangerine-like. This can be established (if one wanted to take the time!) by identifying the esters and aldehydes present. But also, discussions among wine tasters can expose mistakes. During many a tasting, I have felt that my descriptions were close but not exactly on target, when a colleague offers the spot-on description. "That's it precisely," is my reaction. My initial description was wrong.

So far, then, I am arguing that wine descriptions are grounded in physical and perceptual fact, hence making them, to that extent, object-ive, but also fallible, as most judgments are. But things get complic-ated. I have been talking about literal descriptions of the wine's physical features. What happens when we move to more qualified and more aesthetic characterizations, and ultimately to an evalu-ation of the wine? Is objectivity maintained? Let us take this a step at a time.

After perception occurs, what exactly is happening? Do we have objective inferences to the *aesthetic* properties of the wine, or do we have a report of the subjective impressions of a given taster that can be accepted or rejected at will? It is one thing to say a wine is tannic and perhaps another to say it is powerful, muscular, brood-ing, delicate, or dumb. Clearly, we are here working at the level of aesthetic description, involving, as it so often does, the use of metaphor. Are these metaphorical descriptions just the subjective waxings of the critic or are they aesthetic properties really (but metaphorically) true of the wine? Frankly, such descriptions can probably belong to either category: I certainly have read and heard descriptions that I can make little or no sense of. But there is never a guarantee against gibberish. Maynard Amerine and Edward Roessler[1] frown on metaphors as unscientific, and my friend (and co-contributor to this volume) Adrienne Lehrer[2] argues extendedly that there is a serious lack of agreement among individuals regarding the meaning of the words used to describe wine.

---

[1] Maynard A. Amerine and Edward B. Roessler, *Wines: Their Sensory Evaluation* (New York: W. H. Freeman, 1976).

[2] Adrienne Lehrer, *Wine and Conversation* (Bloomington: Indiana University Press, 1983).

I, however, have more faith in metaphor. I believe that it is reasonably clear and communicative to characterize Beethoven's *Symphony No. 6* as "pastoral" and his *Op. 74 String Quartet* as "energetic." They surely are descriptions that must be grounded in the musical details, but it seems to me that they *are*. *Wine Spectator* calls one Mosel riesling "plump and well integrated" and another "lean and racy."[3] I believe I understand this. The first has more fruit extract and glycerol, yet is not, as a result, out of balance (another metaphor), and the second has less fruit intensity and probably more of a spring water flavor, but with considerable acidity. When aesthetic metaphors are grounded in the descriptive vinous facts, they can be powerful, colorful, and elegant ways of getting a point across, and can be *true* of the wine. Nelson Goodman, in his famous *Languages of Art*, says that artworks can metaphorically exemplify properties such as sadness, poised power, and flashing action.[4] I do not believe a wine can be sad, but I do think it can be poised or flashy.

It seems obvious, though, that perception is one thing and aesthetic sensibilities are another. One can perceive the amount of fruit extract in a particular zinfandel, aesthetically describe it as "dense," but then comes the evaluation that it is "overwhelmingly dense." Points get deducted. Descriptions lead to evaluations. What is objective and what is subjective in this complicated process? What is literal and what is metaphorical?

The judgment that the wine is dense is based upon the perception of the levels of extract and tannin and alcohol, and these levels, of course, can be established chemically. If a taster considers one wine more tannic than another, she can be proven right or wrong. If she thinks the residual sugar in the wine is around 2 percent, this can be determined. But when the conclusion arrives that this chardonnay is *too* sweet, making it cloying and lacking in taste-clarity, *standards* have been applied. Can they be established as right or wrong? What when experts agree? Is the wine then objectively cloying?

"Cloying" is certainly a feature of the wine that philosophers and psychologists call a "response-dependent property," meaning that the

---

[3] *Wine Spectator*, December 31, 2005, Vol. 30, No. 14 (New York: M. Shanken Communications), p. 208.

[4] Nelson Goodman, *Languages of Art* (Indianapolis: Bobbs-Merrill, 1968).

wine is physically such that it regularly causes a certain experiential response in normal or qualified observers. Just like being red: a thing is red if it causes that well-known "reddish experience" in those with normal vision. Yet, most of us still think that objects are really, objectively red. So seeing red is not subjective, even though it is response-dependent. If the judgment that a wine is cloying is not only based on the perception of its level of residual sugar, but also is a judgment shared by most experienced tasters, isn't that about as objective as you could want?

Well, the problem is that unlike 'red', which is purely descriptive, 'cloying' is at least partially evaluative. It is what Frank Sibley calls a "merit-quality."[5] This implies that some normative standards are being applied, at least implicitly. It is most likely that these are norms that reflect the taster's past experiences and are essentially comparative in nature; for example:

- "This is too sweet for a chardonnay of this style."
- "Cabernets should always have a touch of dustiness in their aroma and this one does not."
- "Vinification in this Cahors seems too short – classic Cahors are denser and have greater depth."

So if most aesthetic descriptions are evaluatively loaded and are based upon the norms of the taster, then there will pretty clearly be deviations in these descriptions across tasters with different experience. Do we then have nothing but subjectivity and phenomenological reporting in wine descriptions using aesthetic terms?

Not so fast. As philosophers, we must remember the power of argument. Your standard of justice, for example, may not awaken you to what is happening in a certain industrial plant in regard to workload and wages (capitalist pig that you are!), but perhaps when I have a discussion with you, I can persuade you that my norms have more credence. Similarly, there is room for argumentation about wine-tasting standards. Given the fallibility that we acknowledged earlier, everyone should be open to change, refinement, or revision of their

---

[5] Frank Sibley, "General Criteria and Reasons in Aesthetics," in John Fisher (ed.), *Essays on Aesthetics* (Philadelphia: Temple University Press, 1983).

standards. Art criticism in general has as one of its functions to get you to see or hear what you did not before. This can involve a revolution of one's standards. So argument doesn't always mean loggerheads: it can convince. Yes, one person's "bruising" zinfandel may only be another's "full-bodied" wine, but such disputes may well be resolvable.

If someone's first reaction to Maurice Ravel's *Pavanne for a Dead Infant* is that it is overly sentimental and maudlin, while you think that the correct aesthetic judgment is that it is nostalgic and wistful, it is possible to point to musical features of the piece to attempt to discern which judgment is more on the mark. For example, the light orchestration and the flowing character of the melody seem to be reasons for thinking the piece is not maudlin but does have a wistful quality. The point here is that, even if you cannot establish chemically that a wine is "bruising," such a description can nonetheless be argued for on the grounds of the basic and non-aesthetic features of the wine.

With the help of appropriate real-life wine comparisons, mightn't I be able to bring you around to see that those classically styled Cahors just have more to offer, and that your standard for a good Cahors needs to be appropriately revised? I can see a dispute, say, between two tasters, being resolved by a rethinking of their standards ("maybe zinfandels *can* carry that huge amount of alcohol with some level of grace"), or a realization on the part of one that they have overstated the case in the particular instance ("well, come to think of it, this wine really doesn't lack fruit, does it?"). Argumentation has results and changes beliefs. There is, at least, the possibility of dialectic regarding standards, which may well lead to a modification of your standards, if you appreciate the force of the other point of view. Perhaps the refinement of standards can be conceived as objective; through argument and a resulting greater acuity, one can become a better taster and make more subtle but also more exact judgments.

My point, then, is that since standards or sensibilities are open to argumentation, they can be judged as more or less plausible or more or less experienced. When it comes to aesthetic sensibilities, one can be convinced to make a change. This process need not be seen as any more "subjective" than a debate over justice is necessarily subjective.

131

Sensitivity and Subjectivity

But is there a point where argument gives out, where there is simply no traction for an argument to claim victory? What happens if our aesthetic disagreements are not a matter of differences in standards but rather differences in physical sensitivity to the properties of the wine that we take to be aesthetically important? If your threshold for smelling lemon or orange is 4,000 times greater than mine,[6] then it seems obvious that when it comes to deciding whether this Savennières is too lemony in its flavor, we are going to have a disagreement. I said earlier that wine descriptions can be precise without necessarily being subjective, but if that precision is based on your judgment of the *degree* to which a wine exhibits a certain property, and that reaction is a function of your particular level of physical sensitivity to the wine's various components, isn't an objectivist in trouble?

There is ample evidence that individuals differ in their sensitivity to perceptual stimuli, but the magnitude of these differences as it impacts wine judgments needs to be emphasized. A person can be ultra-sensitive to sourness and relatively insensitive to sweetness. Will this not inevitably affect their judgment of the balance of the Mosel riesling we are sharing, two of whose most important properties are level of sweetness and acidity? Twenty- to forty-year-olds are more sensitive to sweet, bitter, and salty tastes than are forty- to sixty-year-olds. What if you are a thirty-year-old and on a tasting panel with a sixty-year-old? You cannot tell him to become a thirty-year-old again (much as he might like!). Phenylthiourea (a compound occurring in wine) tastes extremely bitter to two-thirds of the population; nevertheless, one-third is totally insensitive to it.[7]

And then there is the matter of "supertasters." They are not super in the sense of being expert, or being able to guess twenty wines in a row in a blind tasting. Rather, they are blessed with palates

[6] Reported in Alan R. Hirsch, MD, review of Piet Vroon, Anton van Amerongen, and H. de Vries, *Smell: The Secret Seducer, Journal of the American Medical Association* 279 (1998): 1840.

[7] Amerine and Roessler, *Wines: Their Sensory Evaluation*, p. 58.

having 25 percent more taste receptors of various types than the norm. As a result, they react more intensely than others to bitterness, sweetness, and the creamy sensation of fat. They are not lovers of broccoli (way too bitter!), but if you slather it in butter, maybe they would capitulate. How, then, do a supertaster and I (assuming I am not one!) agree about the aesthetic effect of that slightly bitter finish I notice on our expensive Alsace gewürtztraminer? I think it gives the wine nerve, he thinks the wine finishes with a near-metallic taste, which is probably not a good thing. Notice that these local evaluations (i.e., evaluations of singular properties of the wine) have a material impact on the wine taster's all-things-considered judgment of the wine's quality. The final judgment of overall quality must, to be rational, be a summative exercise over the various local evaluations that have resulted from analysis of the wine's properties. They are, therefore, crucial to the entire wine-tasting enterprise.

And yet, disputes like the one between me and my supertaster friend seem completely irresolvable. They are irresolvable both about the wine's aesthetic properties and about its ultimate value. And they are so for reasons of sensitivity rather than sensibility. No one wants a wine to taste literally metallic, so my cohort and I do not have a disagreement over standards or sensibilities. But he is so much more sensitive to tannin or bitterness than I am that he says "overly tannic," and therefore also says "inelegant and unbalanced finish," and then concludes, "a wine marred by its awkward, off-putting finish; 84 points." I, on the other hand, say "a bitter hint on the finish," and then say "firm, bracing, and clean at the end," and conclude, "this is a wine taster's wine – perhaps not a wine for everyone, but excellent – 90 points." What do we do now?

Sensibilities are perhaps best seen as abilities for identifying certain features of a wine or work of art as aesthetically significant. *Sensitivities*, on the other hand, are the physical capacities to react to certain properties. And here, questions of intensity are central. Greater sensitivity is ascribed to one person over another when the first either reacts *more* intensely to a certain property, or reacts to *lower* intensities of some quality. Is there a *right* level of reaction? Can my friend just be overly sensitive or I just be numbingly insensitive?

133

It is interesting to note that from "the inside," as it were, the perceptual judgments that ground the disparate aesthetic and evaluative conclusions made by my friend and me will be judged by each of us to be as objective as any perceptual judgment can be. The supertaster says to himself, "I know tannin when I taste it, and this gewürtztraminer is much too tannic. Don't you get that?" The answer is that no, I literally do not get it. And yet, from my point of view, I believe I have attentively perceived all there is to perceive in the wine, and the level of bitterness is fine.

But if we have an irresolvable dispute here, based on physical differences, there is a reasonably clear sense in which the judgments are *subjective*. Not that they are reports of the phenomenological and imaginative whimsy of the tasters, but that there is significant variation from subject to subject. Variations that lead to manifestly different aesthetic judgments. A rather odd conclusion, then, seems to be forming. Where we first suggested that a wine taster's perceptiveness rather than his imagination and vocabulary was the guarantee of objectivity, I am now arguing that, because of *variations* in perceptiveness, subjective disputes are ineliminable.

The Argument: "No Argument-No Objectivity"

That is my claim, but what is the argument? After all, one can follow David Hume about *sensibilities*, believing that interpersonal variations are a matter of experience, education, attention, and so forth. But, Hume thought, with the "right" backgrounding, our aesthetic judgments should coalesce.[8] As I said earlier, one can be convinced into accepting certain standards of taste, and here lies the difference: there is no arguing about sensitivities.

I may try and even succeed in changing your sensibilities and your subsequent judgments about what is aesthetically important in a given wine or style of wine. I think, for example, that you *ought* to pay more attention to the silkiness of the texture of pinot noir, because, by my standards, a pinot noir cannot be first rate without that

[8] David Hume, *Of the Standard of Taste and Other Essays*, ed. John W. Lentz (Inglewood: Prentice-Hall, 1965).

134

textural quality. But, in contrast, there *simply is no room for argument* when it comes to sensitivities. We would never (and logically cannot) think it appropriate to suggest that tasters with divergent sensitivities *ought to be* coming to the same conclusions about the same wine.

Perhaps you think that there is one optimal level of sensitivity, and it is that from which correct descriptions and evaluations flow. This would be a mistake. Not only are levels of sensitivity for the most part not under voluntary control but, more importantly, there just are no grounds for privileging one level over the other. Yes, we want a good taster to be maximally *aware* of the properties exhibited in a wine – let no property go unperceived! – but no, that does not mean that maximal sensitivity (whatever, if anything, that might mean) is optimal.

And notice that you would agree that, if you were forty times more sensitive to acidity than you are, you would then be *justified* in finding the wine edgy and sharp, rather than crisp and refreshing as you do now. Consequently, you cannot very well say that the taster with forty times more sensitivity than you is just *wrong* when he finds your refreshing wine sharp and edgy. There is, therefore, no force to the idea that, when disputes about a wine's value are based upon differences in sensitivity, only one disputant's claims can be warranted.

Hey, It's Objective *and* Subjective

So, in the end, are wine tasting and wine criticism objective or subjective? Like so many other philosophical problems, we find that when we delve into the matter, all the easy answers recede into oblivion. I certainly believe that qualified tasters can accurately perceive many of the physicochemical properties of a wine, and also that those with aesthetic leanings can "interpret" a wine correctly, just as a painting or piece of music can be interpreted. Correctness conditions for aesthetic descriptions surely are looser and more indeterminate than they are for a judgment that the wine has 3 percent residual sugar. Still, I have had wines that I think are *truly* describable as "forceful and powerful," for example.

135

John W. Bender

I cannot deny that a degree of subjectivity might well be lurking in the divergent standards that wine tasters may be applying, but I have a perhaps overly optimistic idea that these are negotiable. What are not negotiable, however, are the physical differences that each of us brings to the tasting table. Consequently, my conclusion is that the most interesting form of subjectivity in wine appreciation is grounded in our own objective differences. Cheers!

9

Experiencing Wine
Why Critics Mess Up
(Some of the Time)

Jamie Goode

Introduction

What is it about wine that sets it apart from other beverages and foods? It is hard to single out just one aspect since there are so many. First of all, there is history. Wine has been with us for some 7,000 years and has been an enduring facet of many cultures. It has religious significance in that the Christian church uses it as the symbol of Christ's blood in celebrating the Eucharist. It is also relatively "natural," in that the properties of the grapes are crucial for determining the characteristics and quality of the wine they make, in a way not seen with more "manufactured" drinks such as beer and whisky. Then there is diversity, the result of a bewildering array of grape varieties coupled with differences in winemaking technique, vineyard characteristics, and climatic influence. But for the purposes of this book, perhaps the most remarkable thing about wine is the way that a culture has developed around it where enthusiasts and professionals frequently share their sensory perceptions by means of words. I cannot think of many other fields of human endeavor where active sharing of people's private sensory experiences is practiced to such a degree.

In this essay, I am going to rather bravely try to pull together some quite disparate threads to weave a common story about our perception of wine, and how this relates to wine criticism and rating. After a brief overview of the practice of wine criticism, I look at the nature of our experience of wine drinking, reviewing recent biological insights into the biology of flavor perception. The next stage is the translation of this conscious representation into words, which is not as straightforward as we like to think. What are the most effective ways of describing wines in terms of words? And does our vocabulary for wine in any way shape our tasting experience? Finally, I tackle the thorny question of individual differences in wine perception. When we taste a wine together, are we all having a common experience?

Wine Tasting in Practice

At the heart of the wine trade lies the assessment of wine quality and style, and the sharing of that assessment in words. As a professional wine writer based in London, I have the opportunity to attend tastings on most working days. For various reasons, I have to turn most of these opportunities down, but I still attend perhaps forty significant tastings each year. The number of wines offered on such occasions varies, but individual tasters would usually sample between fifty and 120 different wines. These events are not all for the benefit of journalists; perhaps the majority of attendees are people involved in the selling of wine. Nonetheless, almost all participants will be taking notes, which in the main are an attempt to put down in words the sensory experience they are having as they swirl, sniff, and slurp.

This assessment of quality is important. An exceptional wine will retail for hundreds of dollars, a humble one for perhaps five. To be sure, some of the appeal of the super-expensive trophy wines lies in their scarcity, aspirational marketing, and a human penchant towards conspicuous consumption. But if the emperor really did have no clothes – and there was no widely agreed qualitative distinction between cheap and expensive wine – then the whole system would have collapsed long ago.

That is not to say that there are not fault lines developing in the wine world, largely generated by different ideas about what constitutes quality among influential critics. There is a clash of cultures. Fine wine as we know it grew up and developed as an aesthetic system based on the idea that it is possible to differentiate quality in wines in a way that is largely objective. Through a process of benchmarking and consensus among key figures in the wine trade, the classic European wine styles became established; the wine trade developed its own codified language for describing wine, and a self-consistent "system" of wine was the standard by which all wines were judged. The existence of New World wines was acknowledged by the fine wine world, but these were largely outside the established system. However, things have now changed. The classic fine wine standard has been called into question, and there is a degree of schism between those who see themselves as guardians of this traditional system and those who challenge it as being restrictive and outdated.

The key reason for this conflict has been the emergence of wine ratings and of critics who have approached fine wine from a different qualitative standard to that of the establishment. It is hard to overstate the way that wine ratings have changed the world of fine wine. Thirty years ago, they did not exist – if you wanted to choose a good bottle, you trusted your merchant, bought on the reputation of the producer, or spent many years acquiring the detailed knowledge needed to navigate the complexities of the fine wine market on your own. Then along came American critic Robert Parker, who many consider to be the most powerful person in the world of wine today. As a lawyer with a passion for wine, in 1978 he began publishing the *Wine Advocate*, a simple publication but one that was to revolutionize the fine wine market. Parker's approach was to position himself as a consumers' advocate, and his aim was to give people the sort of impartial guidance that would help them make informed wine buying decisions. His stroke of genius was to score wines on an easily understandable 100-point scale, where anything scoring under 80 was not up to much and anything over 90 was pretty special.

Suddenly consumers were empowered. While tasting notes are an important part of the *Wine Advocate* and his book (*Parker's Wine Buyer's Guide*), it is the scores that make relative performance transparent. "Parker points" offered a way into wine for those daunted by its complexity. They introduced an element of competition in the world of fine wine, and enabled overperforming new producers to rub shoulders with the classics: rather than building a reputation over generations, all that was now needed for entry into the wine world elite was a string of scores in the high 90s. They also allowed wine to be traded by those with no specialist knowledge, because prices track scores, and the highest-scoring young wines have tended to increase in value spectacularly after release.

139

Just as consumers have found Parker points to be a short-cut mechanism for making buying choices, wine merchants have found them equally useful as a sales tool. The way that ratings make fine wine easier to understand and buy has also been a significant factor in the opening up of new markets for fine wine, most specifically in Asia.

Paralleling the influence of wine ratings (or perhaps helped by it), the fine wine market has grown significantly in the last twenty years, and with it there has been a profusion of critics. Many of these also use a 100-point scale, which is now firmly fixed as the standard for wine ratings, although a few stubbornly stick to 5-, 20-, or 25-point systems. Some of these critics, such as James Halliday in Australia, Stephen Tanzer in the United States, and Michel Bettane in France, have an important local influence but are less well known internationally. Others, such as Tom Stephenson (a Champagne expert) and Clive Coates (a Burgundy specialist), have an influence limited to their regions of expertise. Magazines such as the US publication *Wine Spectator*, whose various tasters also issue 100-point verdicts, and British title *Decanter* do have some influence with their readers. But no one comes close to Parker in the arena of fine wine. Of course, there is more to wine writing than rating wines. Hugh Johnson and Jancis Robinson are examples of well-known, highly respected wine writers who tend to write more generally about wine, rather than focus on rating specific bottles. What they say matters, but in a different sort of way.

Unsurprisingly, for one so dominant in his field, Robert Parker has come in for some flak. Criticisms usually come in three forms. First, there are those who object to the practice of scoring wines at all. Second, some people disagree with Parker's taste in wine, arguing that he favors wines made in a more obvious, very ripe style – sometimes at the expense of subtlety. Third, there are those who object to the way that scores are used by consumers, who buy by points rather than develop their own taste, and the corresponding effect that a high rating has on the availability and price of a wine. Perhaps most sinister is the assertion that Parker's preferences have caused producers to change the way they make their wines, so that they will garner the all-important high scores.

While there is undoubtedly some validity to these criticisms, the general feeling in the trade is that, on balance, Robert Parker has been good for fine wine. Probably the most positive effect his ratings have had is that they have given consumers the confidence to trade up in their buying. The existence of a highly influential über-critic, though, raises some important questions, which the rest of this essay will attempt to answer. First, can the existence of clashing critical opinions about wine be explained merely in terms of cultural differences in wine appreciation, or does it reflect some underlying biological differences in wine perception? Second, does what we now know about the biology of flavor perception have anything useful to contribute to how we view wine criticism? And, third, what is the most effective way to share this perceptual experience of wine, and does our language for wine in turn shape our perception of it?

The Taste of Wine: How We Perceive What is in Our Glass

What is the nature of our perception of wine? Most people have a rather simplistic view that takes into account input from just taste and smell receptors in the mouth and nasal cavity. These receptors turn chemical information into electrical signals, which can then be processed by the brain. The tongue and soft palate have taste buds containing receptors for five modes of chemical stimuli: sweet, salty, bitter, sour, and umami. The nasal cavity contains olfactory receptor neurons which express, between them, around 2,000 different receptors, each tuned to recognize different chemical signatures of volatile odorants. The simplistic view sees a linear pathway from the detection of elements of wine by the taste receptors in the tongue and the olfactory receptors in the nasal cavity to the mental representation of the wine's properties. This is wrong, and a much more nuanced and complicated view of the process is needed.

Rather than act as a straightforward measuring instrument, the brain "models" the world around us. Our sensory systems are bombarded constantly by a mass of information, which, if attended to uniformly, would swamp our perceptive and decision-making processes. So the brain is able to extract from this sea of sensory data just those features which are most relevant. This is done by a procedure known as higher-order processing.

We often think that our sensory system is revealing to us the world around us in an accurate and complete way. Actually, however, what we experience is an edited version of reality that is based on

141

the information that is most relevant to our survival and functioning. For almost all purposes it does no harm for us to think of the world around as revealed to us to be "reality" – indeed, life would become quite complicated if we operated any other way – but for the purposes of this discussion it is useful to realize that the version of reality we experience is an edited and partial one.

This can be illustrated in a number of ways. Think about your household pets, if you have any; imagine your friends' if you do not. Dogs live in a smell world that is almost completely closed to us, and which is just as vivid to them as the visual world is to us. Rats and mice, like many small mammals, get almost all the information they need about their environment from a combination of sniffing and using their whiskers: they are nocturnal, and vision is not very useful at night. Now switch on your radio or television, or take a call on your mobile phone: it is clear that the air is full of information that we cannot access unless we have a device to decode it. The information we do access is sufficient to allow us to effectively negotiate the world around us, and while it might be nice to see an extended spectrum of colors, or in the dark, or have the olfactory acuity of a sniffer dog, it is not essential for our daily lives.

The higher-order processing in the visual system is the best understood for any of the senses. Scientists have worked out how visual processing extracts features of the environment that are most likely to be relevant. For instance, our peripheral vision is sensitive to motion: moving objects immediately stand out, because neurons are tuned to respond to them. This motion detection ability is much stronger in the periphery than it is in the central visual field. Look at your computer monitor (as long as it is a conventional tube and not a flat screen), and then look away. As you look away, the screen of your monitor appears to flicker in your peripheral vision; you were not aware of this while you were staring at it. Faces are also likely to be significant cues, so our visual systems have special brain mechanisms for face processing. This is the reason why so many advertisements and magazine covers rely on human faces, even where the face is not particularly relevant.

Although it is less well studied, this sort of higher-order processing is also important in flavor detection. We are bombarded with chemical stimuli all the time and the brain has to filter this information so that only the important bits get through. It seems that much of the brain is dedicated to producing a suitably edited view of reality, just as the staff in a newsroom work hard all day sifting through the output of their journalists to produce a fifteen-minute news bulletin for broadcast that evening.

The senses of taste and smell work together to perform two important tasks: identifying nutritious foods and drinks, and protecting us from eating things that are bad for us. The brain achieves this by linking food that we need with a reward stimulus – it smells or tastes "good" – and making bad or unneeded foods aversive. To do this, flavor perception needs to be connected with the processing of memory (we remember which foods are good and those which have made us ill) and emotions (we have a strong desire for food when we are hungry that then motivates us to seek out a decent meal). Because seeking food is a potentially costly and bothersome process, we need a strong incentive to do it. Hunger and appetite are thus powerful physical drives. They are also finely tuned. It is striking that we are able to eat what we need and not a lot more or less: even a slight imbalance, over decades, would result in gross obesity or starvation.

What we describe as wine "taste" is actually a multimodal sensory experience. Recent work has shown that it is in a brain structure called the orbitofrontal cortex that taste and smell are brought together to form the sensation of flavor.[1] Information from other senses, such as touch and vision, is also combined at this level, to create a complex, unified sensation that is then localized to the mouth by the sense of touch – after all, this is where any response to the food or drink, such as swallowing it or spitting it out, will need to take place. It has also been shown that the orbitofrontal cortex is where the reward value (the "niceness," known more grandly as "hedonic valence") of taste and smell is represented. That's another way of saying this is where the brain decides whether what we have in our mouths is delicious, dull or disgusting. Another study has shown that the brain uses two dimensions to analyze smells, intensity, and hedonic valence.[2]

---

[1] Edmund T. Rolls, "Brain Mechanisms Underlying Flavour and Appetite," *Phil. Trans. R. Soc. B* 361 (2006): 1123–36; published online June 15, 2006; doi:10.1098/rstb.2006.1852.

[2] A. K. Anderson, K. Christoff, I. Stappen, D. Panitz, D. G. Ghahremani, G. Glover, J. D. E. Gabrieli, and N. Sobel, "Dissociated Neural Representations of Intensity and Valence in Human Olfaction," *Nature Neuroscience* 6 (2003): 196–202; published online January 21, 2003; doi:10.1038/nn1001.

The amygdala responds to intensity while the orbitofrontal cortex is the region that decides whether the smell is good or bad.

Some nerve cells in this brain region respond to combinations of senses, such as taste and sight, or taste and touch, or smell and sight. This convergence of inputs, known as cross-modal processing, is acquired by learning, but it is a process that occurs slowly, typically requiring many pairings of the different sensations before it is fixed. This suggests an explanation for why we often need several experiences with a new food or wine to be able to appreciate them fully. It is also at this level where stimulus–reinforcement association learning takes place. This is the situation where, for example, you are faced with a new food (stimulus) which tastes good, but then it makes you violently sick (association). Next time you pop some of this in your mouth, you immediately spit it out in disgust. It saves you the bother of being sick again, and is therefore a protective mechanism. (However, this mechanism evidently can be overridden, as in the case of the binge drinker who throws up in the gutter on Friday night and the next day returns to her or his drink of choice.)

There is a further concept that is of interest here, sensory-specific satiety.[3] This is the observation that when enough of a particular food is eaten, its reward value decreases. However, this decrease in pleasantness is greater than for other foods. Putting it more simply, if you like both bananas and chocolate, and then eat lots of bananas, you cannot stomach the thought of another banana but you will still fancy a chocolate. This clever brain trick makes us desire the particular sorts of foods that we need at a given time, and helps us to balance our nutritional intake. In humans, the response in the orbitofrontal cortex to the odor of a food eaten to satiety decreases, but the response to another odor that has not been eaten does not change. The subjects' perception of the intensity of the smell of the consumed food does not change, but their perception of its pleasantness (hedonic valence) does. Swallowing is not necessary for sensory-specific satiety to occur. This could have some effect during a wine tasting where a taster is repeatedly encountering the same sort of taste or smell. At a large trade tasting it is quite common to taste as many as 100 wines in a session. If these results of sensory-specific satiety are

[3] E. T. Rolls and J. H. Rolls, "Olfactory Sensory-Specific Satiety in Humans," *Physiology and Behavior* 61.3 (1997): 461–73.

extrapolated to this sort of setting, then it is likely that the brain will be processing the last wine you taste differently to that of the first, assuming that there are some components to the taste or smell in common – for example, tannins, fruit or oak.

The fact that we model the world around us, rather than perceive an exact representation of it, has relevance to wine appreciation. A critic's palate is not analogous to a measuring device: his or her evaluation of a wine is not just a matter of an assessment of the wine's properties, as, for example, a spectrophotometer would measure the light transmission characteristics of the said wine in a cuvette. Let us return to Robert Parker and his 100-point scale. If he rates a wine at 94/100, the tendency among wine lovers is to regard this score as a property of the wine ("this is a 94-point wine"). Yet it is more accurate to think of the score as a property of an interaction between Robert Parker and the wine: what he is rating is his perceptual experience, which depends in part on him and only in part on the properties of the wine itself. Critics are reporting on their interaction with the wine; they are rating the conscious representation of that wine in their brain. This leads us on to the related issue of translating wine into words, how this translation brings noise into the system, and also the intriguing possibility that language actually helps mold our representations.

Wine into Words: The Language of Wine

In a recent piece in *The Times* newspaper, Jonathan Meades took a dig at the way language is used in wine descriptions.[4] He pointed out that when Hugh Johnson's iconic *World Atlas of Wine* was first published in 1971, Johnson offered a lexicon of fewer than eighty descriptors for tasting notes. Meades clearly disapproved of the way this list has since burgeoned. "The globalization of wine-making and the type of people now buying it have caused that lexicon to be vastly augmented. A new, qualitatively different language has evolved. The old one, founded in the certainties of St James's and St Estèphe, was a code. It was as hermetically precise and exclusive as the jargon of

---

[4] Jonathan Meades, "Vintage Hyperbole, If I'm Not Mistaken," *The Times* (London), April 30, 2005.

any other self-regarding profession," said Meades. "This has largely disappeared, drowned by a clamorous demotic which, far from being codified, attempts to express (rather than classify) a wine's qualities and, equally, to demonstrate the verbal invention of the merchant, sommelier, writer, buff, casual drinker." Meades added that such talk "is frequently characterized by the hedged bets of jest and self parody."

Meades's unease with winespeak raises an important question. In describing wine, what are we trying to do? Are we using a learned code, where we associate particular standardized terms with physical attributes of the wine? Or do we attempt to describe what is *actually* there in ways that others, unschooled in our "system," can relate to or understand? In practice, it is likely that a bit of both goes on. Nonetheless, it is important to work out which system we are attempting to implement: the code, or the real-life description. This then leads to further questions. Which linguistic tools are appropriate or permissible in descriptions of wine? Some argue that we should go no further than simile; others see metaphor as a crucial tool in our endeavor to share what we are experiencing. Should we be attempting to describe a wine as plainly and accurately as possible, breaking it down in a reductionistic manner into its constituent flavors and aromas, or do we use more figurative and creative language to build a more holistic description?

Frédéric Brochet, a cognitive psychologist, has done some important work that is relevant here. He has studied the practice of wine tasting as carried out by professionals. His claim is that the practice and teaching of tasting rest on a fragile theoretical basis. "Tasting is representing," says Brochet, "and when the brain carries out a 'knowledge' or 'understanding' task, it manipulates representations."[5] In this context a "representation" is a conscious experience constructed by the mind on the basis of a physical experience, in this case the taste, smell, sight, and mouthfeel of a wine. Brochet used textual analysis (which looks at the sorts of words that tasters use to verbalize their representations) and behaviour analysis (inferring cognitive mechanisms from looking at how subjects act) to come up with some fascinating conclusions.

---

[5] Frédéric Brochet, "Chemical Object Representation in the Field of Consciousness," Académie Amorim 2001; www.academie-amorim.com/us/laureat_2001/brochet.pdf#search=%22frederic%20brochet%20amorim%22.

Textual analysis involves the statistical study of the words used in a text. Brochet used five data sets, consisting of tasting notes from *Guide Hachette*, Robert Parker, Jacques Dupont, Brochet himself, and notes on eight wines from forty-four professionals collected at Vinexpo. He studied the way that the different tasters used words to describe their tasting experiences, and summarized his six key results as follows. (1) The authors' descriptive representations are based on the types of wines and not on the different parts of the tasting. (2) The representations are 'prototypical': that is, specific vocabularies are used to describe types of wines, and each vocabulary represents a type of wine. Putting this another way, when a taster experiences a particular wine, the words he or she uses to describe it are those that the individual links to this sort of wine. (3) The range of words used (lexical fields) is different for each author. (4) Tasters possess a specific vocabulary for preferred and non-preferred wines. No taster seems to be able to put aside his or her preferences when his or her representations are described. (5) Color is a major factor in organizing the classes of descriptive terms used by the tasters, and has an influence on the sorts of descriptors used. (6) Cultural information is present in the sensorial descriptions. Interestingly, Brochet states that "certain descriptive terms referring to cognitive representation probably come from memory or information heard or read by the subject, but neither the tongue nor the nose could be the object of the coding."[6]

In the next set of experiments, Brochet invited fifty-four subjects to take part in a series of experiments in which they had to describe a real red wine and a real white wine. A few days later the same group had to describe the same white wine and this white wine colored red with a neutral-tasting food colorant. Interestingly, in both experiments they described the "red" wine using identical terms even though one of them was actually a white wine. Brochet's conclusion was that the perception of taste and smell conformed to color: vision has more of an input in the wine-tasting process than most people would think.

In a second experiment, Brochet served the same average-quality wine to people at a week's interval. The twist was that on the first occasion it was packaged and served to people as a *vin de table*, and on the second as a *grand cru* wine. He analyzed the terms used in

---

[6] Ibid.

the tasting notes: for the *grand cru* wine versus the *vin de table*, "a lot" replaced "a little"; "complex" replaced "simple"; and "balanced" replaced "unbalanced" – all because of the sight of the label.

Brochet explains the results through a phenomenon called "perceptive expectation": a subject perceives what she has pre-perceived, and then finds it difficult to back away from that. For humans, visual information is much more important than chemosensory information, so we tend to trust vision more.

From here we move to the language of wine and to the literary devices used to communicate sensory experience. Let us focus first on written language, where letters, which are visual sensations, are turned into words. We are so familiar with this that to have it pointed out to us seems absurd. As soon as we see words on a page, these visual sensations become loaded with meaning. Think of a love letter, or a tax demand: the visual sensations almost immediately stimulate an emotional response in us. (As an aside, the written word has enabled the development of a complex society. It enables us to use pencil and paper, or laptop computers, as an extension of our mental space. We can share with others our thoughts, and use these devices as tools to store, and then add to, moment-to-moment thoughts, thus in time building an article or idea in a way that would not be possible otherwise.)

In wine writing we do the opposite. We attempt to turn our conscious perception elicited by a flavor, but added to by our memory and learning, into letters on a page, which we hope will in some way convey our perceptions to others who lack the same flavor stimulus. We are attempting to share, in as transparent a way as possible, our own private world of perception. What are the most effective and legitimate ways of doing this? Should we enlist figurative language in descriptions of wine?

A fascinating academic project is underway at the Department of Modern Languages, University of Castilla-La Mancha in Spain, involving Drs. Ernesto Suarez-Toste, Rosario Caballero, and Raquel Segovia, entitled *Translating the Senses: Figurative Language in Wine Discourse*. The initial stage of the project involves collecting a data set consisting of 12,000 tasting notes, from a range of British and American publications (*Wine Advocate, Wine Spectator, Wine Enthusiast, Wine News, Decanter,* and Wineanorak.com). This text is cut, pasted, and cleared of all extra information. The types of metaphors used are tagged, and then a concordance is used to track each instance of any type of metaphor of interest.

"Wine folks use metaphor all the time," says Suarez-Toste. "Aroma wheels are OK for identifying aromas, but the structure and mouthfeel almost always demand the use of figurative language. For one thing we personify wine most of the time. Not simply by saying it has a nose instead of a smell. It has character, it's endowed with human virtues and vices. It can be generous, sexy, voluptuous, whimsical, shy, demure, bold or aggressive. We almost cannot conceive wine without personifying it."[7]

We reach for metaphors because of the impoverished language we have for describing tastes and smells. "Because there is no single lexicon with the expressive potential to cover all the range of sensorial impressions, the intellectualization of sensorial experience is inextricably linked to the figurative uses of language," explains Suarez-Toste. "There is no problem with this as far as such areas of human life as poetry are concerned, but the inherent subjectivity of sensorial experience represents innumerable difficulties when technical discourse is under scrutiny."

What about the good old tasting note? "This relies heavily on a combination of terms articulating the remembrance of the taster's repository of aromas and flavors, connotations and, above all, figurative language which, although may be perceived by the layman as deliberate obscurity, is a valuable tool that allows the (only partially satisfactory) communication of the experience of tasting wine. The vocabulary used points to various figurative phenomena (synesthesia, metonymy, metaphor), all of which are indispensable tools for articulating what is an intrinsically sensorial experience."

So we have wine as a living creature; wine as a piece of cloth; wine as a building; even, in a recent note by Robert Parker, wine as a whore. It is easy to make fun of this sort of description, but such metaphors are born of necessity. While we would like to have a more exact way of sharing our experience of wine in words, such precision does not exist, and those who restrict themselves merely to naming aromas and flavors end up missing out on some of the more important aspects of the character of wines that cannot be described in this way, such as texture, structure, balance, and elegance.

---

[7] Personal communication, 2005.

"Currently we're obsessed with structure and mouthfeel," Suarez-Toste explains. "These usually demand architecture and textile metaphors. One curiosity that our audiences enjoy is that a wine can be described in the same tasting note as silky and velvety. Of course the terms are for them mutually exclusive. The idea is that both are different (but almost synonymous for the critic's purpose) realizations of a textile metaphor. The connotations are smooth and expensive, fresher in silk (more used for whites) and warmer in velvet (more frequent in reds), but essentially the same." Suarez-Toste and colleagues are at the stage where they will soon be presenting their early results at conferences.

Are We All Tasting the Same Wine? Individual Differences in Wine Perception

The third main theme of this essay is whether as wine tasters we all share the same (or, at least, an approximately similar) taste world. This is where we turn to a branch of psychology known as taste psychophysics. This field of study concentrates on how physical taste stimuli are perceived by the mind. Linda Bartoshuk, Professor of Surgery at Yale University, is one of the leading experts in this field. In her work on the psychophysics of taste she has addressed the difficult question of how we can compare sensory experiences among different individuals.

Are two people drinking from the same bottle of wine having a common experience? "In my view, this is one of the most interesting questions in sensory science," responds Bartoshuk. "It taps into an important philosophical issue: since we cannot share experiences directly, is there a way to make comparisons across individuals (or groups) indirectly?"[8] One of Bartoshuk's contributions to this field is that she has devised a reliable scale for making intersubject comparisons that makes use of cross-sense comparison.

Part of the problem of comparing taste experiences among individuals stems from genetic differences. The best known of these genetic mechanisms is that involving PROP (6-N-propylthiouracil). This compound and its chemical relatives contain a group that stimulates a specific bitter taste receptor. Non-tasters of PROP carry two

---

[8] Personal communication.

recessive alleles of a gene that has recently been localized to chromosome 7; tasters carry either one or both alleles. "My lab discovered a large variation among tasters; those with the most taste-buds are called supertasters and those with fewer are called medium tasters," states Bartoshuk. "Supertasters live in a neon taste world; taste sensations are roughly three times as intense to them as non-tasters." But it is not just taste that is affected by these genetic differences. "Since taste buds are surrounded by nerve fibers carrying oral burn/pain, supertasters perceive more oral burn from stimuli such as alcohol, and supertasters also perceive more intense oral touch sensations." Tannic structure in wine is perceived by the sense of touch, so this is highly relevant here. Bartoshuk continues, "perhaps the most important attribute of the sensory experience produced by wine tasting is retronasal olfaction. When we sniff odors from the outside world, this is called orthonasal olfaction. When we put things in our mouth, chewing and swallowing pumps up volatiles up behind the palate into the nasal cavity. This is retronasal olfaction." Supertasters, it seems, perceive more intense retronasal olfaction, presumably because they perceive more intense oral sensations.

Given the individual differences in taste perception, how does Bartoshuk make sensory comparisons among individuals and groups? Initially, she used responses to varying dilutions of salt solutions (NaCl) as a taste standard, but she found that this varied with PROP tasting status. The answer was to take advantage of the surprising observation that experiences from different sensory modalities can be matched for perceived intensity, in a form of artificial synesthesia. Putting this more simply, using appropriate standards from an unrelated sense that shows less individual variation than taste, such as the brightness of a light or the loudness of a sound, can make between-subject comparisons in taste intensity possible. For example, in one experiment, non-tasters matched the bitterness of black coffee to the brightness of low-beam headlights at night, while supertasters matched it slightly above high-beam headlights at night. Without the use of an appropriate standard from another sense, scales labeled for taste intensity produce invalid comparisons across groups and individuals.

There is a lot more to be said about individual differences in flavor perception, but this would require more space than is available here. For a start, how do individuals differ in their suite of olfactory

151

receptors? Then there is plasticity in taste: we know that taste does not show a lot of stability over time. People's preferences can change quite markedly with learning and experience. There are changes with age, and likely sex differences, too. It would also be nice to know more about the contribution of learning and memory to the perception of wine. Could it be that critics who are tasting many wines daily have changed their perception of wine to the degree that their opinions are no longer that useful to the occasional drinker, because they are having a quite different experience of the same wine?

Concluding Remarks

When we try to share our perception of wine by means of words, we are attempting to do something very difficult. As we come to taste a wine, we are bringing a lot of our own "stuff" to the table: our culture of wine, the context of our experience of wine, and our expectations about the tasting experience. Then, as we taste, our experience of flavor is a multimodal sensory experience consisting of taste, smell, touch, and vision inputs, which are frequently bound together at different pre-attentive levels, and which then can even feed back to modify the unimodal sensations themselves.

Taste is imprecise, and shows a lot more individual-to-individual variation than other senses. Thus as we taste wine we use the "stuff" we bring to the tasting experience to help frame our thoughts about the wine. As Brochet has shown, our mental representations of wine are prototypical: as we taste, we decide, from our experience, what sort of wine we are tasting, and this then helps us pick our descriptors. Or we might know that a particular wine we are tasting is a Pauillac, and this will lead our thoughts in certain directions as we taste. It is an intriguing thought that the language we have developed (and each taster will have evolved his or her own lexicon) actually shapes our perception, in part through attentional effects, in part because our language of wine will give us a framework on which to build our descriptions. How do we find something if we are not looking for it? Having a vocabulary for wine will likely direct and shape what we "get" from each wine.

But pointing out the complexity of the tasting process is not meant to be a counsel of despair; writing tasting notes and communicating about wine is still a useful endeavor. Rather, as we understand more about the biology of perception, it helps us to make sense of the results of this process and causes us to be more realistic about the degree of precision or consensus that is possible in assessing wine. While there is such a thing as expertise in wine tasting, we should taste humbly and not seek to champion a uniform, one-size-fits-all model of wine assessment. Incompetence and individual differences in perception are quite separate entities that are often mixed in together. Tasting well is a difficult skill, and some of the anomalies between different tasters' views on the same wine are undoubtedly because some wine tasters are not very good at it. Others are likely due to cultural differences or degrees of experience, and still others may be because of real differences in perception that have a biological basis. There's still an important place for critics; there is no room in this "new synthesis" of wine assessment for the über-critic. However, this new understanding of wine perception emphasizes the importance of a learned culture of fine wine, where what comes next builds on the foundations of what went before. Many of the current conflicts in the world of wine are caused by a failure to recognize that there is a culture of aesthetic appreciation of fine wine that is to a large degree learned by the process of comparison and benchmarking: it is a system of aesthetics. But that is another story.

Is figurative language appropriate in technical tasting notes, or should we aim for more technical and analytical descriptors? I would argue that if we are seeking a communication of our perceptions that is as accurate as possible, then the use of figurative language is essential, simply because we lack any other effective way of communicating vital aspects of wine such as structure and texture. In addition, the move to technical-sounding language is usually accompanied by a reductionist dissection of wine into its component parts. The use of metaphor brings us back to a more holistic description of wine, which is more appropriate because our perception is, after all, a multimodal, unitary one. There is also an important place in wine description for the use of synesthetic descriptions: while these run the risk of sounding somewhat contrived, they can bring a fresh, altered perspective that keeps us from getting into a rut with overreliance on stale tasting note terms.

153

IV

The Beauty of Wine

10

You'll Never Drink Alone
Wine Tasting and Aesthetic
Practice

Douglas Burnham and Ole Martin Skilleås

We shall argue here that wine appreciation is *aesthetic*: that is, it is an activity akin to listening to music or viewing a painting. This argument is not easy to make and, in fact, philosophers in the past have generally dismissed it as quite impossible. An important reason is that we tend to put the objects we appreciate aesthetically into three broad categories. One is the visual, which includes painting and sculpture, but also dance and architecture belong in this category. Another category is the aural, and the only obvious example here is music. The third category is the linguistic, comprising novels, poems, and plays. This means that in our way of thinking about objects we appreciate aesthetically, three of the senses are left out completely: touch, smell, and taste. While vision and hearing work "at a distance," these latter senses are sometimes called "proximal" because they involve our bringing something right up against us to touch it, or even inside us such as for smell and taste. Why are there no major art categories, or even minor ones, that correspond to these excluded senses?

In our essay, we want to expand the range of aesthetic objects beyond those that are traditionally considered art. A philosophical treatment of art tends to focus on the activities and thoughts of an *artist*. We will instead focus on the perceiver, or more precisely, *groups* of perceivers. It seems to be possible for someone to regard an object in an aesthetic manner without there being any question of that object constituting a work of art. The obvious example is nature: there is nothing odd in saying that we see a beautiful landscape. Studying

157

the side of the perceiver thus seems more general than the question of art. This generality may help us to understand how wine, which involves at least two of those three excluded senses, can be aesthetically interesting to us without having to argue that wine is art.

In what follows, we will maintain that wine appreciation can and should be considered an aesthetic activity, but only if we understand 'activity' in the special sense of an 'aesthetic practice'. By 'aesthetic practice' is meant above all that we cannot consider wine appreciation, or even music or visual arts appreciation, from the point of view of an isolated viewer who has an immediate, simple experience of something. We argue that philosophical aesthetics tends to begin (sometimes even when believing it does not) with the isolation, immediacy, and simplicity of aesthetic experience. Our argument continues that *because of this beginning*, it therefore also tends to discount the possibility of a phenomenon like wine being aesthetic. Instead, we must take into account the full context of the perceivers, particularly what they have learned in the past, their skills and competencies, the language they use to describe what they are viewing, and the inter-subjective (involving more than one person) nature of all the above. We will try to capture much of what an aesthetic practice involves, but which would appear to be prior to the immediate experience of a thing, under the heading 'funding'. An aesthetic practice with its 'funding' is a multifaceted phenomenon, and this allows us to answer the objections to considering wine appreciation as aesthetic.

It would appear to be the case, and many would want us to believe, that there are two major barriers standing in the way of wine being a proper object of aesthetic attention. The first is that the response to wine is irretrievably *subjective*, perhaps because it involves the 'bodily' senses of taste and smell. By subjective is meant that whether I like a wine or not is only my own concern, and not a matter others can have a valid view about. On the other hand, we feel it is productive to talk about art, even to the extent of being able to change someone's tastes. Because the proximal senses are often considered the most "subjective" senses, it is likely that their involvement in wine appreciation lies behind the claim that such appreciation is merely

158

"subjective." The second barrier is that, even if the first could be overcome, there would still be the impossibility of *communicating* about our subjective taste sensations to others. The language of wine appreciation, when it leaves the domain of straightforward descriptive terminology, is often considered to be pretentious and perhaps even meaningless. However, here we aim to show not only that both of these barriers are illusory, but also that they are not even different issues. We will do this through showing that wine appreciation is an *aesthetic practice*. A similar claim has been substantiated recently, in a paper in the *Journal of Wine Research*.[1] That it is an "aesthetic practice" means that wine appreciation can be compared fruitfully to listening to symphonies or looking at paintings in a gallery.

A related point we want to show in this essay is that there are two theoretically distinct vocabularies in responding to wine. On the one hand, we have the now established vocabulary used by wine critics in newspapers and elsewhere, typically referring to astringents, fruits, smokes, and stones. On the other hand, we have an aesthetic vocabulary, in which the terminology is strikingly similar to that used in the arts to communicate judgments on paintings, pieces of music, and literary works. For example, professional wine tasters will often use terms like 'balanced' or 'complex' about a wine in a way that does not refer to clusters of particular flavors. It is this latter vocabulary we believe to be poorly understood in the world of wine. Moreover, its use within the field of wine appreciation is almost totally ignored in the community of philosophical aesthetics. Understanding the latter vocabulary – how it arises and how it works – is the key to unmasking the misunderstandings mentioned above.

When tasting a wine, we certainly have the problem of communicating our impressions to others, or indeed recording them for ourselves. It is quite simply very difficult to describe our experience of wine. The sense impressions can be as clear as daylight, yet the words fail to convey what we experience. In his book *The Well Wrought Urn*, Cleanth Brooks dubbed the practice of distinguishing sharply between form and content in a poem "the heresy of paraphrase."[2]

---

[1] Steve Charters and Simone Pettigrew, "Is Wine Consumption an Aesthetic Experience?," *Journal of Wine Research* 16 (2005): 121–36.

[2] Cleanth Brooks, *The Well Wrought Urn* (New York: Reynal and Hitchcock, 1947), p. 201.

A paraphrase is an attempt to capture what the poem means in different words, and in prose. The paraphrase keeps the content, but leaves behind the form (the particular words used in the poem, the sounds, rhythms, rhymes, etc.). According to Brooks, a paraphrase that purports to be the same thing in other words is impossible since the form is not to be "translated" into another form without loss of aesthetic "meaning." Given the difficulties we experience when trying to communicate the experience of tasting a wine, one may feel it to be a heresy, in a related sense, to translate the experience of the wine into language, but there is little choice. The ability to identify and re-identify elements of sensory reactions to wine relies on linguistic terms, and even to compare and contrast, and to bring our knowledge to bear on the experience, is necessarily linguistic in nature. One's *funding*, the knowledge and experience one brings to the encounter with a particular wine, is also inextricably linguistic. In other words, there is not in fact a sharp distinction between tasting the wine and then communicating our reactions. For, by developing the capacity to communicate, we likewise develop the capacity to taste, and vice versa.

'Funding' is the term we use for the knowledge and experience that we "bring to" the appreciation of an aesthetic object. Funding has several aspects, and it is instructive to explore these. It can be conceptual in nature, or at least conceptualizable, so that one can explain how and why this experience of a particular work (*this* painting) has been influenced by previous ones (*other* paintings). This funding can be quite explicit and technical, such as identifying a poem as having the sonata form. This kind of funding we may call *cultural funding*, and it includes, but is not identical to, a more or less standardized typology of forms and descriptions. In wine, knowledge about kinds and styles of wine may easily be seen to form part of this conceptual funding. For instance, this kind of funding will comprise knowledge about the desirable properties of types of wine – such as young Mosel rieslings – as well as knowledge of the effects of vintage, aging, breathing, and so on.

The second kind of funding may be called *practical funding*. This is a developed ability to detect and discriminate the relevant elements of the experience of wine, and to deploy the conceptual knowledge of the first kind of funding. Physiologists believe that so-called "supertasters,"[3] people who are significantly better at detecting trace elements of smell and taste than the average, are not necessarily better at tasting wines: they often just flinch at the astringency and the heat (from alcohol), and do not find wine pleasant at all. This indicates that the practical funding of wine tasting is already more than mere sensory competence. By "sensory competence" we mean the ability to discriminate between flavors and scents. Practical funding is, at the very least, a sensory competence *developed* by experience and one that takes place within the context of intersubjective practices. The two are linked, for in the case of wine appreciation, this development generally takes place in specific contexts (e.g., formal tastings or a course on wine) and almost always with others. There are many widely recognized intersubjective practices of wine appreciation. These include the procedure of "blind" tasting, the careful ordering of the sequence of wines tasted so as to not dull the palate, the restrictions on food eaten, the type of glass, the temperature of the wines, the lighting and ventilation of the tasting room, not consuming too much alcohol (or even spitting out), and so forth. These controlled conditions may be rigidly adhered to in professional circles, but even casual and amateur tasting has its equivalents. The aim is to make possible the kind of close *attention* necessary for appreciation. There is an obvious analogy with the controlling of conditions and variables in a scientific experiment. But this analogy is also misleading. The purpose of a properly designed experiment is to render redundant the judgment of the experimenter, whereas the practices through which wine appreciation happens are designed precisely to enable the exercise of judgment. In the case of an individual, practical funding is developed by way of such repeated activities, but it also consists of the ability to put these activities "to work" so that they are not simply an empty ritual, and indeed to work with others in such contexts to arrive at a compelling account of the wine experience.

The development of sensory abilities is important for a wine taster, just like musicality and the development of this is a great benefit to the critic or appreciator of music. However, again, practical funding

---

is not exclusively sensory. It also involves the accumulated experience of other aesthetically successful objects of the same type. This means that the experience of previously tasted young rieslings from Mosel forms part of this second kind of funding, while we saw that the conceptual knowledge of what the desirable properties of these wines are would more usefully be seen as forming part of the first kind of funding.

When it comes to the ability to discern and distinguish elements of scent and taste in a wine, the most important aspect is the development of a language. As the olfaction researcher Professor Tim Jacob of Cardiff University says:

> The inexperienced person does not have a smell vocabulary. This hugely restricts their ability to describe and define odors. A large part of the wine taster's skill comes from being able to develop some sort of classification system, and then to associate words and categories with smells.[4]

The need for practical funding is also evident in the appreciation of pictorial art, to name but one other aesthetic practice. It is fairly uncontentious that only if you are familiar with the abstract colorist style of painting will you know how to look for the aesthetically relevant features in a painting of this kind. The familiarity, though, is not reducible either to the ability to detect colors and gradations or to conceptual knowledge about the colorists. Instead, it emerges from directed experiences of colorist paintings, seeing over and over again how they "work." In the case of wine appreciation, practical funding will enable you to distinguish between elements of scent and to name flavors. It is demanding to keep in mind subtle odors, their nuances, degrees of astringency, and impressions of kinds of acids, fruitiness, and colors. Indeed, the wine merchant and trader Ronald Avery of Bristol, once deemed to be the most competent taster in England, was asked by a journalist whether he had ever mistaken a Burgundy for a claret. "Not since lunchtime," was his reply.[5] Here, again, our argument is that this ability is not reducible to sensory competence.

[4] Quoted in ibid., pp. 173–4.
[5] In Hugh Johnson's *Wine: A Life Uncorked* (London: Weidenfeld and Nicolson, 2005), this remark is attributed, with a slightly different wording, to Harry Waugh.

162

First of all, not all scents and flavors will be equally relevant to aesthetic judgment, and practical funding would have to include the ability to judge relevance. Moreover, the aesthetic judgment will eventually also involve the *relationships* of scents and flavors to each other, and practical funding must make this possible. For example, a judgment that employs the concept of 'balance' will not be referring to just one scent or flavor but to a set of relationships between them. The ability to experience relations of sensations is different from the simple ability to experience sensations individually. Wines you have tasted before, similar or dissimilar, may be relevant, and experiences of previous vintages of the same wine, or wines from the same producer and *appellation*, would enable comparisons. This "tacit" knowledge is learned by doing, by acquiring a vocabulary, and becomes manifest in practice.

However, the detection of, discrimination between, and even relating different elements of taste to each other are not sufficient to judge wines as aesthetic objects. In his highly influential article "Aesthetic Concepts," Frank Sibley pointed out that concepts such as 'balanced', 'elegant', 'profound', 'harmonious', 'vivid', 'powerful', 'complex', 'unified', 'delicate', and so on, are referring to "emergent properties," and that their use is not entailed by the application of objective criteria.[6] Rather, their use indicates that they are based on aesthetic judgments, which by their very nature are singular. By this it is meant that if one artist paints a picture that is judged aesthetically successful, and then she (or someone else) paints something very similar (same technique, subject, composition, etc.), then the second painting *might or might not* be judged aesthetically successful. The "very similar" involves an attempt to reduce the first painting's aesthetic success to objective criteria, which can be employed in any number of cases. While the conceptual and practical kinds of funding involve transferable knowledge, this third kind of funding does not. Aesthetic judgments are grounded in what is present to mind there and then – the properties that have emerged within the singular act of judgment – and not in the presence or absence of objectively describable and generally desirable elements or clusters of elements. Aesthetic success

---

[6] Frank Sibley, "Aesthetic Concepts," in John Benson, Betty Redfern, and Jeremy Roxbee Cox (eds.), *Approach to Aesthetics: Collected Papers on Philosophical Aesthetics* (Oxford: Oxford University Press, 2001), pp. 1–23.

just cannot be determined by ticking off a series of elements or qualities on a pre-determined checklist. This means that practical funding combined with cultural funding does not necessarily take one to aesthetic judgments. To apply a term most often used in the philosophy of mind, the aesthetic judgments are supervenient. This means that the second kind of funding, while necessary, is not sufficient to engage in an aesthetic appreciation of a wine. However, in the above, when we say aesthetic judgments are grounded in what is aesthetically present "there and then," this does not entail the irrelevance either of objectively describable elements or of funding. On the contrary, it is from out of these sources alone that aesthetic properties can "emerge." The issue, rather, is of the impossibility of providing a general rule that will describe or predict this emergence. Thus, there are no objective criteria sufficient for the attribution of such qualities as "vivid" or relations such as "balanced," and attempts to justify such attributions are normally effected through perceptual guidance. For instance, a description of perceptual elements may be an attempt to indicate the supervenient: "the smell of x balanced by the smell of y." In this case the description that indicates is our intersubjective access to "seeing as," and it is a means of grasping the aesthetically successful whole by way of its elements.

As Stanley Cavell puts it: "it is a matter of the *ways* a judgment is supported. . . . It is essential to making an aesthetic judgment that at some point we be prepared to say in its support: don't you see, don't you hear, don't you dig?"[7] However, it is not only the case that judgments are ultimately justified by the "don't you see?," but this is also how aesthetic abilities are developed. Others help us to "see," although they cannot do so by simply *telling* us what to see. This third kind of funding we may call "emergent perception" or "aesthetic judgment." This funding concerns the ability to move from detectable properties of smell and taste to the presence (or absence) of emergent properties. To know what 'complex' means in a wine is to have sensed it previously – or to have a guide who can help one to "see as." Again, it is acquired intersubjectively. Emergent properties are nevertheless based upon sensed properties. It is *this* set of smells that are harmonious, delicate, etc. – or indeed which have a

---

[7] Stanley Cavell, "Aesthetic Problems of Modern Philosophy," in *Must We Mean What We Say?* (Cambridge: Cambridge University Press, 1976), pp. 73–96 (p. 93).

temporal play. The capacity to appreciate emergent qualities is therefore an additional competence, but one that cannot do without practical funding. It is not enough to be competent in other aesthetic practices, though it is likely to be an advantage. An understanding of how a Renaissance painting is aesthetically "harmonious," or how an Italian Baroque concerto is "delicate," could only ever be analogous to the appropriate use of these terms in wine tasting, because the relationships described thereby emerge through the experience of an entirely different set of sense properties. However, the analogy could be helpful in "indicating." That is, one taster in a group employing the analogy of the emergent quality of "balance" in a painting might serve to help another to perceive a wine "as" balanced. Though seldom used in the score-based wine reviews these days, analogies can also help us communicate the "character" of a particular wine. To say about a high extract Amarone that it is like a Hummer with a Fiat engine may be more revealing than listing the fruits, smokes, and stones detected.

Aesthetic practice aims to produce consensus on interpretation, and this is why judgment leads to "surely you must see it that way too." The condition of such judgment, and also its product, is a community of judgment. By 'community' is meant a group who have not only broadly similar tastes but also similar sets of funding, and therefore also follow similar practices in their tasting (the procedures of wine tasting) and share an appreciative language. Unlike judgments that we ordinarily understand to be subjective or simply culturally relative – such as basic food tastes – aesthetic judgments present themselves as normative. If I identify harmony in wine or a painting then "surely" you will too, if only you perceive correctly. If we do not agree, then we tend to suspect that one of us is being unduly influenced by extraneous factors, or is insufficiently funded, or just has not yet "seen as." But, expressing the normative aspect of aesthetic judgment in this way is misleading. Traditional aesthetics tends to extrapolate outwards from an individual perceiver; if, then, perceivers happen to agree in their judgments, this is perhaps because their perceptual faculties are similar, or some other explanation. Just like the distinction above between sensing something and communicating it, the fact of agreement or disagreement between observers is taken to be subsequent to and dependent upon an individual experience. Accordingly, traditional aesthetics is forced to make

165

rather too much of senses that act at a distance (sight and sound), reproducible objects (paintings that remain the same, music that can be listened to again), and forms (that is, identifiable "shapes" in space or time, in contrast to "qualities" such as color, tone, etc.). Traditional aesthetics thus tends to pass over experiences that involve the proximal senses (taste and smell, especially), transient objects (such as a particular vintage or even *this* bottle of wine), and qualities. In short, by starting with the individual, some objects and practices, which include wine and wine tasting, are more or less automatically excluded from consideration by traditional aesthetics.

Our claim is that this traditional picture is misleading. Intersubjective practices of tasting (procedures, knowledge, and language) are the condition of an individual person's appreciation. Wine tasting as a particular type of experience, to be sure, belongs to an individual – but only because that individual *already* belongs to an intersubjective community of wine tasters. I broadly agree, so to speak, with the judgment of my community even before I taste the wine, and it is this agreement that makes it possible for me to taste the wine in an appreciative manner. This intersubjectivity does not have to be grounded in similar faculties, but rather in developing similar "tools" of identification and modes of judgment (i.e., funding). The change in emphasis from individual experience to communities of aesthetic practice (a move so obviously required in the case of wine appreciation if it is to have any credibility as an aesthetic phenomenon at all) might also be helpful in traditional areas of aesthetics, though this is too wide-ranging a claim to substantiate fully here.

This third kind of "funding," aesthetic judgment, comes about through becoming part of the relevant aesthetic practice, mainly though practical, first-hand training with others more experienced or competent, though influence from the media (magazines, newspapers, television) may also help along the way. Recall the wine appreciation activities we discussed above as the context of practical funding. It is not uncommon to discourage discussion among the tasters, in this way trying to ensure that each taster reaches his or her own conclusion. To be sure, this practice may ensure that the taster is not influenced by someone perceived as being in a position of power or greater expertise. However, here we have developed a thoroughly intersubjective account of appreciation. The "no discussion" practice may be a relic from the aesthetic tradition that extrapolates outward from the individual taster, and should perhaps be reconsidered in the interests of attaining, on balance, the richest and most revealing results, and not just the most "accurate."

Summing up so far, we think it is fair to say that the appreciation of a wine is quite similar to the appreciation of music or paintings in relation to how the objects engage our faculties. This is also supported by the empirical investigations undertaken by Charters and Pettigrew. However, the similarity in language involved in responding to these two kinds of object is even more important. When appreciating fine wines we tend to use the same, or at least very similar, concepts to those used in the appreciation of abstract paintings, music, or other artworks. That neither abstract pictures nor wine are generally described by concepts such as 'sentimental', 'trite', or 'poignant' is probably due to their lack of narrative or obvious emotional content.

At the initial level, the fact that an object is "aesthetic" is constituted by the activity of appreciation, rather than the other way around. In that sense, the attempt can be made to approach any object aesthetically provided "funding": that is, provided a descriptive language and meaningful intersubjective comparisons are in place, can be put in place, or can at least be borrowed from a sufficiently similar mode of appreciation. Commercial designs, for appliances or furniture say, are often thought of as "crossing over" and that means appreciated in this manner. The question is then whether the experience of the object *rewards* such concentrated attention. Understanding how an object can be rewarding or "aesthetically successful" is accordingly more difficult. Appreciation at this second level gives rise to emergent concepts (balance, harmony, delicacy, etc.) and does so with an integral necessity – the experience seems to demand such concepts from us. The presence of these concepts in the appreciation of the object is considered valuable and meaningful. In short, anything can be appreciated aesthetically, but far from all objects reward such appreciation with the experience of emergent, aesthetic concepts. However, we must not think of this "reward" as the simple presence of something in the object; rather, such features are emergent, and the possibility of this emergence itself is, as we have seen, founded in funding and aesthetic practices.

This means that an investigation of the language, or vocabularies, of wine appreciation *per se* – that is, in isolation from practices and modes of funding – is unlikely to achieve any interesting results. Aesthetic practices are indeed dependent upon linguistic formations, but they are not reducible to "talk." The descriptive mode of language relates to the detection and discrimination of elements of taste.[8] The descriptive language is founded upon the apparently more objective properties of the wine itself: sugars, acids, fruit or herb flavors, etc. The language is intended to be transparent in this sense. However, it is the presence of the aesthetic concepts – the second type of vocabulary – that should alert us to the distinctly aesthetic judgments of wine. This latter vocabulary refers to an aesthetic practice and to an emergent experience, and not to objective criteria. Looking at this vocabulary on its own leads almost inevitably to the conclusion that it is hopelessly metaphorical and thus pretentious or even meaningless. So, neither the taste experience (when, as we have argued above, it is illegitimately isolated from the context of wine appreciation) nor the language used (when likewise isolated) provide anything but misleading pictures.

Accordingly, one may wonder if the widely publicized differences between the style of wine criticism of Robert Parker, Jr. and that of some of the British wine critics, such as Hugh Johnson, may in fact be related to these two levels of judgment: the discrimination of elements and the aesthetic judgment. Parker is known to all with a serious interest in wine. His *Wine Advocate* set out to offer unbiased and no-nonsense advice on wines to consumers, clearly influenced by the likes of Ralph Nader, stating that wine was no different from any other consumer product. His 100-point system of scoring wines has created some controversy, and so has his influence on the style of wines produced. One reason for thinking that this controversy may have something to do with aesthetic judgment is that Parker, but even more so *Wine Spectator* with its tasting panels, tends to describe wines in quantitative terms. Wines that get many points are often described as "big," "massive," and "huge," while more aesthetic terms centering on elegance and subtlety are less in favor. Our suspicion, and it is no more than this, is that Parker and others who want to be the consumer's best friend are wary of using aesthetic judgments because of their very nature. The use of a language referring to *quantities* seems to be more objective, the proper sphere of no-nonsense

---

[8] Still broadly understood to also include olfactory and tactile impressions.

critical attention, and hence quantity is praised in wines. According to Jancis Robinson, this leads "wine producer(s) to make wines they don't actually like themselves, but they make them – much bigger than their own taste – because they think they'll get high points."[9] In a response to Robinson's statement, a reader on a bulletin board on Robert Parker's site on the Internet writes: "when I bring more elegant and nuanced wines to parties with neighbors, I'm not sure most 'get' it. Those seeking more elegant wines are often those who are the real wine gurus."[10] Another commentator states quite clearly what the no-nonsense school of wine criticism believes: "some of the terminology that shows up in tasting notes is fatuous and, frankly, tiresome in its pretentiousness."[11] The latter commentator may very well have a point, but we also suspect that he may be throwing the aesthetic baby out with the pretentious bath water.

This division between descriptive judgments and aesthetic judgments is not confined to wine appreciation. Much of what goes for pretentious babble in galleries around the globe is more likely to be aesthetic judgment, and support for such judgment. To the uninitiated it may well sound pretentious. But as Hugh Johnson writes: "who would think of rating Manet and Monet?"[12] The divide between the American "dictator of taste" (Hugh Johnson's words[13]) and Hugh Johnson and his like may have much to do with using the points system. Together with large tastings, where the syndrome of "taster's palate" – whereby only the most obvious wines tend to get noticed in a major line-up – is likely to occur, the points system invites the notion that there is a template for excellence in wine that the wine under scrutiny measures up, to a greater or lesser degree. Appreciation takes on a more or less mathematical meaning, and this is a major obstacle to considering wine as an aesthetic object, since it easily becomes a matter of measuring a wine against a set of criteria known and knowable by everybody. "Introduce the illusion

[9] Jancis Robinson interviewed in *St. Helena Star*, July 6, 2006. www.sthelenastar.com/articles/2006/07/06/features/food_and_wine/iq_3503367.txt (accessed July 12, 2006).
[10] Peter Baird: dat.erobertparker.com/bboard/showthread.php?t=97998 (accessed July 12, 2006).
[11] Ed Custard: dat.erobertparker.com/bboard/showthread.php?t=97998 (accessed July 12, 2006).
[12] Johnson, *Wine: A Life Uncorked*, p. 43.
[13] Ibid., p. 40.

of absolutes and your tastes have to shape up,"[14] but not only that: the very condition of an aesthetic judgment is that it is singular, and the very idea that wines can be measured against one scale of value obscures and makes impossible this crucial aspect of wine appreciation.

Prior to the American consumer-friendly approach to writing about wines, critics were more likely to use similes and metaphors, particularly anthropomorphic ones. "They tried to express differences, or feelings, for which no technical language existed . . . they could be highly expressive."[15] To understand this, one had to taste the wines and use one's knowledge of human physiognomy and behavior. From time to time a writer or critic would use a term or concept which caught on, and "it is sometimes hard to know whether a new taste has appeared or just a new description become current."[16] This phenomenon shows how the acquisition and application of a terminology are absolutely crucial in having an appreciation of wine, and also illustrates the communal nature of the third kind of funding. It also shows how focusing exclusively on the language of wine appreciation is misleading: such an approach could not but emphasize the apparent pretentiousness, arbitrariness, and subjectivity of this language, and thus reinforce the tendency toward a language of objective quantity.

This essay has shown that wine appreciation is an aesthetic practice. By this is meant two things. First, that wine appreciation must be considered aesthetic, in a way broadly similar to how we treat music or art appreciation. Second, however, that at least in the case of wine this happens only by way of a complex set of activities, competencies, knowledge, and language usage, all of which are originally intersubjective in nature. In turn, our results have had a number of further implications. We must reconsider those "barriers" to wine appreciation that we mentioned in the introduction: that the experience of wine is too individualistic or subjective, and that it is impossible to communicate meaningfully about one's taste or smell experiences. These barriers lend credence to the *Wine Advocate* school of wine appreciation, which tends to reject qualitative judgments and the "pretentious" aesthetic language developed to communicate

---

[14] Ibid., p. 43.
[15] Ibid., p. 47.
[16] Ibid., p. 48.

them, in favor of relatively straightforward flavor words and quantitative judgments. However, it turns out that both of these barriers are misconceptions. These barriers can be seen as the illusions they truly are once we understand that wine appreciation is a phenomenon that emerges from out of various types of funding and in particular through an intersubjective activity. Even the distinction between an individual's experience and the subsequent communication of that experience is misleading. The aesthetic vocabulary that arises to communicate the results of such wine appreciation is not a hopelessly metaphorical attempt to describe merely subjective states. Rather, this language is an element of a coherent and already intersubjective practice of tasting. This practice allows individuals to attend to and share the experience of emergent aesthetic qualities.

Our conclusions suggest that there will be several other fruitful areas for investigation, and we hope, of course, to look at these in our proposed book, *The Universal Nose*. Let us indicate two of these areas here. First, it would seem to be the case that, in traditional aesthetics, the denigration of the proximal senses involved in wine appreciation goes hand in hand with the prominence given to certain aesthetic concepts such as 'form'. If there is a genuine relationship between these two, then our recovery of the proximal senses may in turn imply that certain key concepts in aesthetics should be rethought from the ground up. Second, we think we have solved the apparent problems with considering wine appreciation as aesthetic by way of the concept of aesthetic practice, and especially its emphasis on intersubjective activities of appreciation. This has also meant moving away from the basic status accorded the individual perceiver within traditional aesthetics, upon whom many of the key concepts of aesthetics seem to be built. Thus, the shift of focus onto communities of judgment that has been argued for in this essay should, perhaps, entail a further shift within the basic categories of aesthetics. Far from being a marginal topic, wine appreciation may yet turn out to be the catalyst for a considerable change within philosophical aesthetics.

171

11

Who Cares If You Like It, This Is a Good Wine Regardless

George Gale

Some Prefatory Remarks about Aesthetics

Aesthetic theories have two jobs to do. First, they should undergird and explain the aesthetic judgments that we typically make. Second, they should provide a descriptive apparatus that broadens, deepens, and generally enriches our conversations about our aesthetic objects and judgments.[1] It seems doubtful to me that any aesthetic theory will ever ultimately *settle* the disagreements that we might have among ourselves about our judgments; yet it would be useful if our aesthetic theories enlighten these disagreements by making them both clearer and more precise. That is my hope in what follows: to provide the elements of an aesthetic theory which can serve to enlighten, to clarify, and to make more precise some disagreements in a limited but legitimate aesthetic domain.

My subject is wine, and the aesthetics thereof. There are good reasons for choosing this subject, as opposed to, say, sculpture, painting, or dance. For one, wine is a much simpler object to investigate than any of these other subjects. This follows from the fact that a glass of wine is simpler than, for example, Michelangelo's *David*, Claude Monet's *Water Lilies*, or Peter Tchaikovsky's *The Nutcracker*. First, the senses to which wine appeals – primarily, but not solely, taste and smell – are in important ways simpler than those that evaluate

---

[1] I am grateful to Hank Frankel for his pointing this out to me.

172

other aesthetic objects.[2] Vision, which is essentially involved in these three cases, evinces intrinsically more complexity than taste and smell. Thus, our sensory response to wine is categorically simpler than it is to these other three objects. Second, in terms of the aesthetic object itself, although wine is a complex object, it is by no means as complex as the other three. Time, for instance, plays no part in wine as it does in dance; similarly, three-dimensionality plays no part in wine evaluation, but it is crucial in the aesthetics of sculpture. Visual composition is essential in painting, but it plays no role in wine. For these reasons (and perhaps others), wine is a simpler object of analysis than most other aesthetic objects.

However, even given these significant differences between wine as an aesthetic object and these other cases, there is simply no denying that wine *is* an aesthetic object. My hope is that an effective aesthetic theory for wine might very well give us some clues about how to proceed via extension into other aesthetic domains; into, for example, sculpture, painting, or dance.

My approach in what follows is *naturalistic*. Obviously, this notion is both vague and ambiguous: types, kinds, and styles of naturalism are thick on the ground. But let me try to be a bit more specific about what I intend here. In the first place, I would want to say that certain sorts of aesthetic judgments come naturally to us, as birthrights for all humans. That is, in some of our unreflective activities, we behave, quite naturally and freely, as if we were making aesthetic judgments. For example, extensive (and extensively replicated) experiments with babies show that babies aesthetically judge representations of human faces quite naturally.[3] Moreover, they exhibit quite straightforward preferences: babies from all cultures prefer faces with regular features, regular shapes, and particular expressions. Interestingly enough, the sorts of preferences babies have seem to extend into adult life; many of the same features, shapes, and

---

[2] This case is most easily made in terms of the information that can be carried by the sensory channel. Cf. George Miller, "The Magical Number Seven, Plus or Minus Two: Some Limits On Our Capacity for Processing Information," *Psychological Review* 63 (1956): 81–97.

[3] Anna Gosline, "Babies Prefer to Gaze Upon Beautiful Faces," *New Scientist*, October 6, 2004; Judith H. Langlois, Lori A. Roggman, Rita J. Casey, Jean M. Ritter, and Loretta A. Rieser-Danner, "Infant Preferences for Attractive Faces: Rudiments of a Stereotype?" *Developmental Psychology* 23.3 (1987): 363–9.

expressions preferred by babies are judged by adults to be "pleasing," "attractive," etc.[4]

It is clear that we humans make these sorts of judgments quite naturally and, indeed, automatically.

A second, and counterpart, aspect of my sort of naturalism relies on the simple point that the aesthetic objects which concern us are objects with natural properties. This is not to say that the objects are not *artisanal*. Obviously *David* and a glass of pinot noir are equally artifacts insofar as they are products of human artifice. Yet, the properties which they express are natural properties, whether simple or complex. I rely upon this fact directly in my analysis of what goes on in the aesthetic evaluation of wine. Put quite simply, my view is that the natural properties of wine are intrinsically, essentially, and necessarily elements in the aesthetics of wine. But I need to be quite clear what I mean here.

Hume is famously claimed to have held that "is" does not imply "ought" or, more generally, that facts do not imply values.[5] I quite agree with Hume: in any given case of a value judgment – whether that be a moral judgment or an aesthetic judgment – there is no set of facts *sufficient* to lead to that value judgment. However, I think it quite clear that there are certain facts which are *necessary* to a given value judgment. That is, the value judgment holds only if certain facts are true. If the facts are not there, then the value judgment cannot be there, either. That this is a naturalistic claim should be obvious. But I hope that it is equally clear that there is no evident fallacy here, either.

One final point. It is often claimed that, in matters of taste, it is *all* a matter of taste. Thus, when one says, "This is a fine wine," one is only saying, "I prefer the taste of this wine." But this most certainly cannot be the case. On the account which I present below, any attempt to explain why "This is a fine wine" is correct will refer to the properties of the wine and not to details about the judger. But, on the hypothesis that this judgment ultimately means only that

---

[4] I am not claiming that adult judgments are not significantly impinged by cultural learning. Rather, I here make the simple (and weak) claim that there is a discernible consistency in the judgments across time. Cf. Judith Langlois, "The Question of Beauty," www.utexas.edu/opa/pubs/discovery/disc1996v14n3/disc-beauty.html.

[5] David Hume, *A Treatise of Human* Nature, eds. L. A. Selby-Bigge and P. H. Nidditch (Oxford: Oxford University Press, 1978), pp. 469–70.

"I prefer the taste of this wine," it is clear that any explanation of the purported correctness of *this* judgment must, at some point, refer to personal, autobiographical features of the judger. In the end, the two judgments refer to two quite different categories of explanation; hence, they are two quite different categories of judgment. On my account, "This is a fine wine" says absolutely nothing about the personal attributes or the history of the judger. Rather, the claim is one about the *wine*.

Let us now take a look at my account.

Empirical Constraints on Aesthetic Judgments

If I say, "This is a fine wine," what do I mean? Clearly this is an aesthetic judgment. But are only aesthetic values involved in its making? Or are other factors, empirical factors in particular, also relevant? It seems to me that empirical factors *are* intrinsically involved in this aesthetic judgment: were certain of these factors to be true, the judgment would be false, and demonstrably so. My thinking is that a number of empirical elements (e.g., *terroir*, physiological, biochemical, perceptual, and legal) act as constraints upon aesthetic judgments about wine; violations of any of these constraints makes it impossible for the judged wine to be a fine wine. Put most simply, these constraints act as necessary conditions for the judgment "This is a fine wine." If the constraints are violated, then the judgment is false.

One of these factors (viz., *terroir*) in addition sets up specific requirements about a judged wine's *type*. Since, in any fair wine evaluation, the judgment about a wine's type is a theoretical hypothesis based upon empirical observables, one which is a necessary element of ultimately being able to say, "This is a fine wine," we see here a very strong empirical constraint upon the ultimate aesthetic judgment.

Let us look now at how these constraints impinge upon the aesthetic evaluation of wine, beginning with the legal ones.

Legal constraints

Legal constraints upon wine are the most conventional of the lot. However, they are also extremely useful in revealing what the target of our analysis is. All wine-producing countries, as well as larger political bodies such as the European Union, have complicated regulations regarding wine. These regulations consist of definitions, "theorems" deriving from the definitions, cautions, prohibitions, and recommendations. Since wine, its production, its distribution, its consumption, and its quality, are significant elements in the agricultural, economic, and behavioral activities of any wine-producing country, the regulations can not be less complicated than the product, its distribution, consumption, and quality itself – which are themselves extremely complicated, to say the least.

The United States, to choose a country from among the group, is no exception. Wine production etc. in the USA is regulated under *27 CFR* (Code of Federal Regulations), a separate, and quite long, booklet published by the government, a dirty, stained, much-abused copy of which will be found in the library of any winery in the United States. According to *27 CFR, wine* is the product of the alcoholic fermentation of grapes. Products of the alcoholic fermentation of other fruits, vegetables, blossoms, honey, and so on either have their own special names (apples make *cider*, pears make *perry*, honey makes *mead*), or else are given "qualified" names, such as elderberry wine or dandelion wine. We shall concern ourselves with 'wine', simpliciter.

An interesting number of wine's properties follow from its being made from grapes. For example, *table wine*, the most common category of wine, is constrained by law to contain from 12 to 14 percent alcohol. This range of legal values is neither arbitrary nor conventional. Ripe wine grapes in average growing areas produce from 22 to 26 percent soluble sugar, and yeast can convert about 55 percent of that sugar into alcohol. Hence, table wine is simply the normal product of normal fermentation of normal ripe wine grapes.

Physiological constraints

The simple fact that wine interacts with its drinker's physiology places severe empirical constraints upon its properties and qualities. Whatever fine wine is, it most certainly can *not* be a whole bunch of things. Two dimensions come immediately to mind: tartness from acids and astringency from tannins. Both of these are natural components of grapes, hence they are natural components of table wine.

Grapes naturally contain a blend of acids, chief among which is *tartaric acid*. When grape juice is fermented, the acids, for the most part, remain unchanged in the resulting wine.[6] Acidity is measured by the *pH scale*, which ranges from 1 to 14, where 1 is basically battery acid and 14 is drain cleaner. Wine can be quite tart, as tart as little green apples. But it cannot have a pH of 1. Completely aside from the fact that grapes do not get this acidic, it is clear that human physiology cannot drink battery acid. On the other hand, wine cannot have a pH of 14; humans would not do much better with drain cleaner than with battery acid. My point here is a quite general one: the fact that wine is consumed by humans sets inviolable limits on the wine's properties. This point has nothing to do with the different point that most wines *naturally* range in pH from 2 to around 4, a range set by the physiology of the grape and not by the physiology of the human drinker.

Astringency behaves similarly. Tannins are a natural component of plant surfaces such as leaves, bark, and fruit skins. When tannin interacts with human physiology, the interacting flesh puckers, and astringency is perceived. Astringency varies from none to too much. Think about brewing tea: the original water has no astringency, a moderately steeped tea causes noticeable pucker, and a too-strong tea is nearly undrinkable. A naturally occurring fruit example of too much tannin is the *chokecherry*, a small fruit indigenous to North America. As its name indicates, ingestion of the chokecherry fruit causes a choking reaction, with the result that the fruit cannot be swallowed.

Obviously, human physiology constrains us from drinking something with such a high level of tannins.[7] In the end, the judgment "This is a fine wine" can be true only if it is also true that its pH is in some appropriate range and if its tannin level is nowhere similar to chokecherry. I here mention only two constraints, acidity and astringency, though there are others which function similarly (e.g., alcohol content, volatile acidity, etc.): each places a purely natural, empirical constraint on the aesthetic virtue of the wine.

---

[6]   One exception is the tart malic acid that is often transformed into a milder lactic acid through a microbially induced malolactic fermentation.

[7]   Chokecherry seeds and wilted leaves contain cyanide as well. The fruit is a well-recognized danger to livestock. Yet, with suitable dilution with water, and blending with domesticated – and far less astringent – chokecherry juice, a decent and interesting wine can apparently be made from the wild chokecherry (University of Saskatchewan, www.gardenline.usask.ca/fruit/choke.html).

177

But there are other constraints operating as well, ones which focus upon neither the wine simpliciter nor *de jure*, nor upon its drinker's physiology, but rather upon the elements of the winegrowing and winemaking process.

Tradition and practice-based constraints: Terroir

Although grapes grow essentially everywhere in the sub-Arctic Northern Hemisphere, no single variety can grow everywhere. And every variety flourishes only in some particular place or, at most, some fairly limited subset of places, each with its very own particular soil, climate, and terrain. Given some basic precepts of evolutionary biology, none of this should be the least bit surprising to us. Over the millennia, the main project of winegrowers has been, among other things, to achieve the greatest degree of ripeness for the greatest number of their grapes. This has meant thousands of years of experimentation and selection with varieties, with agricultural variables, with pruning techniques, with training structures and technologies, all in aid of presenting the winemaker (who throughout most of Western history has also been the winegrower) with sound, ripe grapes ready for fermentation. In the end, the result of all this experimentation and selection has been the gradual settling down of winegrowing and winemaking into a vast number of divergent *terroirs* – tight clusterings of varieties, terrain, soils, climate, and tradition-based production techniques.[8]

For example, you do not grow the pinot noir in France's Provence because it is too hot there: the grape ripens in the heat of summer, and the delicate flavors get cooked. You do grow pinot noir in Burgundy, where it is much cooler and harvest beats the first frost by a matter of a few weeks, if at all. On Santorini, in the middle of the Aegean, grapes are trained into basket shapes close to the ground. If the grapes were trained into something like six-foot bushes, as they are most other places, the violent spring winds would thrash the vines into pieces. In desert areas, such as Algeria,

---

[8] In most winegrowing regions, the features of traditional practice – which obviously are rooted deeply in the terrain, soils, and climate of the region – are very tightly controlled by law. France, for example, has its *appellation contrôlée*, Italy its *denominazioni*, and so on.

178

the vineyard floor around the vines is piled with stones, which both keeps shallow roots cool and cuts down water evaporation. Each of these three features is an aspect of *terroir*.

Every winegrowing region in the Old World developed wines closely matched to its *terroir*, which had the result that a splendid variety of styles and types of wines came into being. In the end, *terroir* puts an extremely strong empirical constraint upon aesthetic evaluation of wine. Thus, "This is a fine Burgundy" is false in the case where the wine is not a Burgundy. More deserves to be said about this sort of judgment.

Perceptual and Theoretical Judgments

Judging "This is a fine wine" is the last stage in a process which begins with low-level perceptual observations such as "This wine is red," passes through more complex judgments such as "This is a Burgundy," until the final evaluation stage "This is a fine wine" is reached. At each stage of the analysis, different factors come into play, but at no time is the empirical domain absent. There are close parallels between this process of developing an aesthetic evaluation of wine and the process of developing a scientific theory. That is, both processes begin with low-level observations, move on to more complex judgments, until the final stage is reached. For example, when Copernicus developed his theory that the solar system was heliocentric – all the planets went around the sun – he started out with low-level observations about, say, the relative motions of Mars and Venus. He then moved to more complex observations such as that Venus had phases, just like the moon. Only at the end of this long chain of increasingly sophisticated factual judgments was he able to make his theoretical claim, "This is a heliocentric solar system." In my view the claim "This is a fine wine" is also a theoretical claim – an aesthetic-theoretical claim – based, like Copernicus' claim, upon an integrated set of factual judgments. Let's look at the beginning of the process.

Low-level/observational judgments

Wine is an excellent example of a "multimodal perceptual object": it appeals to vision ("red," "clear," "cloudy"), taste ("sweet," "tart"),

179

tactile ("thin," "full-bodied"), and smell ("floral," "stinky"). Many attempts have been made to render the perceptual dimensions of wine not just tractable but rational. An early, and quite successful, attempt is the "20-point scale" developed at University of California, Davis.[9]

Table 11.1

• Appearance/Clarity	(possible 2 points)
• Color	(possible 2 points)
• Aroma/Bouquet	(possible 4 points)
• Total Acidity	(possible 2 points)
• Sweetness	(possible 1 point)
• Body	(possible 1 point)
• Flavor	(possible 2 points)
• Acescency (Bitterness)	(possible 1 points)
• Astringency	(possible 1 points)
• Overall Quality	(possible 4 points)

Here, "Appearance/Clarity" and "Color" are visual descriptors; "Aroma/Bouquet" is olfactory; "Total Acidity," "Sweetness," "Acescency," and "Astringency" are taste factors; and "Body" is tactile.[10] It is evident that this chart treats each of these perceptual categories as a simple observable. Within each scale-value, observables have been subdivided into a rank-order for scoring. Here, for example, is the breakdown of appearance scores:

Table 11.2

Brilliant, near-sparkly, clear with no haze or particulates	(2 points)
Bright, some sparkle, clear with no haze or particulates	(1.5 points)
Dull, mostly clear, perhaps a hint of haze or particulates	(1 point)
Cloudy, unclear with a distinct haze or particulates	(0 points)

In the end, the final score received by the wine is a total of the simple observables.[11]

There are some obvious problems with the conceptual foundations of this method of evaluating wines. With one exception – the category

---

9   www.musingsonthevine.com/tips_rate.shtml.
10   What about "Overall Quality"? Interesting question. More anon.
11   www.musingsonthevine.com/tips_rate.shtml.

"Overall Quality" – the categories are rigorously, indeed heroically, empiricist – they refer to simple observable properties, singly and separately. Underlying the whole project is the notion that wine is a complex observable object, constituted by an integrated set of simpler observables. When one has summed up the evaluations of the constituent observables, one has the final evaluation in hand. But there is a fundamental flaw in the whole scheme: wine is not *simply* an observable object. While it is clearly an observable, perceptual object, quite true, that is not *all* that wine is. Wine is also a *theoretical* object, an object necessitated in an explanatory sense by the observables. It is precisely here that the constraints demanded by *terroir* enforce their limits.

Theoretical judgments

It is obvious that no wine is *just* wine, plain and simple. Wines are particular objects, not general objects. Thus, at every level of analysis, they are instances which belong to categories, ranging from simple observable categories (e.g., "red") to very complex and subtle – indeed *theoretical* – categories. For example, under suitable conditions, "This is a Burgundy" is a theoretical judgment; indeed, under certain very interesting (not to mention instructive) conditions, this judgment is quite straightforwardly a genuine, explicitly theoretical hypothesis. More on this shortly.

The properties which make a wine precisely what it is (e.g., Burgundy, California pinot noir, etc.) are those that derive from its *terroir*. Burgundy and Burgundy-style wines are made from pinot noir grapes, grown in a specific climate, on specific terrain, in a certain specific fashion. The dimensions which comprise a *terroir* have values that have evolved over centuries of experiment and selection. There is a set of principles and a philosophy – hence a theory – which underlies the concept of any given *terroir*, and it is precisely this theory which is invoked when one judges "This is a Burgundy."

Let me be quite clear about this. To claim "This is a Burgundy" is relevantly similar to claiming "This is a heliocentric system," as Copernicus did.[12] Both of these judgments require empirical observations

---

[12] George Gale, "Are Some Aesthetic Judgments Empirically True?" *Amer. Phil. Qtly.* 12.4 (1975): 341–8.

as foundational. Moreover, these observations are determined by certain specific constraints: just as no wine can have a pH of 1, no heliocentric system can have an inner planet without phases.

However, just as in scientific theories, the observable data *under-determine* the theory. Thus, while the UC Davis 20-point observational scale provides necessary data for the theoretical judgment "This is a Burgundy," these data do not fully determine that judgment.[13] Taking the various observed properties, the evaluator reaches the theoretical judgment "This is a Burgundy," something which goes beyond the observed data.

One interesting feature of this process is that the conjunction of the two judgments "This is a Burgundy" and "This is a fine wine" would seem to imply "This is a fine Burgundy wine," a result that seems intuitively satisfying.[14] Further, it would seem that any judgment "*This* is a fine wine" requires first a judgment that "This is a fine X-type of wine." In other words, "This is a fine wine" only if "This is a fine X-type of wine." Since this wine's being of a certain type is judged via an empirically based theory, it is clear that we are here faced with an ultimate and inescapable empirical constraint on the aesthetics of wine evaluation.

This discussion seems a bit theoretical itself. Let me at this point provide an actual practical example of how "This is a Burgundy"-type judgments occur.

Slinging: An existence proof of wine type-evaluation

In the mid-1970s, my home of Kansas City, Missouri was one of the hottest new wine centers in North America: the market was opening up, wild growth in sales and consumption was observed, and an enormous buzz around wine and everything connected with wine swept the city. At the center of this excitement was a core of a dozen or

---

[13]   I think that it is this inferential move which is hidden in the "Overall Quality" category in the Davis 20-point scale: smuggled into the judgment of quality is the notion "for the kind of wine that it is," e.g., "This is a pretty good wine of its type – Burgundy, I think – so I'll give it 3.5 points."

[14]   As Hank Frankel has noted, however, there are exceptions. It might be a bad year in Burgundy, which would allow "This is a fine wine" but only "This is an OK Burgundy." But such a case inevitably requires subsidiary explanations as to why the intuitive inference doesn't go through.

182

so young wholesalers, retailers, restaurateurs, hoteliers, and one winegrower-winemaker who was also the wine columnist for the *Kansas City Star*.[15] Needless to say, with such energy and passion available, the group soon developed a competitive sport focused on wine: *slinging*. Just as in its namesake – gunslinging – the new sport involved challenge and duel, but with bottles of wine as the weapons rather than guns. The sport worked like this.

Your doorbell would ring, and there would be two or three of the group, with one or more bottles of wine hidden away in brown paper bags. "Consider yourself slung" someone would say, and the group would barge into the room. Wine glasses were fetched, and the slingee would then be faced by "The Three Questions": what is the grape, appellation, and vintage? After a suitable amount of tasting and sloshing around in the mouth, the slingee would have to stand and deliver, making a stab at answering the questions.

Of course, after this initial round, it was entirely possible (indeed expected) that the slingee would become the slinger, making a visit to his own cellar, selecting a bottle, and then hiding it in its own brown paper bag for presentation and consideration of the others. Sometimes the sport went public, with the crew assembling at one of the restaurants or hotels represented in the group. Again, the three questions would be asked, and then most likely some further queries would emerge: "Is it a good example?" "Is it fine?" "Do you know who made it?" And so on.

Needless to say, names were taken and scores kept at all events. Over time, individual "batting averages" varied quite a bit among the members, but not much within members. On average, scores for most of the group ranged from the high 30s to the low 60s; I was around 60 percent. But two of the group had phenomenal averages, one fellow in the low 80s, and the other in the low 90s.

What can we learn from the results of this "sport"? Several things seem clear to me. First, that wine provides the human taster a very rich observational situation, one that reliably connects to its elements and *terroir*. Second, that there is a reliable link between these observational properties and theoretical elements which characterize the wine as to type and origin. Third, that human evaluators can

[15] Yours truly. At least three of these dozen or so wine fanatics have gone on to prominence on today's national and international wine scene.

reliably utilize the observational data to make correct theoretical hypotheses about the type and origin of the wine. Taken together, these three points argue strongly for the ultimate empirical constraints upon aesthetic evaluation of wine. In the end, X can be judged to be a fine wine only if X is a wine of a particular type. But since distinguishing X's type is a theoretical judgment, a judgment based upon empirical observations, a guarantee is provided that ultimately, aesthetic judgments have empirical aspects as constraints, as necessary conditions.

Aspects of aesthetic methodology

Slinging, of course, must be done double-blind. It is well known that factual knowledge about wine (and, indeed, any other foodstuff) can shift the perception and hence the observations and hence the aesthetic evaluation of the tasted sample.[16] In the business, one is warned "don't drink the label!" A properly conducted double-blind tasting provides the very best circumstance for aesthetic evaluation of wine. Many tastings, especially competitions such as at state fairs, invitationals, or, as I recently witnessed, the Canadian National Amateur Winemaking Competition, do not even allow *table talk*, discussions among the tasters about the observations that they are making or about the theoretical judgments that they have reached. Taste and smell are just simply too susceptible to suggestion to allow any danger from outside information to intrude upon the tasters' experiences of the wine.

Conclusion

Any theory of aesthetics has two totally interrelated tasks to accomplish: first, it has to attempt to make sense of aesthetic judgments we in fact make; second, it has to facilitate, extend, enlarge our aesthetic discussions, make available to us the theoretical tools which will prolong and enrich the conversations we have with one another about the fine things which engage us. The approach taken

[16] Maynard A. Amerine and Edward B. Roessler, *Wines: Their Sensory Evaluation* (New York: W. H. Freeman, 1976).

by this essay seeks to make some progress on both points. By demanding that empirical considerations, considerations grounded in the natures of both aesthetic object and aesthetic judger, enter our discussions about wine from the very start, and remain until the very end, an enormous enlargement of the universe of wine discourse is achieved. Although some of my specific claims might be wrong, the approach, I think, is not in the least wrong-headed.

185

12

Listening to the Wine Consumer
The Art of Drinking

Steve Charters

Introduction

Is there any relationship between the judgments we make about wine and the way we view art forms? Can we say the taste of a good wine has the same impact on us as the sound of a beautiful piece of music? David Hume, one of the earlier commentators on aesthetics, felt there were some similarities, using a story from the novel *Don Quixote* to exemplify the role of "good taste."[1] In the tale, two men were asked to assess a wine; one tastes and claims it is good but for a hint of leather, the other agrees but notes a distinct flavor of iron. When the barrel was emptied, an old key on a leather thong was found in the bottom. This evaluative subtlety, Hume argued, acts as a metaphor for how the "mental" faculty of taste operates; a good judge can make finely nuanced distinctions about a wine or about a work of art. This essay examines the synergy of wine and aesthetics by considering the perspective of wine drinkers themselves. It is based on a study that considered how drinkers engage with the drink, and the similarities or differences there may be with other, more traditional forms of aesthetic experience, such as listening to music.

This essay is based on a previous article jointly written by the author: Steve Charters and Simone Pettigrew, "Is Wine Consumption an Aesthetic Experience?" *Journal of Wine Research*, 16.2 (2005): 37–52. The permission of the editors of the *Journal of Wine Research* and Simone Pettigrew to use this article as the basis of the present essay is gratefully acknowledged.

[1] David Hume, *Selected Essays* (1757) (Sydney: Oxford University Press, 1998).

Nevertheless, the use of wine tasting as a metaphor for the aesthetic process, as was done by Hume, does not mean that drinking wine itself can be considered an aesthetic experience. As will be seen, some philosophers have explicitly discounted this possibility. Yet drinking wine still excites comments such as "beautiful" or "awesome," terms associated with an aesthetic response. Indeed, a few writers on wine have considered that it is, at least when high quality, an artwork and thus that it can be evaluated aesthetically. Maynard Amerine and Edward Roessler,[2] who wrote a classic text on wine tasting, make these points:

> Aesthetics has to do with the subjective and objective appraisal of works of art: music, art, architecture – and wine. (p. 3)

> The components [of wine] must complement one another synergistically and excite our aesthetic appreciation. (p. 8)

Additionally, wine professionals use the association of wine with art and the aesthetic as a way of understanding – even promoting – their product, linking it to art or music, and by sponsoring artistic events.

However, the perspective that wine consumption is an aesthetic process has not been developed within any consistent theoretical framework. This essay attempts to remedy that lacuna by examining whether or not wine consumption can be considered an aesthetic experience. To provide context, the essay reviews how the Western philosophical tradition understands the aesthetic and then presents the results of a research project which examined the relationship between wine and the aesthetic experience within the framework of the social sciences. The focus is thus on drinkers' views about the aesthetic nature of wine consumption.

The Aesthetic Tradition

Can wine consumption be an aesthetic experience?

There is a long philosophical tradition which maintains that the consumption of food and drink is not susceptible to aesthetic

---

[2] Maynard A. Amerine and Edward B. Roessler, *Wines: Their Sensory Evaluation* (New York: W. H. Freeman, 1976).

187

evaluation. This was clearly delineated by Immanuel Kant,[3] who was known to enjoy wine. The most recent development of the argument that food and wine are incapable of providing an aesthetic experience has been made by Roger Scruton.[4] His argument is threefold. First, he claims that, since St. Thomas Aquinas, philosophers have distinguished the upper senses of sight and hearing, which may allow for "objective contemplation," from touch, smell, and taste. These latter "lower senses" are primarily used for utilitarian purposes. A further distinguishing feature is that, in tasting, both the object and the desire for it are steadily consumed. No such thing, Scruton argues, is true of genuine aesthetic attention. Finally, he argues that the concentrated focus required by aesthetic objects is of a different, more cognitive, nature from the focus demanded of food and drink.

A sustained rebuttal of the traditional perspective was made by Frank Sibley.[5] He notes that, while Scruton claims there is a difference between the lower senses and the higher senses, the latter acknowledges that this difference is "hard to describe."[6] Sibley suggests it is hard to describe because it is non-existent. Additionally, Sibley points out that the argument about the consumption of the aesthetic object also counts for little, for we consume all products – including music or a picture – without necessarily ingesting them. Moreover, he adds, music dies away, and pigment fades. Finally, both types of sense, he claims, can have utilitarian and "baser" elements, and both are capable of sustaining aesthetic interest – that is, of providing the basis for cognitive evaluation of the aesthetic product.

It is also worth adding another criticism of the notion that food and wine can be aesthetic objects. Carolyn Korsmeyer, for example, has noted that the physiological sense of taste "is not only subjective but also relative. It depends on factors idiosyncratic to the taster."[7] By contrast, Korsmeyer claims, true aesthetic objects have no physiological impact on their audience. However, in reply it could be

---

[3] Immanuel Kant, *Critique of Judgment* (1790), trans. Werner S. Pular (Indianapolis: Hackett, 1987).

[4] Roger Scruton, *The Aesthetics of Architecture* (Princeton: Princeton University Press, 1979).

[5] Frank Sibley, *Approach to Aesthetics: Collected Papers on Philosophical Aesthetics* (Oxford: Oxford University Press, 2001).

[6] Scruton, *Aesthetics of Architecture*, p. 113.

[7] Carolyn Korsmeyer, *Making Sense of Taste: Food and Philosophy* (Ithaca: Cornell University Press, 1999), p. 100.

argued that the response to a specific melody, or a line, or a color, may also be idiosyncratic and have relative dimensions.

A number of other recent philosophers have also maintained that food or drink is capable of providing an aesthetic experience. Francis Coleman[8] comments that food and drink may be capable of offering the complex sensations necessary to provide cognitive stimulation. Crucially, Harold Osborne[9] has noted that the distinction sometimes made between the mere "sensuous" pleasure of taste or a smell and the "cognitive" pleasure in the appreciation of high art is a false dichotomy; he analyzes in detail what we see in an artwork, including hue and color, then points out that the components of a smell can be far more complex than either aspects of a visual response. It is thus clear that whilst there may be a long tradition which excludes wine from aesthetic appreciation, it is not a tradition which is universally accepted.

A final point relates to the idea of wine as an "artwork," with the winemaker as artist. A full analysis of this debate is beyond the scope of this essay, which seeks to focus on the consumer's experience rather than the nature of the aesthetic object. However, it is enough to note that there are those who would argue that wine (like, perhaps, a great meal) is capable of being considered a work of art.[10] Nevertheless, Korsmeyer, in a recent, comprehensive philosophical engagement with food and wine, has argued that both products must be seen in a much wider symbolic context rather than merely as artworks or capable of aesthetic evaluation. They have "a symbolic function that extends beyond even the most sophisticated savoring."[11] Other philosophers, like Sibley,[12] have suggested that if wine is capable of aesthetic appreciation, it is irrelevant whether or not it is an artwork.

The nature of the aesthetic experience

In order to explore whether or not wine can be a stimulus for an aesthetic experience, it is useful to attempt to crystallize some of the

---

[8]   Francis J. Coleman, "Can a Smell or a Taste or a Touch be Beautiful?" *American Philosophical Quarterly* 2.4 (1965): 319–24.

[9]   Harold Osborne, "Odours and Appreciation," *British Journal of Aesthetics* 17 (1977): 37–48.

[10]   Korsmeyer, *Making Sense of Taste.*

[11]   Ibid., p. 103.

[12]   Sibley, *Approach to Aesthetics.*

core elements of that experience. Given the disputes that have raged between philosophers for the past three hundred years, this may seem to be a vain exercise, but without engaging in the detail of those disputes, a tentative summary of aesthetic processes can be offered.

At the core of aesthetics at the beginning of the eighteenth century was the notion of beauty; and it is still accepted by most aesthetic thinkers that the beautiful, the sublime, or that which is moving is central to the aesthetic experience.[13] Beauty, however, must be interpreted in a broad sense and covers products beyond the merely visually appealing. Traditional aesthetic thought has considered music, poetry, and often novels and plays to be potentially beautiful products.

Having established beauty as a core concept for aesthetics, the next stage in the development of aesthetic thought was to determine how the beautiful could be appreciated. This debate centered on two issues: how aesthetic judgments could be validated and how the individual made those judgments. Thus, on the former issue, early theorists sought to establish how judgments of taste could be justified, but after Kant the focus shifted from this issue with the assumption that any response is merely personal and incapable of objective justification. Later aesthetic thinkers, however, have revisited the issue of how aesthetic objects can be assessed, and have also returned to the debate about whether or not aesthetic appreciation is objective or subjective.[14]

As well as considering the validity of aesthetic judgments, philosophers of aesthetics are also concerned with the nature of the individual's aesthetic response; how precisely is aesthetic engagement experienced? Some philosophers have argued that the experience is entirely cognitive, and emotion plays no part in it.[15] Others argue that feeling is essential to the experience, or that it is primarily a sensory response.[16] This relates to the debate about the role of pleasure in aesthetic engagement. Some maintain that any pleasure taken in

---

[13]   Simon Blackburn, *Dictionary of Philosophy* (Oxford: Oxford University Press, 1994).

[14]   For recent examples see Monroe C. Beardsley, *Aesthetics: Problems in the Philosophy of Criticism*, 2nd ed. (Indianapolis: Harcourt, Brace, and World, 1980); George Gale, "Are Some Aesthetic Judgments Empirically True?" *American Philosophical Quarterly* 12.4 (1975): 341–8; and Peter Railton, "Aesthetic Value, Moral Value and the Ambitions of Naturalism," in Jerrold Levinson (ed.), *Aesthetics and Ethics: Essays at the Intersection* (Cambridge: Cambridge University Press, 1998), pp. 59–105.

[15]   See Scruton, *Aesthetics of Architecture*, for a clear exposition of this.

[16]   Harold Osborne, "Some Theories of Aesthetic Judgment," *Journal of Aesthetics and Art Criticism* 38 (1979): 135–44.

the process is entirely cerebral; others allow it a more visceral or emotional dimension.[17] However, the increasing interest psychologists have shown in aesthetics has meant that this issue has been revisited. This is particularly evident in the work of Mihaly Csikszentmihalyi and his collaborators,[18] where the concept of "flow" is developed. Flow represents the individual's complete involvement in an activity or product and encompasses mental, emotional, and sensory processes.

One can therefore summarize this review of the literature by suggesting that some of the major aesthetic debates center on three issues. The first is the nature of the aesthetic response, including the nature of pleasure in the experience, and whether or not it is primarily cognitive, emotional or sensory. Second is the role of the aesthetic object, including the elements of beauty and the nature of artworks. Third is how aesthetic judgments can be established – and specifically, whether they tend to be objective or subjective. Each of these will be considered in this essay.

Exploring the consumer response

This essay results from an empirical study examining the Australian consumer's engagement with wine.[19] The study, which was framed within the marketing subdiscipline of consumer behavior, focused not only on wine consumers but also on producers and those involved in wine distribution (including judges and critics). Because it was dealing with previously unexplored phenomena, the research was considered exploratory and adopted qualitative methods using interviews and focus groups (which used a "blind" wine tasting as a stimulus to discussion). The potentially aesthetic dimension was one topic raised with the informants, although the topic was addressed obliquely by asking them if they felt that there were any similarities between wine and music or with art generally. On occasions, the aesthetic perspective on wine was raised voluntarily by informants.

[17] Eva Schaper, "The Pleasures of Taste," in Eva Schaper (ed.), *Pleasure, Preference and Value* (Cambridge: Cambridge University Press, 1983).
[18] Mihaly Csikszentmihalyi, *Flow: The Classic Work on How to Achieve Happiness* (London: Rider, 2002); and Mihaly Csikszentmihalyi and Rick E. Robinson, *The Art of Seeing: An Interpretation of the Aesthetic Encounter* (Malibu: J. Paul Getty Trust, 1990).
[19] Full details of the methodological approach can be found in Charters and Pettigrew, "Is Wine Consumption an Aesthetic Experience?," on which this essay is based.

What Consumers Think

As noted earlier, an examination of the aesthetic experience involves the exploration of three aspects: the nature of the aesthetic response; the features which define an aesthetic object (including its beauty and the concept of the artwork); and the criteria used to establish aesthetic judgments. Consumer views on the aesthetic nature of wine are examined below in the context of each of these aspects. Before addressing each of these, however, it is important to note the differing perspectives amongst informants about whether or not wine does have an aesthetic nature.

Does wine have aesthetic dimensions?

Overwhelmingly (by a ratio of about three to one), informants considered that the consumption of wine shows some similarities to the appreciation of "pure" art forms. Only a very few informants were uncertain about their response, either because they failed to grasp the concept involved or because they were unable or unwilling to reach a final conclusion. In its most extreme form the case for the similarity between wine and artworks was made as follows:

> *Simon*[20] (consumer): Fundamentally, you can make the connection between music, literature, art, and wine. Without them, life wouldn't be worth living. I think that's the fundamental thing. You can certainly drop one or two of them but if you didn't have any expressive qualities in your life then there would be no . . . way of growing as a human being.

This sentiment was repeated, although usually with a less metaphysical tone, by most others. One exception was a focus group participant who discounted any similarity on the grounds that wine – unlike artworks – conveyed no message:

> *Alison* (consumer): But [wine] doesn't tell me anything deep or meaningful. A good artist will be often conveying a view about something. A wine isn't a social comment. You either enjoy it or you don't.

---

[20] All informants have been given pseudonyms.

192

Alison developed her argument more comprehensively than most other informants. As well as the lack of a message, she commented that wine for her had a social function, promoting human interaction, rather than being something that one spent time evaluating closely. Additionally she noted:

> I will appreciate something that aesthetically I might not find pleasing. But I can appreciate it. If I don't find the wine pleasing I don't like it.

She observed that one can appreciate aesthetic objects without liking them (a point made by other informants about wine evaluation generally). However, she did not accept that preference could be divorced from evaluation with wine; rather, she felt that liking and appreciation were unified when drinking.

For the majority of those informants who considered that the response to wine involves similar processes to the response to artworks, three key reasons were offered, of broadly similar weight. The most significant of these seemed to be the pleasure afforded by aesthetic processes. Nearly as important was the nature of the individual's aesthetic experience, and especially the similarity of evaluative methods adopted (involving cognitive processing, the importance of learning and education in developing evaluative skills, and the focus required). The third key likeness revolved around the relevance of personal taste in response to wine and to artworks. Each of these reasons is discussed in greater detail below.

Wine, pleasure, and aesthetic experience

The main similarity offered by drinkers between the experience of wine and music (or any other artwork) was that of the experiential similarities between the consumption of wine and consumption of the arts. Critically, pleasure, as a response, was seen as a common link between the two.

> *Sue* (consumer): It doesn't matter [as long as] you enjoy the music. You don't have to know the ins and outs of it, if you just enjoy listening to it. And it's just [the same] enjoying wine. It's just a pleasurable pursuit.

193

This was a perspective shared by some members of all reference groups. For much of the time that experience seems to fit with a general sense of pleasure; however, occasionally it can become much deeper, and operate as a "profound experience." An exchange in a focus group of winemakers exhibited this perspective using terms that very closely reflect the concept of the "flow" experience.[21]

> *Hal*: It's those great wines that you've had in the past that have had such an emotional effect on you that that's what you're aiming for.
> *Maria*: That's true.
> *Hal*: Great wines that flow through you like nothing else. It's an amazing, heightened experience that you've never had before. And you say that's all just coming from this thing in the glass. I mean that's very intoxicating, morish, you want more of that.

This idea that the experience of wine could be uplifting or profound in its impact was mentioned by a number of other informants, but, invariably, they were frequent and interested drinkers, tending to respond to a wine in both sensory and very cognitive, evaluative terms. Less committed and less interested drinkers appeared not to have had wine consumption experiences which they could articulate beyond the description of general hedonic pleasure.

Some drinkers see the aesthetic response to wine and artworks as being primarily sensory. Thus one interviewee when asked about the similarity between the appreciation of wine and of music responded as follows:

> *Ursula* (consumer): [They're] sensuous. Music can make you feel pretty jumpy. Some art can make you feel pretty sick. I suppose it all requires a sensual response as opposed to just an intellectual response.

For other informants the key similarities between the response to wine and to artworks were emotional. Just before the following extract Mary had been asked if she saw similarities between the experiences of wine and of music:

> *Mary* (consumer): Yeah I do . . . All of those sorts of things that you do because it makes you feel good. Or you listen to because it makes you feel good. It's similar in that respect.

[21] Csikszentmihalyi and Robinson, *The Art of Seeing*.

For Mary, the key link between wine and music was their affective impact. Both can make you feel good. However, for most informants the key form of response was cognitive. This in turn leads on to the next similarity offered between wine and artwork: the importance of aesthetic evaluation in the response to both of them.

Whether sensory or affective, for many informants the consumption of wine and the consumption of artworks are similar because both involve an evaluative process:

> *Diana* (consumer):   There is a point of similarity there. Music or art, theater or all those sorts of things – you're making a judgment and deciding what you want.

These processes – evaluation and judgment – meant that some informants stressed that a key similarity between wine and artworks was the reliance on cognition:

> *Martha* (wine educator):   Yes, I like to think of wine appreciation as cerebral. . . . And so I would think of art.

In turn, this cognitive process of evaluation was seen by informants to comprise three elements. These are the need for focus, the importance of education and expertise, and the impact of exploration and challenge. Each of these is discussed below.

A number of informants developed the idea of aesthetic evaluation to suggest that both wine and artworks require focus. Thus, comparing wine and paintings:

> *Tina* (consumer):   You need to pay attention, to take time to get into them. I take time, as I don't want other people to influence me. I try and try again, and ensure that I'm complete with it . . . I think if you like looking at paintings, you will like drinking wine as well.

For Tina, this focus requires time and the expenditure of emotional energy. It is not something that should be influenced by others, but a practice which she considers her own responsibility. She argued that if you are prepared to undertake concentrated attention with art, then you will probably enjoy doing it with wine as well. This need for focused concentration would be recognized by many psychologists and philosophers of aesthetics as typical of aesthetic engagement.

195

For informants who considered aesthetic evaluation to be part of the response to wine, the gaining of knowledge and skill was often perceived to be important. Knowledge and skill are what give the informed critic the ability to detect the fine nuances necessary for effective evaluation:

> *Hal* (winemaker):   At the high end [consider] the difference between two great tenors. A highly educated musician would be able to pick the subtle differences and say "well this one was quite cluey [competent], better than this one for these reasons." Whereas I'd say "well they were both pretty fabulous." That's where we come to. I guess our expertise is in being able to say "this bottle of Château Margaux . . . is better than this bottle of Mouton" – or something. And some people mightn't be able to see that.

This ability to appreciate is based on two related factors: the detailed knowledge accumulated by years of study and the experience in seeing "subtle differences" gained from considerable application of that knowledge. Note that Hal, as an expert, made the point that he had the ability to evaluate the nuances of his chosen field (viz., wine), whereas he would not have similar skills in other fields of aesthetic consumption.

For many informants the enjoyment of the process of evaluating wine and artworks seemed to be rooted in the challenge of the works and the chance to explore them, processes which engage their knowledge and skill:

> *William* (consumer):   If it's art there's a wide range of choice there. And a lot of people like the experience of everything – so that they can find their preferences.

William saw the experience of a range of aesthetic experiences as positive, implying that people enjoy the process of making decisions about their predilections. As well as the exploration of that diversity, there is the challenge of understanding. What follows is from an interviewee who raised the similarities between wine and music without prompting:

> *Gerhard* (consumer):   I think in both cases you need to know what makes it tick. In music you need to know how music evolved, what's behind it. The link between mathematics and music is an obvious

one. And once you understand certain things like that you can appreciate music, even if it's not to your liking. Sometimes you find if you realize the amount of work that has gone into growing the wine, that's gone into making the wine, that's gone into storing the wine – you can appreciate it for its quality even if you don't like its style.

The challenge, for Gerhard, is to know what makes both wine and music "tick." Processes and philosophy seem crucial to his aesthetic appreciation of the product.

For many informants, a key element of the aesthetic experience, and another major similarity in the response to both wine and artworks, was personal taste. The latter was almost as significant to informants as pleasure and the processes of evaluation as an indicator that wine consumption has an aesthetic dimension. Thus:

> *Hetty* (consumer): If I was looking at art or music I think it would come down to my personal taste. Which is the same as wine – so in that way, I think, [they are] similar.

Hetty makes the point clearly that one's response to artworks is subjective and individual, and her viewpoint was commonly echoed by other informants.

A contrast to this emphasis on the relevance of personal taste as a link between wine and other aesthetic products was the perspective of a few informants that there exists a "commonality of response" to wine and other aesthetic products. The effect of this was to suggest that wine and artworks were similar not because they rely on an individual's personal taste, but because there is a common awareness of how good they can be. This recalls the philosophical perspective on the objectivity of aesthetic judgments.[22] Thus, in one focus group of wine producers, Roger and Maria considered that there are similarities between wine and artworks:

> *Roger*: Often a hallmark of a good work is that it's appealing to everyone regardless of their level of expertise. A painting might be appealing to everyone. [They] will go "wow that's really good, obviously someone's talented, they've put a lot into it. There's no way I could do that – it looks really impressive." Off they go – the punter

[22] Hume, *Selected Essays*; Railton, "Aesthetic Value, Moral Value and the Ambitions of Naturalism."

– and an expert comes along and goes "wow that is amazing . . . their use of shadow and line and light and all of that sort of thing. . . ." Similarly with wine.

Maria: And if you took something that's considered to be high quality into a primitive, naïve group they would still recognize the quality from the rubbish.

Roger maintained that the quality of an aesthetic product can potentially be recognized by anyone, whether experts or amateurs, even though the former are more easily able to rationalize or explain their responses (the "use of shadow and line and light"). This is the opposite of the approach which dismisses aesthetic taste as no more than personal preference and was a perspective held by a few informants.

Wine as an aesthetic object

As outlined in the review of literature, the second key aspect of the aesthetic experience focuses on the aesthetic object which acts as a stimulus to the experience. Informants in this study suggested two key ways in which wine could be an aesthetic object: the awareness of beauty which it engenders, and its similarities to other artworks.

There was a strong sense in the responses of some informants that wine, as a product, has an element of beauty in the aesthetic sense of the word. This was rarely directly referred to, probably because in common parlance beautiful is a term most generally used for what is visually appealing. However, it remained implicit in much of what was said, and with one informant it emerged explicitly:

Wendy (winemaker): [At a concert, art gallery or wine tasting] you're looking for something that's going to be inspiring and beautiful. Yeah, I guess beauty can be seen in all things. And I see [that] wine production – perhaps not the commercial end so much – should be creative . . . Special bottles of wine, certainly I'd rate in that category [as beautiful].

There is a tension in what Wendy is thinking through. She is not sure where to place mass-produced wine styles as objects of beauty. Nevertheless, special bottles – ones which are not necessarily drunk on a day-to-day basis – should be considered inspiring and beautiful, just as a concert could. Although not articulated as clearly, Wendy's perspective was shared by a few other professional informants.

198

However, it became more apparent as an implicit perspective, as in a previous comment by winemaker Tom, that there are some wines which "just like 'bang' [make his] hair stand on end."

Whereas most informants considered that the consumption process of wine and artworks had similarities, a few also made a direct link between wine as a product and other aesthetic products. This point was generally made by suggesting that wine is an artwork itself. Thus:

> *Ellie* (consumer): It involves creating something, if you're creating music or you're creating art or you're creating a wine.

This perspective was held by a range of informants but as one might expect was best formulated by the "artists" themselves, the winemakers:

> *Danielle* (winemaker): I really think there's a huge similarity between art and wine, I really do. I just think it is a true artist that comes up with a very good quality, unique wine . . . So the way I see it is you use like a palette and a canvas. And something that is unique in the art world is not dissimilar to a bottle of wine in the wine world.
> [later]
> *Danielle*: Well I think of Torbreck wines. The guy who makes Torbreck wines, he's an artist. He hasn't had much training or whatever. He's done lots of vintages but . . . apparently he hasn't done a wine science degree or anything. But his wine is just amazing to me.

Danielle was explicit that a good wine is like a good work of art, created from a palette of material (grapes), and unique. She used as a specific example a current Australian wine with cult status, and noted, approvingly, that the winemaker does not actually have a formal winemaking education. There is possibly an implicit suggestion that this freedom from the constraints of being trained in a particular way has allowed the winemaker's artistic side to flourish.

There were, however, dissenting perspectives, even amongst winemakers. Not all of them saw their role as identical to that of the artist:

> *Clive* (winemaker): Art is more an expression of emotions, whereas wine is more scientific, or agricultural or industrial. It's got creative elements in it but also at the end it's pragmatic.

199

By "pragmatic" Clive seems to mean crafted. He accepts that there is an element of creativity in what he does, but he works in a more scientific way than the artist. He fabricates a product which has, in his perspective, less emotional content than a work of art. Another winemaker, however, when asked about the similarities between wine and music, viewed the wine/art link as less one of creativity than of interpretation:

> *Mark* (winemaker): I was thinking about this the other day when I was listening to [some music] . . . Yeah, you can get 20 different musicians and you ask them to interpret one piece of music and they'll all do it fairly differently. But there might be only two or three that you really like personally.

Mark's view is that the impact of wine and the impact of music are similar because, in each case, one is responding to an interpretation of art. Winemakers "interpret" the grapes (and perhaps the vineyard) in what they make, as musicians interpret a piece of music, but the consumer may make selective evaluative judgments about that interpretation. This idea – that the similarities lie in interpretation, not creation – was repeated by consumers as well as professionals.

Discussion and Conclusions

Informants generally saw similarities between the consumption of wine and the consumption of aesthetic products, notably music. This does not necessarily qualify wine as an aesthetic object, yet the experiences and responses offered by informants on the subject of wine tended to match generally the criteria set down for aesthetic consumption as outlined in the literature review.

Most notably, the correspondences observed by informants cover three main areas. Some informants considered wine to have the elements of a work of art. However, more widely noted was the fact that wine, like artworks, can invoke a sense of pleasure – focusing on an awareness of the beauty of the product. This includes both a general awareness of pleasure and a deeper, more profound aesthetic experience. Such a perspective, which sees the intensity of the aesthetic experience as being on a continuum, is not necessarily accepted philosophically, but is perhaps more generally acknowledged by social scientists.

Second, it has been noted that there is a debate about the sensory, cognitive, and/or emotional nature of the aesthetic response, with at least some research suggesting an interaction of all three.[23] This inter-active process was implied in the data provided by informants. However, just as the weight of philosophical analysis has tended to focus on mental activity, so these informants emphasized the cognit-ive evaluation of both wine and music. This cognitive attention in turn seemed to comprise a number of elements. Crucially, and in reflection of the common philosophical view that aesthetic "consumption" requires concentrated aesthetic attention,[24] a number talked about the focus that was needed when evaluating wine.

A third issue is that, as with the appreciation of art, there seems to be a paradoxical response to wine. It can be seen to reflect not just personal taste – a subjective reaction – but also a shared evaluative response, reflecting the idea that everyone may appreciate both its quality and its qualities. This in turn mirrors the classic philosophical debate about the subjectivity or objectivity of aesthetic judgments.[25]

Finally, there seems to be the perception of an element of beauty in wine, although few informants directly referred to it. Some wines may have such an impact on drinkers that they are considered "inspiring or beautiful." Other drinkers, without being so explicit, could still refer to special bottles or being lost for words – both con-cepts which are suggestive of a sense of the beauty of the object. This again reflects the focus of aesthetics on the response to the "mov-ing, or beautiful or sublime."[26]

Where informants did not perceive similarities between wine con-sumption and more formal aesthetic experiences, two reasons tended to be given. The first was that wine conveys no message, whereas art does. This is predicated on the idea that artworks have a meaning, a strongly held view by some philosophers of aesthetics.[27] Nevertheless,

[23]   Csikszentmihalyi and Robinson, *The Art of Seeing*.
[24]   George Dickie, *Aesthetics: An Introduction* (New York: Pegasus, 1971); Scruton, *The Aesthetics of Architecture*; Sibley, *Approach to Aesthetics*.
[25]   George Dickie, *Introduction to Aesthetics: An Analytic Approach* (Oxford: Oxford University Press, 1997).
[26]   Blackburn, *Dictionary of Philosophy*, p. 8.
[27]   Nelson Goodman, *Languages of Art* (Indianapolis: Hackett, 1968).

this argument is not universally accepted by aestheticians. It could be that the mere portrayal of beauty may preclude the need for a message and the "intention" of the artist may have no bearing on the aesthetic experience.[28] Indeed, academics from non-philosophical traditions can find substantial aesthetic meaning in the experience of a meal or a wine.[29] The second reason given by informants for discounting the similarities in the experience relate to the more social nature of wine consumption compared with assumption of the more "private" experience of "high art." There may well be some validity in this perspective, although one can note that even for high art there is a range of ancillary social experiences, from the public reading of a poem through to a group tour of an art exhibition.

As already noted, the perspective of a range of consumers neither proves nor disproves that wine consumption is an aesthetic experience. It does, however, shed new light on the debates about what constitutes such an experience, and crucially the informants' views offer some essential similarities between the two. The specific social function of wine may mark it out from more obvious art forms (or from high art), so a solution may be to consider wine (and perhaps by extension food, and maybe clothing) as a quasi-aesthetic object. Nevertheless, its appreciation seems to have much in common with that of music or the arts in general.

---

[28] Dickie, *Introduction to Aesthetics*.

[29] Mary Douglas, "A Distinctive Anthropological Perspective," in Mary Douglas (ed.), *Constructive Drinking: Perspectives on Drink from Anthropology* (New York: Cambridge University Press, 1987), pp. 3–15; Jukka Grunow, *The Sociology of Taste* (London: Routledge, 1997); Dwight B. Heath, *Drinking Occasions: Comparative Perspectives on Alcohol and Culture* (Ann Arbor: Taylor and Francis, 2000).

V

Wine & Metaphysics

13

Is There Coffee or Blackberry in My Wine?

Kevin W. Sweeney

In the popular mind, wine tasting has often been thought of as a sub-jective, idiosyncratic experience, masquerading behind a false façade of expertise. Who is to say that the Napa Valley cabernet sauvignon that I am swirling in my glass has, in fact, the flavors of coffee or black-berry? Does that Sonoma sauvignon blanc that I have poured for you really possess a mineral middle range of flint and steel? Does the wine's flavor profile actually begin with a grapefruit crispness? Are these claims anything more than personal opinions or idiosyncratic associations?

Philosophers, too, have often been skeptical of claims about a wine's aesthetic character. While acknowledging that a glass of wine could contribute to our enjoying the conversation of others, Immanuel Kant thought that the pleasures of tasting wine were only personal and idiosyncratic.[1] If someone thinks that canary wine – a sweet dessert wine from the Canary Islands – is exquisite, Kant claims that such a judgment is no more than a personal preference. Others need not share that view.[2] Since wine is an ingestive pleasure, he also thought that wine drinkers could never be disinterested, a requirement for a true aesthetic experience: wine drinkers and the Iroquois *sachem*, who preferred the Parisian rôtisseries to the palaces, were alike in that their pleasures satisfied an appetite.[3]

---

[1] Immanuel Kant, *Anthropology from a Pragmatic Point of View* (1798), ed. and trans. Robert B. Louden, introduction by Manfred Kuehn (New York: Cambridge University Press, 2006), pp. 46, 51, 63–4.
[2] Immanuel Kant, *Critique of Judgment* (1790), trans. Werner S. Pluhar (Indianapolis: Hackett, 1987), sect. 7, p. 55.
[3] Ibid., sect. 2, p. 45.

One of the reasons Kant held that critical judgments about food and drink registered only personal preferences is that he thought that our senses of taste and smell were "more subjective than objective, that is, the idea obtained from them is more a representation of *enjoyment* than of cognition of the external object."[4] According to Kant, matters of gustatory taste – our sensory acquaintance with what we orally ingest – were matters of personal pleasure: our judgments about wine and food were not cognitive appraisals of objects but indicators of our individual pleasurable experiences or taste preferences. Even with recent aestheticians' interest in gustatory taste and smell and in alimentary experience in general,[5] there are still philosophers who believe that wine tasting is concerned with the taster's own subjective enjoyment rather than with an aesthetic object. For example, Roger Scruton has argued:

> Vision and hearing, unlike taste and smell, may sometimes be forms of objective contemplation. In tasting and smelling I contemplate not the object but the experience derived from it. A further distinguishing feature might also be mentioned, which is that in tasting, both the object and the desire for it are steadily consumed. No such thing is true of aesthetic attention.[6]

Wine tasting, on Scruton's view, is excluded from being an aesthetic activity because it yields an "object-less" pleasure. Vision and hearing offer cognitive and aesthetic encounters with their respective objects, but taste and smell, Scruton claims, do not.

There is something very counter-intuitive about Scruton's Kantian position that in wine tasting there is no aesthetic consideration of an object. Wine is something tangible; the wine I taste is an empirical object. Perhaps not *all* wines can be said to be objects of appreciation, and not *all* quaffers are aesthetes, but certainly *some* wines are appreciated by *some* people. Can it really be the case that we do not appreciate the wine we see in our glass and taste on our palate? When we sniff the complex aroma of a Puligny-Montrachet and

---

[4] Kant, *Anthropology*, p. 46.

[5] The foremost recent work on gustatory taste is Carolyn Korsmeyer, *Making Sense of Taste: Food and Philosophy* (Ithaca: Cornell University Press, 1999).

[6] Roger Scruton, *The Aesthetics of Architecture* (Princeton: Princeton University Press, 1979), p. 114.

register its developing character on our palate, are we not appreciatively encountering an object? I think that we are; however, the appreciative encounter with wine poses some problems at which Scruton might be hinting. I want to explore the nature of this object that we swirl in our glasses and register on our palates, yet react to in our individual gustatory ways.

To introduce this project of examining the aesthetic object of the wine that we ingest and savor, let me make a preliminary observation. I will usually use the term 'taste' to refer to our acquaintance with the full range of ingested qualities, not just the narrow sensing of sweet, sour, salt, and bitter on the tongue and palate. Much of what we taste is olfactory, depending on our retronasal ability to smell what we ingest, and usually referred to as a perception of "flavor." So sensory qualities of narrow tasting, smelling, touching, and temperature sensing – I do not pursue the question of the importance of hearing what we ingest – I will generally refer to as qualities of tasting. I take this general perspective because I am worried about breaking up the encounter with wine into various different and discrete categories of sense data. I prefer thinking about our acquaintance with a wine as a phenomenological encounter with an object in the world, a complex encounter that I generally refer to as tasting a wine.[7]

That some contemporary philosophers might seem reluctant to recognize wine as an aesthetic object is surprising given that many eighteenth-century philosophers held that our critical appreciation of art and natural beauty – often referred to as "critical taste" – was patterned on alimentary experience, on gustatory taste. David Hume claimed that critical taste as a sensibility of refined appreciation was metaphorically based on gustatory taste.[8] Other "pre-aesthetic" thinkers also drew parallels between "literal" and critical taste, at least in some respects. A basic reason was that gustatory taste, like critical appreciation, was held to be naturally hedonic: we rarely just sense what we ingest; instead, our sensing amounts to a pleasurable

---

[7] Good overviews of the physiology of our sensory acquaintance with wine can be found in Andrew Sharp, *Winetaster's Secrets* (Toronto: Warwick Publishing, 1995), pp. 14–49; and Marian W. Baldy, *The University Wine Course*, 3rd ed. (San Francisco: Wine Appreciation Guild, 1997), pp. 14–43.

[8] David Hume, "Of the Standard of Taste" (1757), in *Essays, Moral, Political, and Literary*, ed. Eugene F. Miller (Indianapolis: Liberty Classics, 1987), p. 235.

or displeasurable experience of what we have ingested. Gustatory taste was also thought to involve an unconsidered "quick discernment," as when we immediately sense that the coffee is sweet or the tea bitter.[9] So, Voltaire noticed a

> striking resemblance between the intellectual taste and the sensual one; for as a nice palate perceives immediately the mixture of different wines, so the man of taste will quickly discern the motley mixture of different styles in the same production; and, let the beauties and defects be ever so closely blended in an object, will always be capable of distinguishing the former from the latter.[10]

Yet, there was a problem in accepting the parallel between gustatory and critical taste: some were concerned that one seemed to be accepting an inherent critical subjectivity. If gustatory taste allowed for individual preference, was critical taste also just a matter of personal preference? If there were no disputing about taste, then taste as a critical sensibility that met certain conventional standards might be acquired as a non-cognitive habit but it could not be objectively based on a knowledgeable perspective. Yet some thinkers rejected the subjective or skeptical part of the parallel. It might be true that one could not rationally persuade or teach someone to like spinach or riesling if she or he had earlier detested it; however, it was hoped that our critical taste could be improved rather than one set of preferences being replaced by another.

One of Hume's intentions in "Of the Standard of Taste" was to show how one might improve one's critical acumen. One could become a better judge of objects of critical appreciation ("a true judge in the finer arts") if one emulated the qualities Hume advocated in his famous little summary: "Strong sense, united to delicate sentiment, improved by practice, perfected by comparison, and cleared of all prejudice, can alone entitle critics to this valuable character."[11] For example, in critically judging a piece of music, one should have a sensitive musical ear to pick up all the subtle tonal nuances of the

---

[9]   Voltaire, "An Essay on Taste," translated from Voltaire's article on taste in Diderot and D'Alembert's *Encyclopédie* (1757), in Alexander Gerard, *An Essay on Taste*, 2nd ed. (1764; rpt. New York: Garland, 1970), p. 209.

[10]   Ibid., p. 210.

[11]   Hume, "Of the Standard of Taste," p. 241. Further page references are given in the text.

piece. The exemplary critic should have "strong sense," which, for Hume, meant having the practical intelligence and critical background to discern the work's genre and to be able to see what generally to expect in such a piece. One also needed to hone one's appreciative skills by practice and comparison and be unbiased in approaching the music.

If, by practice, comparison, freedom from prejudice, and all the rest, one could improve one's critical acumen about works of art, and if there were a parallel between critical and gustatory taste, might there be a comparable regimen to improve one's gustatory skills and critical judgment about wine? Or does gustatory experience by its nature have that ingrained subjectivity which would resist some cognitive practice aimed at general improvement in appreciation? Is Scruton right that gustatory experience is just a hedonic reflex? When we encounter and ingest the wine, are there no objects to compare, practice on, or exercise our good sense about?

Fortunately, a good place to start to address these issues is with one of Hume's examples: the wine-tasting example he adapts from *Don Quixote* about Sancho Panza's wine-tasting kinsmen. I take it that in the following example one of Hume's goals is to counter a skepticism about the possibility of making objective evaluations of wine:

> It is with good reason, says Sancho to the squire with the great nose, that I pretend to have a judgment in wine: This is a quality hereditary in our family. Two of my kinsmen were once called to give their opinion of a hogshead, which was supposed to be excellent, being old and of a good vintage. One of them tastes it; considers it; and after mature reflection pronounces the wine to be good, were it not for a small taste of leather, which he perceived in it. The other, after using the same precautions, gives also his verdict in favor of the wine; but with the reserve of a taste of iron, which he could easily distinguish. You cannot imagine how much they were both ridiculed for their judgment. But who laughed in the end? On emptying the hogshead, there was found at the bottom, an old key with a leathern thong tied to it. (pp. 234–5)

Let me say right off that I think that in many respects Hume's example is bizarre as far as wine tasting is concerned. Nevertheless, in its peculiarity it invites questioning about the fundamental aesthetic character of wine tasting and prompts us to search for a more adequate response to the wine skeptic.

209

The example is troublesome for the following reasons. Hume offers the example as an illustration of what he refers to as that "delicacy of imagination" necessary for sound critical judgment (p. 234). Yet, it is not clear from the example, and from Hume's later discussion of the example, that Sancho's kinsmen exercise their imaginations. Certainly, each respectively senses a minute quantity of leather or of iron in the wine; however, what makes that sensing an act of imagination? Furthermore, Hume claims that the mark of a good palate is the ability to sense minute quantities of ingredients and to make fine discriminations among the varied ingredients of what one tastes. "A good palate," he says, "is not tried by strong flavours; but by a mixture of small ingredients, where we are still sensible of each part, notwithstanding its minuteness and its confusion with the rest" (p. 236). Yet Hume does not explain how the sensing of minute ingredients fits into the overall evaluation of a wine. How is sensing iron or leather related to judging a wine to be good-but-for-the-taste-of-*x*? How does sensing leather or iron connect with recognizing these qualities to be faults and with judging the overall evaluative quality of the wine?

Hume's apparent answer is that the "true judge," possessing a practiced skill, fine sensory ability, and unbiased outlook, can taste a wine and after due consideration render an objective evaluative judgment. Yet the example also gives a very unusual proof of that expertise. Sancho's kinsmen are laughed at because they offer differing verdicts about the wine, when objectivity would seem to require a uniform judgment. What the kinsmen's differing verdicts show, the skeptic would like to claim, is that there is no expertise in wine judging, only subjective opinion. However, the proof that vindicates the kinsmen's judgment, the key with the leather thong, gives a generally misleading account of the nature of warranting a judgment about wine.

The key-with-the-leather-thong proof is misleading because it suggests that exercising a delicacy of the imagination, or sensing a delicate quality in a wine, will have an objective correlate which will support a claim that the wine has that delicate quality. However, can we expect that a claim to taste a grapefruit quality in a sauvignon blanc will be supported by a grapefruit section or peel either being in or at one time having been in the wine? Hume's proof seems to take a very unusual situation – the key with the leather thong supporting the kinsmen's judgments – as a paradigm for the kind of support usually available for verdicts about wine.

In the example, the form of the proof seems to be that there is some substance in the wine which the wine judges sense and identify. If one independently finds that substance in the wine or its container, one has confirmed the wine judge's claim or verdict. So, one kinsman, on the basis of tasting the wine, claims the wine to have a taste of iron, and a piece of iron is found in the wine barrel confirming the judgment. The other kinsman tastes leather, and a piece of leather is found confirming his judgment. (There is also the suggestion that iron and leather are extraneous elements that are not natural components of wine.)

Although I have found Hume's example to be troublesome, there is some initial plausibility to the view that there is this kind of objective support for our claims about what we taste in a wine. For example, imagine that you taste a chardonnay and say, "This wine is very oaky. The oak dominates the taste of the wine, and I do not taste much else." We come to learn that the wine was stored in new oak barrels, the wine was from a poor year, the grapes did not fully ripen, and so the wine has little extract to counteract the oak. You have tasted the oak in the wine because that quality (the oaky taste) comes from the oak staves of the barrels. Instead of there being a moderate amount of oak, which with another wine might have provided some structure to support the wine's complex qualities, the oak, in this example, obliterates any sense of structure and overwhelms whatever qualities the wine might have had. In this chardonnay-tasting example, one probably does not need the fine discriminating palate of the kinsmen to taste the oak. (I have heard people say on tasting a very oaky chardonnay that it was like "chewing on boards.") You taste the oak because it comes from the barrel; the kinsmen taste the iron and the leather because it comes from the key and thong. Both of the examples illustrate tasting extraneous qualities, but one can also find examples concerned with tasting qualities intrinsic to the wine.

For example, imagine that you taste a young cabernet sauvignon and say, "I am getting a taste of green pepper in this wine." Unlike the kinsmen example and the oak-in-the-chardonnay example, this example is not about sensing an extraneous element in the wine. No pieces of green pepper have been added to the cabernet; however, there is a chemical in the cabernet, one of the methoxypyrazines, which is also found in green peppers and causes green peppers to taste

211

the way they do.[12] When you taste the cabernet and sense "green pepper," it is quite likely that you are registering the presence of this green-pepper-tasting chemical. Consider another example of intrinsic tasting. You taste a young chardonnay and say, "There is a green-apple crispness to this wine." Very likely this is a wine that has not undergone a full malolactic fermentation, and you are sensing the malic acid in the wine, the same acid that gives apples their crisp apple-like characteristic taste.

Let us call this view of tasting *analytic realism*. According to analytic realism: in tasting, the taster believes, on the basis of experiencing a sensed gustatory quality which admits of a certain label, that she or he is registering the actual stimulus agent that produces that quality. And, the taster believes that the stimulus agent can be accurately identified with the label. One need not be able to label the component scientifically – one does not have to know that one is sensing malic acid – but it should be clear from what you say that you believe that the sour taste you are experiencing is produced by a stimulus agent in the wine. Furthermore, you believe that the stimulus agent is sour. Of course, making these discriminations requires some sensory acuity and some familiarity with the qualities sensed. Thus, Sancho's kinsmen are exercising a realistic analytic ability in tasting the hogshead. They respectively sense iron and leather, and what they sense is actually in the wine. The analytic realist might very well recognize that our sensory impressions can be illusory or that we might be flat out mistaken in our sensory report. So, someone says, "I taste vanilla in this pinot noir," and on the basis of that sensory report claims that someone has put vanilla extract in the wine. This person has not realized that some oak barrels impart a vanilla quality to the wine.

The problem with analytic realism is that not all the qualities that we impute to the wine when we taste it are qualities that accurately share a label with the stimulus agent in the wine. In fact, there are a great many qualities that we claim to sense in a wine which have labels that do not accurately describe the stimulus agents that produce the taste qualities. Consider the following fairly usual example of wine tasting which resembles, yet is quite different from, the

[12] The chemical is 2-methoxy-3-isobutylpyrazine. See Baldy, *The University Wine Course*, p. 39, and Sharp, *Winetaster's Secrets*, p. 88. I have benefited from lectures on wine tasting given by John Buechsenstein and Ann C. Noble, University of California-Davis, May 6, 2006.

212

example of Sancho's kinsmen. Someone says, "When I taste this wine, I taste 'leather.' I am getting a metallic taste as well." Now sometimes there is copper or iron in a wine, and one might taste it, in which case we have an instance of analytic realistic tasting; however, usually there are not any noticeable metals in a wine when one claims it has a metallic taste. So, let us suppose that there is no metal or leather in the wine or in the barrel in which the wine was stored.

Should we immediately dismiss this report as lacking objectivity? I think not. There might be justification for making this claim even though there is no metal or leather in the wine. First of all, there is an accepted view that low-alcohol wines harvested from unripe grapes will often have a "metallic" taste. It is the tannin from these unripe grapes that we taste as being metallic. "Tinny" is the label that wine tasters usually reserve for this quality.[13] Second, "leather" is not an unusual quality to taste in red wines, particularly in some wines made from Rhône varietals and, especially, in some nebbiolos from Italy's Piedmont region. The taste of leather is produced by the extract in the wine made from grapes from those varietals. Both sensed qualities, "leather" and "metal," are not caused by leather or metal but by other agents that we would not label as "leather" or "metal."

This is not an unusual example in wine tasting. Wine tasters regularly report all sorts of tastes for which there is no actual stimulus agent accurately describable with that same qualitative label. They taste white or black pepper, licorice, mint, melon, figs, cherries, strawberries, blueberries, lichee nuts, coffee, cedar, tar, violets, and a great many others. Young high-extract rieslings are often claimed to have a "petrol" character, yet there is no petrochemical agent which causes the taster to register that quality. Tasters regularly report sensing grass, flint, and a "feral" quality often identified as "cat pee" in sauvignon blancs from the Loire.[14] Other tasters report what some have euphemistically

[13] "When tannins are green, from unripe grapes, or are at aggressive levels in a wine that is fairly young, and the wine is acidic and thin, a metallic taste can easily be generated. Though no metals are involved, the wine can actually become 'tinny' to the taste." Sharp, *Winetaster's Secrets*, p. 100; see also p. 187.

[14] In her book on Loire wines, Jacqueline Friedrich writes: "Ever since I began tasting wine seriously I have felt that many Sauvignon Blancs had an aroma of cat's pee. As revolting as this sounds, it is not a disagreeable scent in a wine. It's a pungent, vegetal aroma with a bit of something feral in it. If you've ever had a close relationship with a cat, you'll probably agree that the image is apt" (*A Wine and Food Guide to the Loire* [New York: Henry Holt, 1996], p. 62).

referred to as "barnyard" qualities – the standard French label is *merde de cheval* – in red Burgundies from Nuits-Saint-Georges.

None of these labeled sensed qualities can be said to identify accurately a stimulus agent in the wine, and wine tasters rarely believe that such qualities accurately identify a substance in the wine. One is not going to hear tasters who have identified a wine as having a "cat pee" quality report that: "They need to keep the kitties out of the *chai* where they store the wine barrels." Or, after noting a "barnyard" quality in a young Burgundy, say: "I think that this vineyard has gone overboard with its organic fertilizer program." And one should not jump to the conclusion that these sensing reports amount to negative evaluations of the respective wines. These terms are not usually used as abbreviated negative evaluations. They are usually used to pick out a quality in the wine. Of course, if these qualities dominate and overwhelm a wine's other sensory aspects and if they occur in wines that do not conform to the regional stylistic parameters appropriate for that wine, they might very well be sensed as faults.

One should not conclude that what these examples that fall outside the scope of the analytic realistic perspective on wine tasting show is that there is no cognitive basis for such sensory reports and judgments based on such reports. In many cases these are not baseless claims. There is some cognitive basis for these particular sensory reports. Nevertheless, with examples like these, one should be prepared to accept them as occurring with a range of similar sensory qualities produced by a stimulus agent rather than restricted to a single sensory effect. For example, someone might report sensing a blackberry quality in a wine, and one would probably be responding to the fruity character of the wine. Others might report blackcurrants, cassis or even raspberries, all qualities that fall within a range of generally similar-tasting fruits. There have been several different proposals for grouping similar tastes together in distinctive categories. For example, some schema distinguish among other qualities a wine's floral, woody, vegetative, spicy, and different kinds of fruity (berry, citrus, tropical, dried) qualities.[15]

[15] A popular and easy-to-use schematic aid to identify ranges of taste qualities is the Wine Aroma Wheel, pioneered by Ann C. Noble and others. See Baldy, *The University Wine Course*, p. 33, and John W. Bender, "What the Wine Critic Tells Us," Chapter 8, this volume. The classic ten-category schema is that proposed by Emile Peynaud, *The Taste of Wine: The Art and Science of Wine Appreciation*, trans. Michael Schuster (San Francisco: Wine Appreciation Guild, 1987), p. 48.

I am going to label this second group of examples as instances not of analytic realism but of *analytic interpretivism*. Under analytic interpretivism, a taster might attribute a sensed quality to a wine yet that quality might not be an actual quality of the wine. That is, the labeled quality would not also accurately label the stimulus agent in the wine. One might say, "I taste lichee nuts or grapefruit in this sauvignon blanc." Yet there might be no stimulus agent that is common to both the wine and to lichee nuts and to grapefruit. I call these examples instances of analytic interpretivism because they call for an imaginative act on the part of the taster. The taster must come up with an imaginative interpretation that is apt, that fits within the correct sensory category, but within that category there is room for interpretation. For example, when a wine, say a chardonnay, undergoes malolactic fermentation, the crisper malic acid changes into the softer lactic acid. One of the byproducts of malolactic fermentation is a chemical substance called "diacetyl," which tasters often register as having a buttery taste. Diacetyl is not butter, but when butter starts to turn rancid diacetyl is produced. Diacetyl is often used as an artificial butter flavoring. So, in the context of other flavors and qualities of the wine, a taster might interpret a wine with diacetyl as having a buttery taste. Yet, depending on the concentration of the chemical, some tasters might not taste the wine as being buttery but instead label the taste as caramel or butterscotch or even honey.[16] However, if a taster seemed to identify diacetyl as having a minty taste, a taste well out of the range of flavors usually associated with diacetyl, one would question the taster's sensitivity or acumen.

Although Hume introduces his example of Sancho's kinsmen in order to illustrate "delicacy of imagination," the example does not show the kinsmen as exercising any imagination, just a fine "realistic analytic" acuity. However, if realistic analysis is not the single major model for wine tasting as an appreciative activity, then Hume's example is not very informative about critical judgment with respect to wine. Yet Hume's example poses the problem of what exactly is the object of appreciation when we critically taste a wine. Is it an object discriminated by realistic analytic acuity? Is it an imaginative or interpretive object? Or, is it some combination of the two? I think it is the

---

[16] "A little imagination can find a wide range of rich, complex and familiar smells in wine" (Peynaud, *The Taste of Wine*, p. 48).

latter. Perhaps the skeptic about wine appreciation focuses exclusively on the imaginative aspect of tasting and concludes that these interpretive efforts show up the personal, idiosyncratic character of taste. Believing that wine tasting involves a personal interpretation, the skeptic might conclude that there is no public object of appreciation – wine appreciation is an object-less pleasure.

Nevertheless, our appreciative tasting is not unrestricted, free-associational interpretation. There is a base of realistic identifications that tasters make, and a taster's interpretations should be both consistent with those realistic reports and fall within a particular range of appropriate qualities. Yet, I do not think that when we interpret what we taste, such an interpretive activity should count against our having an aesthetic encounter with the wine. In our experience with most artistic genres, we believe it appropriate to interpret the works of art we experience. We interpret novels, poems, plays, movies, paintings, sculptures, and so on. Works in these genres and media have realistic bases in accordance with which we build our interpretations, and so do wines.

The overall problem with Hume's example as a model for appreciative wine tasting is its exclusive analytic realistic perspective on wine tasting. There is no question that an analytic attitude aimed at identifying the qualities we taste is an important part of our whole tasting experience; however, it is not the sole major activity of appreciative ingesting. Analytic imaginative tasting also has a significant role to play. Appreciative tasting is not restricted to finding one or more components, in great or minute quantities, which are faults, or even positive elements, in the wine. Neither is our pleasurable experience with a wine nor the wine's overall evaluative quality simply due to its having particular identifiable components. Consider the presence of volatile acidity (i.e., vinegar) in a wine: this usually is a major fault in a wine, but not always. Artisanally crafted wines from the Langhe region in Italy's Piedmont, classic old-style Barolos, sometimes have a little volatile acidity in their extravagant middle range of violets, leather, tar, and a variety of red and dark fruits. The presence of volatile acidity adds to the complexity of the wine.

Wine tasting is a temporal activity that requires one to take a *synthetic* attitude to what one ingests. One needs to taste in a way which synthesizes or brings together the variety of tastes that are registered at different stages of the gustatory experience. These various stages of the ingesting process one links together to form the aesthetic object of the wine. The process of wine tasting follows no one particular track that exhibits a single stylistic character.[17] Nevertheless, our common organs and processes of alimentary ingesting (i.e., our tasting and swallowing what we ingest) dictate a certain general sequence of encounters with a wine. Before the wine enters one's mouth, one engages with its color as one looks at it in the glass and with its aroma as one lifts the glass to one's lips. As one sips the wine, there are three major stages of the tasting experience: the initial encounter with the wine, primarily in the front of one's mouth; the middle stage in which the bitter or phenolic qualities of the wine come out in the back of one's mouth; and finally the finish, after one swallows, in which the wine's flavors often change and develop as they linger.[18] Despite the uniform sequence of ingesting and tasting, there is no single tasting template to which all wines conform, and there is no single standard by which all wines should be judged. There are stylistic differences among wines that have to be recognized in our tasting experience and in our assessment of them. Wines of different styles are ingested and experienced in different ways on one's palate.

The aesthetic ingesting of wine is more like attending to music than contemplating a painting. In tasting a wine of a particular sort, we follow a physiological prescription as to the order in which we encounter the flavors and other aesthetic features of what we have ingested. A painting can have a form or structural organization independent of the structural organization of our experience in contemplating the painting. Yet the wine we taste, however visually

---

[17] For a more developed account of this synthetic character of wine tasting, see Kevin W. Sweeney, "Alice's Discriminating Palate," *Philosophy and Literature* 23.1 (April 1999): 17–31.

[18] I need to clarify that I am not urging a "tasting map" theory of gustatory experience. That is, I am not claiming that we taste particular qualities at and only at particular sites on our palate. A tasting map account would claim, for example, that we taste sweet qualities on the tip of our tongue and bitter qualities at the back of our tongue. This is a scientifically discredited theory. We taste the range of basic qualities all over our palate. We do not just taste sweet qualities on the tip of our tongue. One can also taste the bitter qualities of aspirin on the tip of one's tongue. See Baldy, *The University Wine Course*, p. 24. Nevertheless, we register basic tastes at different temporal rates: we taste sweet qualities sooner than bitter qualities, which take some time to develop on our palate. See Sharp, *Winetaster's Secrets*, p. 47.

appealing, is presented to our palates in a specific temporal sequence that is dependent upon the physiological character of our organs of alimentation. Rather than a quick hedonic reaction, our experience with wine requires an extended encounter, of greater or lesser duration, depending on the particular type of wine. On bringing the wine to our lips, we proceed through an ordered ingesting sequence. For example, a Spanish albariño from Galicia starts off with a series of floral notes; there is a mineral range in the middle; and it ends with a dry finish.

Because of the way a wine of a particular style registers on the palate as one proceeds through the ingesting stages, one can prescribe how one should taste the wine. For example, a white wine like a Muscadet from France's western Loire presents itself initially as a light crisp taste that is followed by a middle range of mineral qualities. It is a wonderful wine with shellfish because it cleanses the palate without dominating the subtle tastes of the seafood. Food and wine complement each other. To taste the wine expecting great complexity and a long and evolving finish would be to misperceive the wine's functional character.

These different stylistic qualities and distinctive functional characteristics need to be acknowledged in our experience and evaluation of wine. The skeptic who thinks that the pleasure we take in wine is either an idiosyncratic preference or an object-less reflexive experience does not recognize the stylistic parameters and functional nature of the wine being ingested. The skeptic also fails to recognize the legitimate but measured nature of our imaginative investment in what we taste, an investment in a distinctive temporal object, realistically analyzed, imaginatively interpreted, and synthetically unified. Wine tasting is not an object-less pleasure; it is a realistic and imaginative encounter with a gustatory object.

14

The Soul of Wine
Digging for Meaning

Randall Grahm

This subject matter may strike you as a bit odd. We do not as a rule talk about the soul of a wine. Instead, we tend to address the less arcane issues of drinkability, varietal typicity, or how clever we have been to have ferreted out this or that rare specimen and for such a deal, no less. If we are particularly unreconstructed, tedious wine bores, we will talk about how *Monsieur Parcaire* or the *Expectorator* has rated the wine or we will talk about all of the different vintages we have consumed in our long and distinguished wine-drinking career and under what circumstances, in which restaurant, accompanied by which dish, and was the pairing palate-bendingly felicitous or not, and so on ad infinitum. In these cases, we are not really attending to the wine itself: it is merely a pretext for us to strut our human, all too human, stuff.

But I would like to talk about wine in a very different way, and that is to try to explore what we mean when we say a wine has soul. I have been brooding about this subject for a long while and have framed the question to myself in a variety of ways.

It was just the other day I had the opportunity to taste a wine – it was a recent vintage of riesling from the Münchberg vineyard made by my friend André Ostertag, consumed in the whatever-the-opposite-of-august-is company of a number of young California wines, among them some of my very own – when I experienced the "Aha!" moment, which was the precipitating event, the proximal cause, as

Randall Grahm, "The Soul of Wine: Digging for Meaning," reprinted from *Decanter* 25.4 (1999).

219

the scholastics would say, of this piece. In this Aha! event, it was abundantly clear that there was something very different going on with André's wine relative to the others. It was not simply that it had *more* of one particular quality than the California wines but the wine seemed to possess a very different order of qualities, as if it might have come from another planet (and I know how *that* feels). It was ontologically different, of a different order of being. Without becoming overly anthropomorphic, it was as if the California wines were enveloped in a sort of pleasant but diffuse fog, whereas the riesling had a sort of stoney resoluteness at its very core – the impression one sometimes gets in shaking the hand of a particularly willful or rugged individual . . . one could be shaking the hand of a mountain.

The California wines were all winningly exuberant: they had a sort of the eager-to-please, puppy dog-like quality to them. André's wine was indeed very pleasing but *it was not there to please*. I'm sure that if André were pressed to characterize the difference, he would gently and respectfully suggest that perhaps his wine was expressing *terroir* and the others, well, no offense intended (André is very much the gentleman) – the others were absolutely charming and possessed other very useful qualities. *Terroir*, for those of us following at home, is that almost mystical quality that the French ascribe to their most special wines. It is the quality that Matt Kramer very poetically described as somewhereness,[1] the distinctiveness of a wine that derives from the place where it is grown, transcending the personal *imprimatur* of the winegrower. I think that the sense of belonging-ness, of coming from somewhere, is very much connected to the idea of soulfulness of a wine.

But before we talk any more about wine-soul, I would like to tell you about *qi gong*. *Qi gong* is the Taoist practice of the skillful movement of *qi*, which is the life force that we share with all beings – ones that we label, Taoists might argue (though argumen-tation is not really their forte), somewhat arbitrarily, either animate of inanimate.

I had attended a *qi gong* class not long before the wine tasting in question and during the class, in one of the exercises, we were asked

---

[1]   See Matt Kramer, "The Notion of *Terroir*," Chapter 15, this volume.

to stand very still and become attentive to the *qi* of the trees that were all around us – to absorb their qualities by breathing them in not just through our lungs but with all of our attention. The notion is that if we slow down enough and open our attention, many orders of beings – animals, trees, and even stones – can speak to us, if we are willing to listen.

I am not sure how well I did with the trees but later when I was tasting André's wine, the report from the glass was absolutely deafening. It was as if it were sending out a beacon, a sort of vinous public address announcement – "I am from Münchberg. I am from Münchberg. I am from *Münchberg*!" – to whomever was capable of hearing its eloquent message. This, for me, was a poignant moment – a bit like standing out on a moor and hearing a mysterious and soulful voice in the distance. I do not know if I am being overly subtle or overly obvious but the point I am making is that I fear that we as a culture have largely grown deaf to this very refined and delicate speech.

If we believe that the discovery of *terroir* in wine – as a meditation for the wine-maker as well as for the wine drinker – may be the clearest path to the revelation of the soul of the wine, the French, it would seem, have attained a level of spiritual evolution far exceeding ours at least in this particular arena. Perhaps the French possess slightly more than their fair share of human weakness and frailty – they can be rather petty and venial at times – but when it comes to wine. I think that they have rather old souls. Their language in describing pursuit of *terroir* is quite evocative of the language of spirituality. To embark upon the spiritual path is to embrace renunciation and to sincerely pursue *terroir*, one must, as a winemaker, learn to subordinate one's ego, to put one's own stylistic signature at the corner of the wine-painting rather than squarely in the middle. To produce a wine that expresses *terroir*, one must adopt an "I–Thou" relationship to the wine and let the wine speak in its own voice. (I might remark parenthetically how difficult this discipline is for New World winemakers. If we were not already in hormonal over-drive to "make a statement," our Mephistophelcan marketers continually coo in our ears about the need for "stylistic differentiation.")

What is a "soul" anyways, as it pertains to wine? We think about the soul as the part of ourselves that is abiding, never changing the

221

part somehow hidden beneath the surface, representing our truest self, the part beyond public ascription. It strikes me that when we talk about wine, especially in the wine press, especially in the case of New World wines, we tend to confuse "personality" with soul. The obvious attributes we perceive in wine, much like the attributes we perceive in our public figures, these days tend to be more of the cosmetic or superficial variety. As a culture, we have gradually grown far more interested in appearances, in the outward appearance of things – which can cloak or disguise the inner essence as often as reveal it. We are far too easily taken in by glitz and glitter, the pulchritudinous Pomerol, to use a crass example.

Continuing that theme, we have a tendency to anatomize wine, to consider it as a collection of elements rather than as an indivisible whole – this is a habit particularly ingrained in the American wine press to which I take great exception. Awarding a wine a "100" is not unlike giving Bo Derek a "10." It is easy, it is lazy, and is utterly beside the point. This deconstruction, if you will, is ultimately a violation of the integrity of the wine, its essence, and is as pornographic as some of the movies I saw in Viciculture class when I was a student at UC Davis, of the early mechanical harvesters – these were essentially vitaceous "snuff" films, wherein the bejesus was just whomped out of the vines. The absolutely best way to overlook the soul of a wine is to break it down into its parts: nowhere will "soul" appear on the laundry list of elements. Yes, we respond well to wines that have a deep saturated color, rich body, a strong tannic profile, some flashy new wood, but do these elements form an integral unity that speaks to us with a distinctly unique and poetic voice?

In wine as well as in virtually every other domain, we tend to make snap judgments and not look past the blatantly obvious. We value style over substance, surface over depth. How else to explain the phenomenon of Keanu Reeves or of California merlot? "Modern" New World style wines are to Old World classics what Keanu Reeves is to Laurence Olivier or what watching television is to reading books. And my deepest fear is that the value that the New World places on "surface" has already begun to infect the wines of the Old World. I fear that Old World is learning out world-view much more rapidly than we are learning theirs and that many great Old World wines are in danger of losing their quirky distinctiveness, their uniqueness, their *terroir*, their soul.

When we are frightened or anxious or distracted we tend to cling to the familiar. We will pull in for a Big Mac or order a glass of merlot because we want to or need to play it safe. But in our secret hearts we long to be thrilled by the mysterious Rhône Stranger. We are habituated, inured to new oak in the same way we experience our own disfunctional families: they may strike us as odd or inappropriate but we can hardly imagine a different world or a world in which chardonnay is decidedly a minor varietal. Our habits and compulsions direct us to repeat the same patterns again and again but we secretly yearn to break into another universe. It is our role as winemakers to create alternative universes for our customers, to touch their souls with wines that are themselves ensouled.

I have mentioned a number of epiphenomena that may resemble wine-soul but are not and I have said that the soulfulness of a wine is somehow related to the expression of *terroir*. However, the creation of a wine is an essentially human enterprise and the wine-soul must be linked to the soul of its producer. But how might one set out to make a wine with soul in the New World for example, in the absence of special knowledge of *terroir*? Finding *terroir* in the New World is as tricky and frustrating as attempting to track down the elusive J. D. Salinger. You wonder along the way if you are not in search of a phantasm. The question may be posed Socratically: as a winemaker in search of *terroir*, how would you even know you have found it, if you did not know precisely what it looked like, felt like, tasted like?

I think that ultimately the creation of a soulful wine is about the winemaker's intent. He must always be ready to admit the possibility of the unknown, the very strange into his winemaking life. If he is always on familiar ground, mystery will never leap out and touch him. He must learn to cultivate his intuition, to always reach out towards that which he doesn't quite understand. Mostly, he must go into his own soul and listen for resonance, for harmony. Also very important, he must ignore received wisdom and be prepared to go against the grain. One of the very strange things about the wine business is that there exist certain "immutable" paradigms – a great vineyard in Châteauneuf-du-Pape, it is believed, must be well littered with stones and be created from multiple *cépages*, almost by definition. And yet the finest Châteauneuf-du-Pape vineyard, Château Rayas, contains nary a stone and is believed (though one never really knows) to be composed of 100 percent grenache. Grenache, as everyone knows, is a non-noble *cépage*, congenitally incapable of producing a truly great, classic wine, except under certain poorly understood "boundary" circumstances when it strangely does.

Whether we succeed or fail, the intent to make a wine with soul ennobles our own souls and we must be grateful for that precious opportunity.

15

The Notion of *Terroir*

Matt Kramer

"Always the beautiful answer who asks a more beautiful question"

e.e.cummings[1]

The "more beautiful question" of wine is *terroir*. To the English speaker, *terroir* is an alien word, difficult to pronounce ("tair-wahr"). More frustrating yet, it is a foreign idea. The usual capsule definition is site or vineyard plot. Closer to its truth, it holds – like William Blake's grain of sand that contains a universe – an evolution of thought about wine and the Earth. One cannot make sense of Burgundy without investigating the notion of *terroir*.

Although derived from soil or land (*terre*), *terroir* is not just an investigation of soil and subsoil. It is everything that contributes to the distinction of a vineyard plot. As such, it also embraces "microclimate": precipitation, air and water drainage, elevation, sunlight and temperature.

But *terroir* holds yet another dimension: It sanctions what cannot be measured, yet still located and savored. *Terroir* prospects for differences. In this it is at odds with science, which demands proof by replication rather than in a shining uniqueness.

Understanding *terroir* requires a recalibration of the modern mind. The original impulse has long since disappeared, buried by

---

[1] *Collected Poems: 1922–1938* (New York: Book of the Month Club, 1977), p. 462.

commerce and the scorn of science. It calls for a susceptibility to the natural world to a degree almost unfathomable today, as the French historian Marc Bloch evokes in his landmark work, *Feudal Society*:

> The men of the two feudal ages were close to nature – much closer than we are; and nature as they knew it was much less tamed and softened than as we see it today. . . . People continued to pick wild fruit and to gather honey as in the first ages of mankind. In the construction of implements and tools, wood played a predominant part. The nights, owing to wretched lighting, were darker; the cold, even in the living quarters of the castles, was more intense. In short, behind all social life there was a background of the primitive, of submission to uncontrollable forces, of unrelieved physical contrasts.[2]

This world extended beyond the feudal ages, as rural life in Europe changed little for centuries afterward. Only the barest vestiges remain today, with the raw, preternatural sensitivity wiped clean. The viticultural needlepoint of Burgundy's Côte d'Or, its thousands of named vineyards, is as much a relic of a bygone civilization as Stonehenge. We can decipher why and how they did it, but the impulse, the fervor, is beyond us now.

The glory of Burgundy is its exquisite delineation of sites, its preoccupation with *terroir*: What does this site have to say? Is it different from its neighbor? It is the source of Burgundian greatness, the informing ingredient. This is easily demonstrated. You need only imagine an ancient Burgundy planted to pinot noir and chardonnay for the glory of producing – to use the modern jargon – a varietal wine. The thought is depressing, an anemic vision of wine hardly capable of inspiring the devotion of generations of wine lovers, let alone the discovery of such natural wonders as some of the great Burgundian wines, such as Montrachet or La Tâche. *Terroir* is as much a part of Burgundy wines as pinot noir or chardonnay; the grape is as much vehicle as voice.

The mentality of *terroir* is not uniquely Burgundian, although it reaches its fullest expression there. It more rightly could be considered distinctively French, although not exclusively so. Other countries, notably Germany and Italy, can point to similar insights. But

[2]   Marc Bloch, *Feudal Society*, trans. L. A. Manyon (Chicago: University of Chicago Press, 1964), p. 72.

France, more than any other, viewed its landscape from the perspective of *terroir*. It charted its vineyard distinctions – often called *cru* or growth – with calligraphic care. Indeed, calligraphy and *cru* are sympathetic, both the result of emotional, yet disciplined, attentions to detail. Both flourished under monastic tutelage.

Italy, for all of its ancient winegrowing tradition, never developed a mentality of *terroir* to the same or even similar extent as France. It lacked, ironically, the monastic underpinning of the Benedictine and Cistercian orders, which were represented to a far greater degree in France and Germany. An ecclesiastical map of Western Europe during the Middle Ages shows hundreds of major monasteries in France and Germany, nearly all of them Benedictine or Cistercian.[3] In comparison, Italy had fewer than a dozen.

The phrase "mentality of *terroir*" is pertinent. The articulation of the Burgundian landscape increased steadily long after the decline of the feudal ages. Ever-finer distinctions of site mounted along the Cote d'Or through to the Revolution of 1789, when the church lands were confiscated and publicly auctioned. The monks and nuns, whose wines and vineyards remained the standard for nearly a millennium, never wavered in their devotion to *terroir*. If only by sheer longevity, their vision of the land became everyone else's. Wherever the church shaped the viticultural landscape, *terroir* was the means by which that world was understood.

But in France there exists, to this day, a devotion to *terroir* that is not explained solely by this legacy of the church. Instead, it is fueled by two forces in French life: a longstanding delight in differences and an acceptance of ambiguity.

The greatness of French wines in general – and Burgundy in particular – can be traced to the fact that the French do not ask of one site that it replicate the qualities of another site. They prize distinction. This leads not to discord – as it might in a country gripped by a marketing mentality – but consonance with what the French call *la France profonde*, or elemental France.

This is the glory of France. It is not that France is the only spot on the planet with remarkable soils or that its climate is superior to all others for winegrowing. It is a matter of the values that are applied

---

[3] William R. Shepherd, *Historical Atlas*, 9th ed. (New York: Barnes and Noble, 1964), pp. 94–5.

to the land. In this, *terroir* and its discoveries remind one of Chinese acupuncture. Centuries ago, Chinese practitioners chose to view the body from a perspective utterly different than that of the dissective, anatomical approach of Western medicine. Because of this different perspective, they discovered something about the body that Western practitioners, to this day, are unable to independently see for themselves: what the Chinese call "channels" and "collaterals," or more recently, "meridians." The terminology is unimportant. What is important is that these "meridians" cannot be found by dissection. Yet they exist; acupuncture works. Its effects, if not its causes, are demonstrable.

In the same way, seeking to divine the greatness of Burgundy only by dissecting its intricacies of climate, grape, soil, and winemaking is no more enlightening than learning how to knit by unraveling a sweater. Those who believe that great wines are made, rather than found, will deliver such wines only by the flimsiest chance, much in the same way that an alchemist, after exacting effort, produces gold simply by virtue of having worked with gold-bearing material all along.

Today, a surprising number of winegrowers and wine drinkers – at least in the United States – flatly deny the existence of *terroir*, like weekend sailors who reject as preposterous that Polynesians could have crossed the Pacific navigating only by sun, stars, wind, smell, and taste. *Terroir* is held to be so much bunk, little more than viticultural voodoo.

The inadmissibility of *terroir* to the high court of reason is due to ambiguity. *Terroir* can be presented, but it cannot be proven – except by the senses. Like Polynesian seafaring, it is too subjective to be reproducible and therefore credible. Yet any reasonably experienced wine drinker knows upon tasting a great and mature Burgundy, such as Corton-Charlemagne or Chablis "Vaudesir" or Volnay "Caillerets," that something is present that cannot be accounted for by winemaking technique. Infused in the wine is a *goût de terroir*, a taste of the soil. It cannot be traced to the grape, if only because other wines made the same way from the same grape lack this certain something. If only by process of elimination the source must be ascribed to *terroir*. But to acknowledge this requires a belief that the ambiguous – the unprovable and unmeasurable – can be real. Doubters are blocked by their own credulity in science and its confining definition of reality.

The supreme concern of Burgundy is – or should be – making *terroir* manifest. In outline, this is easily accomplished: small-berried clones; low yields; selective sorting of the grapes; and, trickiest of all, fermenting and cellaring the wine in such a way as to allow the *terroir* to come through with no distracting stylistic flourishes. This is where *terroir* comes smack up against ego, the modern demand for self-expression at any cost. Too often, it has come at the expense of *terroir*.

It is easier to see the old Burgundian enemies of greed and inept winemaking. The problem of greed, expressed in overcropped grapevines resulting in thin, diluted wines, has been chronic in Burgundy, as are complaints about it. It is no less so today, but the resolution is easily at hand: lower the yields.

But the matter of ego and *terroir* is new and peculiar to our time. It stems from two sources: the technology of modern winemaking and the psychology of its use. Technical control in winemaking is recent, dating only to the late 1960s. Never before had winemakers been able to control wine to such an extent as is available today. Through the use of temperature-controlled stainless steel tanks, computer-controlled wine presses, heat exchangers, inert gases, centrifuges, all manner of filters, oak barrels from woods of different forests and so forth, the modern winemaker can insert himself between the *terroir* and its wine to a degree never before achieved.

The psychology of its use is the more important feature. Self-expression is now considered the inalienable right of our time. It thus is no surprise that the desire for self-expression should make itself felt in winemaking. That winemakers have always sought to express themselves in their wines is indisputable. The difference is that today technology actually allows them to do so, to an extent unimagined by their grandparents.

Submerged in this is a force that, however abstract, has changed much of twentieth-century thinking: the transition from the literal to the subjective in how we perceive what is "real." Until recently, whatever was considered "real" was expressed in straightforward mechanical or linear linkages, such as a groove in a phonograph record or a lifelike painting of a vase of flowers. Accuracy was defined by exacting, literal representation.

But we have come to believe that the subjective can be more "real" than the representational. One of the earliest, and most famous,

229

examples of this was expressionism in art. Where prior to the advent of expressionism in the early twentieth century, the depiction of reality on a canvas was achieved through the creation of the most lifelike forms. Expressionists said otherwise. They maintained that the reality of a vase of flowers could be better expressed by breaking down its form and color into more symbolic representations of its reality, rather than by straightforward depiction.

How this relates to wine is found in the issue of *terroir* versus ego. The Burgundian world that discovered *terroir* centuries ago drew no distinction between the *grand cru* vineyard that they discovered and called Chambertin and the idea of a representation of Chambertin. Previously, there were only two parties involved: Chambertin itself and its self-effacing discoverer, the winegrower. In this deferential view of the natural world, Chambertin was Chambertin if for no other reason than it consistently did not taste like its neighbor Latricières. One is beefier and more resonantly flavorful (Chambertin) while the other offers a similar savor, but somehow always is lacier in texture and less full-blown. It was a reality no more subject to doubt than was a nightingale's song from the screech of an owl. They knew what they tasted, just as they knew what they heard. These were natural forces, no more subject to alteration or challenge than a river.

All of which brings us back to Burgundian winemaking. In an age where the subjective has been accepted as being more "real" than the representational, the idea of an immutable *terroir* becomes troublesome. It complicates ego-driven individualism, the need to express a personal vision. In an era of relativism and right of self-expression, Chambertin-as-*terroir* has given way to Chambertin-as-emblem. The notion of *terroir* as an absolute is rejected. All Chambertins therefore are equally legitimate. We have come to accept that a grower's Chambertin is really only his or her idea of Chambertin. The vineyard name on the label is merely a general indication of intent.

How, then, does one know what is the true voice of the land? How does one know when the winemaker has interposed himself or herself between the *terroir* and the final wine? Discovering the authentic voice of a particular *terroir* requires study. The only way is to assemble multiple examples of a wine from a particular plot and taste them side by side. Ideally they should all be from the same vintage. This eliminates at least one distracting variable.

In seeking to establish the voice of a *terroir*, one has to concentrate – at least for the moment – not on determining which wines are best, but in finding the thread of distinction that runs through them. It could be a matter of structure: delicate or muscular; consistently lean or generous in fruit. It could be a distinctive *goût de terroir*, something minerally or stony, chalky or earthy. Almost always, it will be hard to determine at first, because the range of styles within the wines will be distracting. And if the choices available are mostly second-rate, where the *terroir* is lost through overcropped vines or heavy-handed winemaking, the exercise will be frustrating and without reward. *Terroir* usually is discovered only after repeated attempts over a number of vintages. This is why such insight is largely the province only of Burgundians and a few obsessed outsiders.

Nevertheless, hearing the voice of the land is sweet and you will not easily forget it. Sometimes it only becomes apparent by contrast. Take a wine such as a Meursault "Perrières," for example, and, in the good ones, you find a pronounced minerality coupled with an invigorating, strong fruitiness. You do not realize how stony or fruity, how forceful, until you compare Perrières with, say, Charmes, which is a contiguous vineyard. Then the distinction of Perrières clicks into place in your mind. It is never so exact or pronounced that you will spot it unerringly in a blind tasting of various Meursault *premiers crus*. That's not the point. The point is that there is no doubt that Perrières exists, that it is an entity unto itself, distinct from any other plot.

Such investigation – which is more rewarding than it might sound – has a built-in protocol. When faced with a line-up of wines, the immediate impact is of stylistic differences, a clamor of producers' voices. Once screened out, the lesser versions – the ones that clearly lack concentration and definition of flavor – are easily eliminated. Some are so insipid as to make them fraudulent in everything but the legal niceties. Then you are left with the wines that have something to say. At this moment, you confront the issue of ego.

The ideal is to amplify *terroir* without distorting it. *Terroir* should be transmitted as free as possible of extraneous elements of style or taste. Ideally, one should not be able to find the hand of the winemaker. That said, it must be acknowledged that some signature always can be detected, although it can be very faint indeed when you reach the level of producers such as Domaine Chevillon in Nuits-Saint-Georges, Domaine Marquis d'Angerville in Volnay or Domaine

231

Vincent Dauvissat in Chablis, to name but a few. The self-effacement of these producers in their wines is very nearly Zen-like: their "signature" is an absence of signature.

Such paragons aside, the presence of a signature is not intrinsically bad, as long as it is not too expensively at the cost of *terroir*. A good example of this is the winemaking of the Domaine de la Romanée-Conti. The red wines of this fabled property – Echézeaux, Grands-Echézeaux, Romanée-Saint-Vivant, Richebourg, La Tâche, and Romanée-Conti – all share a stylistic signature that becomes immediately apparent when the wines are compared with other bottlings from the same vineyards. (Only two of the properties are exclusively owned or monopoles, La Tâche and Romanée-Conti.) All of the wines display a distinctive silkiness, almost an unctuosity, as well as a pronounced oakiness.

Nevertheless, the wines of the Domaine de la Romanée-Conti do overcome this stylistic signature to display a full measure of their particular *terroirs*. This is confirmed when tasting other good examples of Richebourg or Grands-Echezeaux or the other properties. The reason is that the yields are admirably low; the clonal selection is astute; the harvesting punctilious in discarding rotted or unhealthy grapes; and the winemaking – stylistic signature aside – devoted to expressing the different *terroirs* to the fullest degree. The wines could be improved if the signature were less pronounced, in the same way that a beautiful dress could be improved if the designer's initials were eliminated.

This matter of signature only becomes apparent when tasting multiple examples of the same *terroir*. Although the ideal is what stereo buffs call a "straight wire," where the signal goes through the amplifier without any coloration, this simply is impossible given the intervention of both grape and grower. In this, winemaking in Burgundy really is translation. The poet W. S. Merwin maps out the challenge:

> The quality that is conveyed to represent the original is bound to differ with different translators, which is both a hazard and an opportunity. In the ideal sense in which one wants only the original, one wants the translator not to exist at all. In the practical sense in which the demand takes into account the nature of translation, the gifts – such as they are – of the translator are inescapably important.[4]

---

[4] *Selected Translations: 1968–1978* (New York: Atheneum, 1979), p. xi.

A good example of this would be the various Meursaults of the Domaine des Comtes Lafon and those of Jean-François Coche-Dury. Stylistically, the Lafon wines are more voluptuous, more apparently oaky when young, but impeccable in their definition and separation of flavors. There is no mistaking one *terroir* with another when tasting their wines. The same may be said of Coche-Dury, except that his style is more austere and somehow leaner, with distinctions of *terroir* that are almost painfully precise. The depth and concentration are the equal of Lafon, yet the delivery is slightly different. In both cases, the distinctions of site are preserved at all costs. Both accomplish what W. S. Merwin intends when translating someone else's poetry: "I have not set out to make translations that distorted the meaning of the originals on pretext of some other overriding originality."[5]

Awareness of the existence of signature in a Burgundy is critical, if only because it is easy to be seduced by style at the expense of *terroir*. A surprising number of Burgundies, especially the white Burgundies, do just that. Character in a white wine is much more hard won than in a red, if only because white wine grapes usually have less intrinsic flavor than red wine grapes. This is very much the case with chardonnay compared to pinot noir.

Moreover, much of the flavor in a wine is extracted from the skins during fermentation. Where many red wines, and certainly pinot noirs, are made with extended skin contact, most white wines see little or no skin contact. This is true for chardonnay as it is produced in Burgundy, although there are exceptions. At most, a white Burgundy will see no more than 24 hours of its chardonnay juice fermenting or simply macerating in contact with its skins; most pinot noirs are given anywhere from seven days to three weeks on the skins.

Because of this, the temptation is strong for the winemaker to infuse flavor into white wines by means of various winemaking techniques in lieu of winning it in the vineyard. The most common of these is the use of brand new oak barrels, which provide an immediately recognizable scent of vanilla and toastiness. Another approach is to leave the young but fully fermented wine on its lees or sediment while aging in the barrel and stir up this sediment from time to time. Here the winemaker is seeking to capitalize on the subtle flavorings of

---

[5] Ibid.

autolyzing or decomposing yeasts. Sometimes, though, the result is a wine with off-flavors from microbial deterioration.

Too often, signature substitutes for insufficient depth. It is easier, and more ego-gratifying, to fiddle with new oak barrels and wine-making techniques than to toil in the vineyard nursing old vines and pruning severely in order to keep yields low. Character in a white Burgundy, even in the most vocal of sites, does not come automatically. One need only taste an overcropped Montrachet – it is too common – to realize how fragile is the voice of the land when transmitted by chardonnay. As a grape, it is surprisingly neutral in flavor, which makes it an ideal vehicle for *terroir*, or for signature.

Character in a red Burgundy is just as hard won as in a white, but its absence is not as immediately recognizable because of the greater intrinsic flavor of pinot noir. That said, it should be pointed out that flavor is not character, anymore than a cough drop compares with a real wild cherry.

Whereas chardonnay is manipulated to provide an illusion of depth and flavor, the pursuit with pinot noir is to make it more immediately accessible and easy down the gullet. An increasing number of red Burgundies now are seductively drinkable virtually upon release only two years after the vintage. Such wines can be misleading. Rather than improving with age, their bright, flashy fruitiness soon fades, like an enthusiasm that cools. The wine drinker is left stranded, stood up by a wine that offered cosmetics rather than character.

All of which underscores why *terroir* is the "more beautiful question" of wine. When the object is to reveal, to amplify, and to transmit *terroir* with clarity and resonance, there is no more "beautiful answer" than Burgundy. When it is ignored, wine may as well be grown hydroponically, rooted not in an unfathomable Earth that offers flashes of insight we call Richebourg or Corton, but in a manipulated medium of water and nutrients with no more meaning than an intravenous hook-up. Happily, the more beautiful question is being asked with renewed urgency by both growers and drinkers. A new care is being exercised. After all, without *terroir*, why Burgundy?

VI

The Politics & Economics of Wine

16

Wine-Tasting Epiphany
An Analysis of the 1976 California vs. France Tasting

Orley Ashenfelter, Richard E. Quandt, and George M. Taber

Introduction

It has been called the most famous organized wine tasting in history as well as the most discussed wine event of the twentieth century. This was the Paris Tasting of May 24, 1976. Steven Spurrier, an Englishman who owned both a wine shop and wine school in the heart of Paris, organized an event that pitted some of France's best-known wines against their little-known California counterparts. For the French reds, there were icons like Château Haut-Brion and Château Mouton Rothschild among the Bordeaux-blend reds, and Bâtard-Montrachet Ramonet-Prudhon and Puligny-Montrachet Les Pucelles Domaine Leflaive among the white Burgundies. On the other hand, the California reds carried names like Mayacamas Vineyards and Ridge Vineyards and the whites came from wineries such as Veedercrest Vineyards and Chalone Vineyard. At the end of the day, though, California wines won in both the cabernet sauvignon and chardonnay categories. The winners: Stag's Leap Wine Cellars in red and Château Montelena in white.

For the past thirty years, heated discussions have taken place on both sides of the Atlantic over whether the Paris Tasting proved anything or was even fair. There has never been any debate, though, about its impact on the history of California wine. Spurrier's event literally put California on the map. Before that day in May, California was an also-ran in the world of wine. In 1976, there were only about forty wineries in the Napa Valley. A few newcomers were striving to make quality wine, using as their models of excellence the great French wines. But no one paid them much attention because the world's image of California wine had been established by the Gallo brothers, and that meant mass-produced, low-quality, inexpensive commodity wines.

Immediately after the Paris Tasting, both American and global wine enthusiasts gave California wines a second look, and they began drinking them more frequently. The California wine business was soon flourishing, and its winemakers began charging prices more comparable to those being demanded by top French wineries. Many of the Californians plowed back their new profits into new equipment and new plantings. Today there are more than 400 wineries in California, due in part to the Paris event.

Some Historical Context

With the current French wine industry in crisis due to declining local consumption and increased global competition, it is hard to remember what the wine world looked like in 1976. In those days, France literally ruled the world. Sure, wine was made in other countries, as it had been for centuries, but France was predominant and unchallenged. Consumers around the globe generally believed that it was only in France that all the things that make great wine – the best grape varieties, ideal soil, perfect climate, skilled craftsmanship, age-old tradition – came together.

If that widespread belief were going to change, the stimulus had to come from France itself. The fact that the tasting was in Paris, that the wines tasted were outstanding examples of French enology, and that the judges were French were all absolutely crucial factors for changing the then conventional wisdom. Everything that day was in France's favor, yet the California wines had held their own against the best that France had to offer. Ironically, the revolution against French wine had to start in Paris to be credible.

The Paris Tasting also came at a time of dramatic changes in the wine world. Consumption in traditional wine-consuming countries, such as France, Italy, and Spain, was undergoing a long, slow decline that continues to this day. Annual French per capita wine consumption, for example, peaked in 1926 at 35.9 gallons, but is now less than half that level.[1] On the other hand, wine consumption in such places as Britain, the USA, and Australia, which had previously drunk little, was on the upswing. Consumers in those countries were less tradition-bound and more open to new wines from different places, especially their own local production. Moreover, the New World wineries were anxious to tailor their product to the tastes of the new wine drinkers.

Staging the Tasting

Steven Spurrier has often said that if he had known that the world would still be examining and critiquing his informal little wine tasting thirty years later, he would have done a lot of things differently. No one, though, has ever seriously accused him of playing favorites. He has often said that he selected French red and white wines that he was sure would beat the Californians. After all, he owned a wine shop and wine school in Paris. There was no need for him to insult his hosts or to make them look silly by losing to the Americans.

Spurrier was actually very careful to have a level playing field for his event. The wines, for example, were decanted into neutral bottles because he was concerned that the knowledgeable French judges would spot the minor difference between French and California containers and score the French wines high and the Americans low. He also determined the tasting order by having the names of the wines drawn out of a hat.

However, his decision to have six California and four French wines was clearly a mistake because it gave a statistical advantage to the Americans; the proper mix should have been five of each. He explains the choice of having more California wines by saying that his primary goal was not to have a Franco-American confrontation but to expose these eminent French judges to an interesting collection

---

[1] George M. Taber, *Judgment of Paris: California vs. France and the Historic 1976 Paris Tasting that Revolutionized Wine* (New York: Scribner, 2005), p. 280.

of California wines.[2] Since he had the extra California ones, it seemed only natural at the time to put more of them into the tasting so that the judges could try more.

He also made no attempt to weigh the judges' scores to make the results more statistically accurate. Rather, Spurrier simply followed the procedure he had experienced at many French wine tastings in which he had participated. He asked the judges to score the wines based on 20 points, ranking them on the basis of four criteria: eye, nose, mouth, and harmony. And then he added up the individual scores. Again those were the standard procedures used in French tastings at the time.

Spurrier's tasting, though, has been studied carefully over the years to determine if indeed it had been statistically accurate and whether a more rigorous judgment might have resulted in a different result.

Analyzing the Results

In their pioneering book, *Wines: Their Sensory Evaluation*, Maynard Amerine and Edward Roessler set out the details of how one should summarize the results of a wine tasting and draw conclusions from it.[3] The basic scientific presumption from which they start is that *human behavior is not perfectly predictable.* Among those with considerable experience with wine tasting, this is hardly a controversial assumption. As Spurrier stated after the event, "the results of a blind tasting cannot be predicted and will not even be reproduced the next day by the same panel tasting the same wines." The primary goal in the analysis of a wine tasting is to determine the extent to which the conclusions that have been drawn are likely to be reproduced on another occasion. The key requirements that Amerine and Roessler establish for determining the internal validity of a wine tasting can be summarized in a simple set of rules: the tasting of the wines should be blind; the judges should arrive at their views independently; and the results should be analyzed statistically.

(1) *Taste the wines blind.* As any experienced taster will admit, identifying wines blind is an incredibly difficult thing to do. As a result,

[2] Ibid., p. 185.
[3] Maynard A. Amerine and Edward B. Roessler, *Wines: Their Sensory Evaluation* (New York: W. H. Freeman, 1976).

there is no doubt that tasting wines blind is a humbling experience. Perhaps this is why it is resisted, but the failure to taste wines blind leads to terrible biases. Indeed, one of the primary purposes of an independent wine tasting is to test whether common perceptions are really correct. Doing this requires that extraneous information *that reflects the opinions of others* be kept from biasing the tasters. Otherwise, what is the point of creating the wine tasting? You might just as well read the score a wine has received in a wine publication and parrot it to everyone who will listen (something which, in our experience, happens all too often!).

(2) *Keep the tasters' opinions independent.* Wine tasting is a very subjective experience. As a result, even when wines are served blind, the opinions of others often serve as focal points for agreement. For example, a very noticeable feature in many large wine-tasting events is the presence of "table effects." What seems to happen is that one or two individuals have strong opinions at a table, and this crystallizes the opinions of others. Move the same people to a different table and they may have a completely different opinion!

There was actually quite a bit of talking among judges during the 1976 event, perhaps because they were nervous. Separating the California wines from the French ones turned out to be much more difficult than had been expected. Judges at one end of the table would say that the wine currently being tasted was French, while those at the other end would say that it was definitely from California. The most telling result of the event – and the clearest sign that California wines had made great progress from the days of jug wines – might be that the judges that day could not clearly distinguish between the American and French wines. It is doubtful, however, that this group of strong-willed, self-confident, and independent judges were much swayed in their voting by the high level of table chatter.

To combat the problem of dependence of tasters, some very professional groups do not permit anyone to speak about the wines until after they have written down their ranking of them. In other groups, including one that two of us participate in regularly, independence does not seem to require such extreme measures. Perhaps this is because the tasters in our group revel in disagreement, but even we exercise some discretion in what we say (i.e., somebody might say, "I think one of the wines is slightly oxidized" rather than "wine C is slightly oxidized").

(3) *Analyze the results of the wine tasting systematically*. As mentioned above, this topic is discussed at some length in Amerine and Roessler's seminal work. Again, the key goal that they postulate for analyzing a wine is the reproducibility of the analysis.

The judges. The complete details of the cabernet sauvignon tasting, including the scores awarded by each judge to each wine, are contained in the table in the appendix to this essay. (We transcribed the original data from the *Connoisseurs' Guide to California Wine*, July 1976.) The wines were marked against a maximum score of 20. The judges were a distinguished group. Apart from Spurrier and Patricia Gallagher, whose Académie du Vin sponsored the event, it included Odette Kahn, editor of the *Revue du Vin de France*; the distinguished Jean-Claude Vrinat of the restaurant Taillevent; Raymond Oliver of the restaurant Le Grand Vefour; the sommelier Christian Vannequé of La Tour d'Argent; Aubert de Villaine of the Domaine de la Romanée-Conti; Pierre Tari of Château Giscours; Pierre Bréjoux of the Institute of Appellations of Origin; Michel Dovaz of the Académie du Vin; and Claude Dubois-Millau of the eponymous restaurant guide.

The results. The first thing to notice about this event is that the scores of both Spurrier and Gallagher are reported in the table, but these scores were not, in fact, counted in arriving at the results. Since both of these organizers of the event tasted the wines blind, there is really no reason to exclude them from the analysis, and in the table we have chosen to include their scores with the group. It turns out that this has very little effect on the results, but it does permit us to examine whether their scores are systematically different from those of the French judges.

The second thing to notice is that the scoring is based on a simple averaging of the numerical grades. As Spurrier acknowledged in *Decanter* magazine in August 1996, he tallied the winners by "adding the judges' marks and dividing this by nine (which I was told later was statistically meaningless)." The problem with this approach is, of course, that it may give greater weight to judges who put a great deal of scatter into their numerical scores and thus express strong preferences by numerical differences. It is for precisely this reason that, in a typical athletic competition with multiple judges, the judges' numerical scores are converted to ranks *before* the winners are tallied. Converting the grades to ranks guarantees that each judge has the same influence on the outcome. Absent this, the judge who grades wines from, say, 1 to 20 will have a far greater influence on the outcome than a judge who grades the wines on the same scale but uses only the scores 19 and 20.

To see the problem, suppose there were two wines, A and B, to be scored by two tasters. Suppose the first judge scored wine A with a 1 and scored wine B with a 20, but that the second taster scored the same wines 20 and 19. The average score of the first wine would be 10.5 and the average score of the second wine would be 19.5. In fact, however, the first wine was preferred by the second taster, while the second wine was preferred by the first taster, so there is no clear group preference.

In the table, we have shown the conversion of the judges' scores to ranks, and we also provide the group ranking. The method recommended by Amerine and Roessler for computing the group ranking is to count the "points against." This is done by simply adding the sum of the rankings for each wine. Since we have used the scores of eleven judges, the best score obtainable would then be eleven first-place votes, or eleven "points against." Since there were ten wines in total, the worst score obtainable would be eleven tenth-place votes, or 110 "points against." As the table indicates, the best score achieved was actually 41 (for the 1973 Stag's Leap Wine Cellars S.L.V. Cabernet Sauvignon). So, it was no mistake for Steven Spurrier to declare the California cabernet the winner. (Whew!) However, the worst score (of 79.5 points against) was for the 1972 Clos du Val California Cabernet Sauvignon, and this is not the wine that was placed last using the average of the judges' numerical grades. As the table indicates, there is a loose agreement between the ranking of the wines using the average grade and the average rank awarded by the judge, but it is far from perfect.

The fact that the most preferred wine did not attain the lowest "points against" is a result of the fact that there was considerable disagreement on the ranking of the wines by the individual judges. This is common in virtually all carefully conducted wine tastings. In fact, to most experienced wine tasters, complete agreement is a suspicious sign of collusion!

Despite the apparent disagreement among the judges, there is also considerable evidence of concordance. Using a common statistical scheme, it is easy to establish that there is enough concordance among

243

the tasters that it makes sense to believe that the resulting ranking is not just a product of random chance. A loose grouping of the wines by these statistical criteria suggests that the wines may be grouped into three categories. At the top are the 1973 Stag's Leap Cabernet Sauvignon and the 1970 Château Montrose. The second group contains most of the remaining wines. It may be noted in particular that the statistical analysis lumps Stag's Leap and Montrose together in the "best" category, but excludes Château Mouton from this top group, even though it is not far behind. This is a consequence of the particular statistical test employed and we would not quibble if someone argued that Mouton belongs in the top group as well.

Judging the judges. It is also useful to consider how successful the judges were in appraising the wines. One measure of the success of a judge is the extent to which an individual judge's ranking is a good predictor of the group's ranking (where the group's ranking excludes the particular judge in question). By this measure the judges would be ordered as follows (from best predictor to worst): Aubert de Villaine (.70 correlation), Jean-Claude Vrinat (.65), Claude Dubois-Millau (.61), Steven Spurrier (.47), Pierre Bréjoux (.46), Christian Vannequé (.42), Odette Kahn (.29), and Raymond Oliver (.25). Ironically, the preferences of the remaining judges (Dovaz, Gallagher, and Tari), two of whom were French, are unrelated to the group preference.

Retesting History

The Paris Tasting has been repeated numerous times over the years, and Spurrier has almost had a second career going around the world reenacting the famous event. After the original tasting, the judges had all said that it was somewhat unfair because French wines were known to take longer to develop and therefore had been tasted too young. Spurrier defended his selection of the wines by saying that he had chosen wines that were then in the market and were of roughly comparable vintages. He bought the California wines directly from wineries during a trip to California in the spring of 1976, and he selected the French wines from those he was currently selling at the wine shop he ran in Paris.

The judges' calls to "Wait 'til Next Year," however, have not turned out to be substantiated. Although there may be different winning wines, the California ones have repeatedly outperformed the French ones. The closest to a rematch took place nearly two years after the original event on January 11 and 12, 1978, at the Vintners Club in San Francisco. Spurrier flew in from Paris to run the tasting, which took place over two evenings, the white wines the first night and the reds the second. In the chardonnay competition, California's Chalone, which had come in third at Paris, beat out Château Montelena, the original winner, by just one-tenth of a point. In the cabernet sauvignon tasting, Stag's Leap again walked off with first place, a half-point ahead of Heitz Martha's Vineyard, which had placed ninth in Paris.

Spurrier organized a retasting at the French Culinary Institute in New York City in 1986 at the time of the tenth anniversary. This time only the red wines were tasted because it was felt that most of the whites were over the hill. Again a California wine, Clos du Val, won. It had been eighth at Paris a decade earlier.

Also at the time of the tenth anniversary, *Wine Spectator* magazine retasted the original red wines. In that competition the Heitz Martha's Vineyard came out on top, while the French wines were scored fairly low. The magazine's James Laube wrote after the event, "The extra decade of bottle aging was kinder to California Cabs than to the Bordeaux."[4]

In May 2006, on the occasion of the thirtieth anniversary, probably the last reenactment of the Paris Tasting took place. It was a complex judging of both the original vintages plus more recent vintages and some different wines. Spurrier and Gallagher again organized this one, which took place simultaneously in the Napa Valley and in London. The judges were a mixture of American, British, and French wine experts. In the historic part of the event, again only the red wines were retasted. The results from both the European and the American judges were overwhelmingly in favor of the California wines. The top five wines were from California, with Ridge Monte Bello taking first place ahead of Stag's Leap. The Californians were followed by the four French wines, and the Freemark Abbey from California placed tenth.

---

4 *Wine Spectator*, April 1–15, 1986.

After more than thirty years and countless retastings, the original conclusions of the Paris judges have passed the test of time.

Further Reading

A complete history of the 1976 tasting is contained in George M. Taber, *Judgment of Paris: California vs. France and the Historic 1976 Paris Tasting that Revolutionized Wine* (New York: Scribner, 2005).

An indispensable analytical book for anyone seriously interested in the sensory evaluation of wine is Maynard A. Amerine and Edward B. Roessler, *Wines: Their Sensory Evaluation* (New York: W. H. Freeman, 1976). Although this book can be tough going, it is an extremely rewarding discussion of many of the most important issues raised in wine-tasting evaluations. A fascinating paper that includes a full Bayesian analysis of wine tasting applied to the 1976 French tasting data is "The Analysis of a Wine Tasting" by renowned Bayesian statistician Dennis Lindley (Imperial College, London, emeritus). A companion, frequentist approach is taken by renowned econometrician Richard Quandt in his "Measurement and Inference in Wine Tasting," prepared for presentation at the Meetings of the Vineyard Data Quantification Society in Ajaccio, Corsica on October 2–3, 1998. Both papers are available in the *Journal of Wine Economics*, published by the American Association of Wine Economists, Vol. 1, No. 1, May 2006 (email to jwe.whitman.edu). They are also available online at www.liquidasset.com.

The two most popular and influential wine publications, *Wine Spectator* and *Wine Advocate*, do not use analytical methods to determine the validity of their tasting results, although, it should be admitted, the latter relies on only one taster for each group of wines judged so that there is no question of internal validity. A twenty-eight-year-old newsletter that uses good analytical practice in reporting the results of its wine tastings is the *California Grapevine*. See www.calgrapevine.com. (The authors of this essay have no financial interest, direct or indirect, in this publication.)

Appendix

THE FAMOUS 1976 TASTING: CALIFORNIA CABERNET SAUVIGNON VS. BORDEAUX

Number of judges = 11
Number of wines = 10

Identification of the wine: The judges' average grade

	(out of 20)
Wine A is Stag's Leap Clr. '73 (CA)	14.14
Wine B is Mouton '70 (FR)	14.09
Wine C is Montrose '70 (FR)	13.64
Wine D is Haut-Brion '70 (FR)	13.23
Wine E is Ridge Mt. Bello '71 (CA)	12.14
Wine F is Léoville-Las-Cases '71 (FR)	11.18
Wine G is Heitz Martha's '70 (CA)	10.36
Wine H is Clos du Val '72 (CA)	10.14
Wine I is Mayacamas '71 (CA)	9.77
Wine J is Freemark Abbey '69 (CA)	9.64

The judges' grades

	Wine									
Judge	A	B	C	D	E	F	G	H	I	J
Pierre Bréjoux	14.0	16.0	12.0	17.0	13.0	10.0	12.0	14.0	5.0	7.0
Aubert de Villaine	15.0	14.0	16.0	15.0	9.0	10.0	7.0	5.0	12.0	7.0
Michel Dovaz	10.0	15.0	11.0	12.0	12.0	10.0	11.0	11.0	8.0	15.0
Patricia Gallagher	14.0	15.0	14.0	12.0	16.0	14.0	17.0	13.0	9.0	15.0
Odette Kahn	15.0	12.0	12.0	12.0	7.0	12.0	2.0	2.0	13.0	5.0
Claude Dubois-Millau	16.0	16.0	17.0	13.5	7.0	11.0	8.0	9.0	9.5	9.0
Raymond Oliver	14.0	12.0	14.0	10.0	12.0	12.0	10.0	10.0	14.0	8.0
Steven Spurrier	14.0	14.0	14.0	8.0	14.0	12.0	13.0	11.0	9.0	13.0
Pierre Tari	13.0	11.0	14.0	14.0	17.0	12.0	15.0	13.0	12.0	14.0
Christian Vannequé	16.5	16.0	11.0	17.0	15.5	8.0	10.0	16.5	3.0	6.0
Jean-Claude Vrinat	14.0	14.0	15.0	15.0	11.0	12.0	9.0	7.0	13.0	7.0
Average grade	14.14	14.09	13.6	13.2	12.1	11.2	10.4	10.1	9.8	9.6

17

The Old World and the New Worlds Apart?

Warren Winiarski

Some recent important comparative tastings between wines of the Old World and the New have challenged the assumption that these wines, arising from such different origins, can be judged by the same standards of excellence. Indeed, notwithstanding the botanical identity of the grape type, a question has been raised about whether the same criteria of excellence can be applied to wines of both worlds, or else whether the "worlds" are so different that their wines must be judged by different standards.

It would appear, then, that the key to this question could be reduced to the topic of "quality," that sometimes mysterious aspect of wine which make some wines stand out from others. What is it, we ask ourselves? All international competitive tastings presuppose that it is possible and desirable to judge the wines of many countries and to identify those which, in the opinion of the judges, possess "quality" to a greater or lesser extent. The judges, in their evaluations, assume that there are standards for wine quality which transcend the particular, national, and regional characteristics of origin and allow the wines to be compared according to those standards. Naturally, we need to reflect on that assumption.

The title of this essay suggests a polarity of approach. Is it really a polarity? Is the difference between the Old World and the New rather a difference of focus or emphasis? In this discussion, I take the point of view that there is a common *unity*. Relatedly, I endorse a viewpoint which says that wines can be understood and appreciated independently of their origin and that the distinction between the Old World and the New World is not as significant as the distinction between the "regional" and "classic wines" from whatever origin.

I use the word 'regional' in a sense a bit different from, but not unrelated to, the typical use in the wine trade today where, it is used to describe a class of wines lower than the classed growers or the top-selling wines from a given winegrowing area. The reader will discover the difference in due course.

The history of wine itself suggests a common origin and an elaboration of the same tradition. It suggests continuity, not disjunction. Where did our history begin? Some place in the East, it is said. How far east is not clear. Egypt certainly; perhaps beyond. There is viticultural evidence suggesting that the ancestors of *Vitis vinifera*, so important to us, reach back to the Orient.[1] Our conscious history of the West seems to begin with Greece and Rome, from Rome throughout the Mediterranean basin, then northward across Europe, even to the "scepter'd isle," and from thence, on imperial prows, to the great colonies in the New World: America, Australia, New Zealand, South Africa, and beyond. I stated colonies but, of course, this is not meant specifically in a political sense. Rather, the colonizers are the bearers of vines and the art of winemaking.[2] They are going forth even today with the former colonials returning to tend the vines of the Old World. And of course, very recently, the Old World Europeans are coming again to the New World to prospect for vineyards, to plant their vines, and to make their wine on soil which has another flavor and flies another flag. They are serving Bacchus, who has been called a wandering god. It is obvious that the sugar of grapes is like the aroma of flowers. It acts as an attractant to promote the spread of the vine's life wherever it can. You can see, then, by this transoceanic dispersion, how much more effective is the transformed sugar of the grapes. In spreading the joy of wine across the great seas, a remarkably satisfactory association of humans and fruit is born. I perceive, then, wherever the vines have spread, modifications of a common stream and not disjunction.

---

[1] See, for example, Patrick E. McGovern, Stuart J. Fleming, and Solomon H. Katz, *The Origins and Ancient History of Wine* (New York: Routledge, 2000); and Patrick E. McGovern, *Ancient Wine: The Search for the Origins of Viniculture* (Princeton: Princeton University Press, 2003).

[2] George M. Taber, *Judgment of Paris: California vs. France and the Historic 1976 Paris Tasting that Revolutionized Wine* (New York: Scribner, 2005).

The same appears to be true if we let our imagination play a bit to consider the first winemakers we can imagine. I suppose they might have been bees and birds. I can assure you that both are remarkably attentive little things. They observe the smallest changes in the vineyard relating to the ripening of the grapes – just as any good winemaker does. And when they discover a certain sugar level in the berries they certainly appear to be able to communicate what is taking place to others who are equally interested in the process. Soon, hordes of fascinated wine lovers are gathering to sample and, no doubt, to pass the word. I have tasted some of their wines. They are not bad at all, but they do not age.

Another thing to observe about the winemaking of birds and bees is that the wines they make are not stored and they do not travel from their place of origin. They are both made and consumed on the spot on the perfect vessel of the grape with its waterproof skin. And last, we may observe that their wines are made in a way that might be called traditional in the extreme. Each year the wines are made in exactly the same way. There are no changes in procedure – as far as she can observe – to accommodate changed circumstances, conditions, and grape character.

Therefore, to gather up these somewhat paradoxical observations, how does human winemaking differ from that of the birds and bees? In the first place, the wine humans make normally lasts for more than one season: there is a preserving aspect to human art. Second, humans are collectors and gatherers: they bring their grapes from the fields and collect them all together in larger waterproof vessels where the wines come to be (i.e., humans increase the batch size). Also part of this second difference, and even more important than mere collection, they select very carefully from the grapes available to them (i.e., they exercise choice in accordance with goals). Finally, they are always changing their actions in accordance with the changing circumstances of the place, the time, and the grape material: they are guided by purpose, vision, and inspiration to modify what is given. They are always deliberating and matching means to ends. These characteristics apply wherever humans make wine, at least to some extent.

The earliest written account of wine we have in the Western tradition is the one in the Bible. The Old Testament tells that directly after the flood waters receded, Noah planted a vineyard.[3] Of course, this was not the first form of agriculture mentioned in the Bible. But the discipline of winegrowing (viticulture) as opposed to the mere gathering of fruit to use in one form or another is a particularly long-range form of agriculture; furthermore, it requires long-term, stable conditions. In the Covenant of the Rainbow, by which it is signified that earth-wide flooding will not reoccur, that needed stability and protection is promised. Now the Bible says that Noah planted the vineyard and drank the wine. It does not say that he made the wine. I puzzled over this curious omission for some time. Some of my friends who understand these things suggested a rule of reading this account which made sense. The rule is this: when the Old Testament is silent about an important topic, the silence is as important as what is said explicitly. They speculated that the silence is meant to indicate that Noah did not make the first wine but that it was a Divine Gift.

Now if the first wine did not come about by human forethought, then the first vineyard was not planted for the sake of wine. Otherwise, this would imply that Noah knew what wine was, and according to this account, he did not. However, afterwards, knowing the character of wine, humans could tend their vineyard both for nourishment from the fruit and to provide for the making of wine, which was another kind of nourishment. There is another question that follows upon this. Was the knowledge, skill or art that made possible the transformation of fruit to wine possessed in a perfect form by Noah in the beginning? Behind this question lies much of the difference between the Old World and the New. I shall mention it again later.

We should also observe that in the course of the biblical narrative, wine did not come in the Garden of Eden. Wine does not belong to humans as humans, but to humanity that has been expelled from the Garden. It belongs to a fallen humanity, which has needs and must toil by the sweat of its brow, in all those places which are *not* the Garden of Eden. Some of us call those places vineyards.

Let us not look at them. Grapes, of all the plant edibles, seem to be unusually sensitive to the region and to the circumstances of their

---

[3] Genesis 9:20–1.

growth. Unlike carrots, which are pretty much the same wherever they are grown, grapes and the wine they produce reflect their origin and their care to a high degree. Thus, in every place where vines are grown, they will express the regional character of soil, the climate, and other natural circumstances. They will also betray the work of the wine grower through his intent and his methods. Furthermore, in some places, favored because of the special character of the soil, climate, and those other natural circumstances, the wines seem to possess another possibility beyond expressing the regional character. These wines seem to lend themselves to the possibility of transcending the merely regional and reach what might be called the classic dimension.

This possibility of ascent might perhaps be the source of a tension between two current, different views of winemaking. First, it is a *useful* art insofar as it is *preserving* – like jelly and cheese making – because it preserves for another year the sunshine and the life of a year before: It later makes that preserved life available as nourishment. Second, it is also something like a fine art because, like music, its product is particularly *evocative*. This is so because it gives pleasure not through the satisfaction of any need but because of things like harmony, balance, complexity, and completeness. There is an old view that distinguishes between pleasures that come about through replenishment (as the pleasure of food seems to come about through removing the pain of hunger) and other pleasures which are not preceded by any obvious pain like hunger. Such pleasures, like those derived from music, were called unmixed pleasures.[4]

And so, from this double root of the art of winemaking, it seems that there come about two alternative ideas about "quality" or "excellence" in wines.

There are the wines which possess "quality" because they seem to represent the character of the soil and the climate of the region. Indeed, by a remarkable power of association, these wines seem to be able to express much about the unique place where they originated. We are attracted to them because they reveal their originality. We do like what is "our own." There is a "comfort" in regional wines because

---

[4]   Aristotle, Nichomachean Ethics, trans. Roger Crisp (Cambridge: Cambridge University Press, 2000), Book X, Chs. 1–5; Plato, *Philebus*, trans. Benjamin Jowett, available at classics.mit.edu/plato/philebus.html (accessed June 20, 2007); John 4:7–16, 6:35.

they conform to what is "our own." They are good, here and now, precisely *because* they are like the here and now. There are charming, intimate associates with local circumstances, not only such as soil and climate, but even steeples, church bells, trees, villages, and history.

On the other hand, in some places where grapes are grown, there exists a potential for the wine to take another direction. For, in addition to liking what is "our own," we are attracted to the "best." I call this the "lure of the classic." In this instance, there is even some negation or moderation of the merely regional qualities of wine in order to avoid parochial associations. These wines possess "quality" because they take their bearings by considerations such as harmony, balance, proportion, scale, magnitude, and euphonic relationship of parts. It is clear from the enumeration of these qualities that there is no attempt, in this class of wine, to focus on or to enhance regional characteristics.

There is a related topic which must be addressed, and that is the perceived conflict between "traditional ways" and the "ways of innovation" in winemaking. The topic is related but is not identical to the one regarding the "regional" and the "classic." Each side to this discussion offers virtues which the other side sees as faults. And the faults on the other side are seen as aspects the other finds worthy of following. In the following description of the two sides, I will make statements as an advocate for each.

What, then, are the virtues of the traditional ways? Tradition, in its purist form, offers stability and continuity. Furthermore, it is inward and rooted. It says that the "old" is the good and the "new" is the bad. As it says this, it acts as a limitation to change, and it would prefer to resist change. It looks backward and beyond that. It says that, if the old is the good, then the oldest is the best – for, "the oldest is older than the old." A simple proof of this is as follows: The classic answer of a traditionalist to the question, "Why do you do it that way?" is, "Our fathers did it that way, and, if it was good enough for them, then it is good enough for us." An even more classic response is, "because we have always done it that way." There can be nothing older than always: always is forever.[5]

---

[5] Consider Shakespeare, *King Lear*, II.2. 278–381.

Now, however salutary and desirable it may be to take one's bearings by tradition in politics, morals, and customs, some reflection will show that the traditionalist view, in its pure form, is a questionable authority in the arts (especially in the useful arts[6]). There are a few arts which are not improved by practice. In fact, the useful arts seem, by their nature, to be progressive: they need tending from successive generations who learn and correct and correct again. If it were not so in winemaking, we would be learning the art from Columella, whose 2,000-year-old writings on wine and vineyards offer astonishing insights but are useful mainly for principles and not for practice.[7] Only those arts which have accomplished their purpose perfectly – without excess of defect, and it is said that there are some of these – can be said to be at an end. A desire to maintain tradition, then (about an art), supposes that tradition supplies *the* truth and the final answer.

Recently, a noted practitioner of the winemaking art in the Old World said: "We do not follow tradition as such, we do not follow bad habits, we do not follow tradition for the pleasure of being traditional, but we experiment so that we can know whether the tradition was right or wrong. And we found that it was right."[8] This appears to say, if I understand the man correctly, that "right" or "wrong" is a higher standard than tradition. His statement suggests that, as far as art is concerned, the traditional must be judged, used or modified in light of the higher standards. And so he appears to have concluded that in this useful art at any rate, what we are seeking is what is "good" and not the "old" as such.

I believe this interpretation of his words may surprise him; but I believe it may also be revealing and helpful. For to take one's bearings simply by the past means that the past must have discovered *everything* which is good and important about a practice or a discipline or an art. It would also mean that there is nothing of importance that is to be found in the present or in the future. That is, it assumes that the past has a fullness and a completeness to which

[6] Aristotle, *Politics*, trans. Trevor J. Saunders and T. A. Sinclair (New York: Penguin, 1981), Book II, Ch. 8.

[7] Columella, *On Agriculture*, 3 vols. (Cambridge, MA: Loeb Classical Library, 1941–55).

[8] Robert D. Drouhin, "Directions in French Winemaking Symposium," American Institute of Wine and Food, 1986 (unpublished).

nothing can be added. It is finished. Such an assumption or conclusion would not appear to provide the impulse to make great wine.

The above conclusion brings us to the innovators' point of view. The innovators seem to take a position diametrically opposite to the traditionalist: the "good" is not in the past, but rather in the *future*. The "now" is but a stepping stone to some future perfection. They seem to say "we can make wines better (at some future time), if we 'know a bit more' or if we gather in the results of more experiments and data." They regard the past and tradition as fetters and shackles to the perfection that might come about through change. They welcome change. Perfection in the arts, they say, comes about by being free to speculate, to wonder and to try new things. Science, they say, is essentially progressive and they use science in the service of improvement. Besides, they ask, "what, essentially, *is* tradition?" And they have their own answer: is it not, they say, essentially the accumulation of trial and error? New things embedded in acceptance? Is it not concretized or sometimes even fossilized innovation?[9]

This innovationalist point of view provides for the relentless pursuit of technological improvement – what some would call, I think, the antithesis of being guided by culture. It is certainly powerful in the New World. But it is not absent in the old. Some of the most far-reaching investigations and discoveries are coming from studies in the laboratories of Old World industry and universities. I mention only the better-known studies of vine and root stock physiology, grape vine canopy management, clonal selection, disease-free cellular propagation, gene splicing, etc.[10] Remember that it was Louis Pasteur, an Old World fellow, who first discovered the mechanism of yeast fermentation.[11] All of this fundamental research supposedly in the service of improving the art of the Old World: science in the service of art. It appears, however, that there is a danger of a certain technological sterility and uniformity from this knowledge when applied. Science, like numbers, is universal: it does not admit of the charms of the local and the here and now. The wines produced by science

[9]   Robert Mondavi with Paul Chutkow, *Harvests of Joy: How the Good Life Became a Great Business* (New York: Harcourt Brace, 1998), pp. 197–8. (Compare the approach between Robert Mondari and Andre Tchelistchef).
[10]   Drouhin, "Directions in French Winemaking Symposium."
[11]   Louis Pasteur, *Studies on Fermentation* (1879), trans. F. Faulkner and D. C. Robb (New York: Kraus Reprint, 1969).

255

as such seem to obliterate the qualities we find endearing and lovable. Perhaps that is why the dyed-in-the-wool traditionalists would prefer to see some so-called "flaws" remain in their work (i.e., the ones they are used to and which are their own). They dread the thought of the success of what has been described as "perfection without a purpose."

In conclusion, I would like for you as the reader to think about this: the contemporary practice of the art of winemaking appears to be a blend which combines elements of both points of view. The Old World appears to emphasize tradition, the New World appears to emphasize innovation.

However, some of the traditionalists of the Old World preach tradition but practice the most rigorous scientific technology behind the casks and the cobwebs. On the other hand, some of the most vociferous innovators in the New World make pilgrimages to the ancestral shrines. And they both do what they do in the service of "quality," that mystery some of whose aspects we have explored.

What of the future for these two points of view and of the Old and New World of wine? I think we may safely surmise that they will draw closer together. The innovators will look to tradition to see if there is not something they have overlooked or forgotten. But they will not look to the past as past and therefore as authoritative. The traditionalist, who strictly speaking must regard the past as authoritative and therefore as embodying wisdom which cannot be exceeded in the present or the future, will nonetheless be looking – perhaps cautiously, distrustfully, reluctantly, even if inevitably – at what is revealed by inquiry. But he will do that in the light of self-confidence in a perfection already attained.

18

Taste How Expensive This Is
A Problem of Wine and
Rationality

Justin Weinberg

For $2,500, you can now buy one bottle of 1997 Screaming Eagle, a cabernet sauvignon-based wine from Napa Valley, California.[1] It is not a large bottle, but the standard 750 milliliter format in which most wine is found. If you have some measuring spoons nearby, take out what is probably the smallest one, the quarter-teaspoon. Now imagine someone eye-dropping a milliliter of wine into this spoon, which would not quite fill it up, and asking $3.33 for it.

Reasonably, you decline. Robert Parker, the world's most famous wine critic, called the 1997 Screaming Eagle "a perfect wine." Giving it his highest rating of 100 points, he added:

> Representing the essence of cassis liqueur intermixed with black-berries, minerals, licorice, and toast, this full-bodied, multi-dimensional classic is fabulous, with extraordinary purity, symmetry, and a finish that lasts for nearly a minute. It has the overall equilibrium to evolve for nearly two decades, but it will be hard to resist upon release. Anticipated maturity: now–2020.[2]

You realize it will be hard to detect the layers of varied flavors Parker describes, let alone the wine's symmetry or finish, in a scant quarter-

I would like to thank Fritz Allhoff, Matthew McAdam, Daniel O'Connell, and Sara Weinberg for comments on drafts of this work, and Joseph Kluchinsky, Hugo Linares, and Martin Reyes for helpful conversations about the wine business.

[1] This price and others throughout the chapter, unless otherwise noted, are actual prices or rough averages of prices obtained from wine-searcher.com for a 750 milliliter bottle.
[2] Robert Parker, *The Wine Advocate* (126), January 1, 2000.

257

teaspoon. Such a paltry volume of liquid will leave the majority of your taste buds uncaressed by its extraordinary purity and multi-dimensionality. You decide you will need a glass of it. That will be $500, please.

You demur. Perhaps, then, some blackberry jam on toast, a cigarette, a licorice whip, and a Centrum? Even in 2020, this will likely cost much less than $500. While you might not be willing to pay $2,500 for Screaming Eagle, plenty of others are, and this is just one example of many wines for which many persons are willing to spend many dollars. Perhaps Screaming Eagle is out of your price range, but you probably have been tempted by wines with prices at the upper end or just beyond what you consider affordable.

In this essay, I examine this attraction to expensive wines. I argue that wines often function as Veblen goods: we desire them more strongly as their prices increase *because* their prices increase. I further argue such desiring is irrational. There are certain aspects of what we can call *wine enthusiast culture* that contribute to wines functioning as Veblen goods. At the end of the essay, I ask what we should think about wine enthusiast culture in light of its capacity for fostering irrationality.

Veblen Goods

Economics teaches us that, in general, as the price of a good increases, demand for that good decreases. As the price of butter rises, I may consume fewer moon waffles,[3] or switch to *I Can Sort of Believe It's Not Butter*. Demand for a good only speaks to consumers' actual actions. But changes in the price of a good may also affect consumers' attitudes. We prefer to spend less on a good rather than more, so as the price of one of two similar goods rises, we may come to prefer the second. Prices can affect desires even when they do not affect purchases. If the price of plastic swords is cut, I may be more tempted to teach my classes dressed as a pirate, even though I ultimately opt to dress as a philosopher.

There are some goods that do not follow normal patterns of inter-actions between prices and preferences. For some goods, as their prices increase, consumer' preference for them also increases. That is, the

---

[3] A moon waffle is a waffle (made from waffle batter mixed with caramel and "liquid smoke") wrapped around an entire stick of butter and served on a toothpick. It was invented by Homer Simpson of *The Simpsons*.

increase in the price of the goods makes the goods more desirable. These are known as *Veblen goods.*

Veblen goods are named for Thorstein Veblen, author of *The Theory of the Leisure Class.*[4] In this work, Veblen coined the idea of "conspicuous consumption," which describes consumer activity intended to display one's high social status. A person might purchase an expensive, flashy sports car known for its commendable performance at very high speeds. But most people, including those who purchase such cars, spend nearly all of their driving time on ordinary roads full of ordinary drivers traveling at ordinary speeds and stopping at ordinary traffic lights; the closest they get to a racetrack on which their own car's finely tuned superiority might be observed is the parking lot at a NASCAR event. And even if they were to drive on the track, most people are not experienced enough to notice the subtle differences in performance for which the car may be known. People know this about their world and themselves, so it is unlikely that the vehicle's performance is the reason for its purchase. But possession of the car indicates to others that you can afford it; according to Veblen's idea of conspicuous consumption, it provides evidence for your economic status, and is an attempt to impress others.

The higher the price of the good, the stronger the signal it sends about the consumer's high status. Thus, conspicuous consumption can serve as an explanation for the existence of at least some Veblen goods. Among the status-seeking, desire for such goods increases as their price increases. Note, though, that while conspicuous consumption can provide one explanation for some Veblen goods, what makes a good a Veblen good is simply that it becomes more desirable as its price increases. There may be other possible explanations for Veblen goods besides status-seeking.[5]

Wines as Veblen Goods

Wines often function as Veblen goods. Initial evidence of this is one likely reaction to the first sentence of this essay: "Oh, how I would

---

[4] Thorstein Veblen, *The Theory of the Leisure Class* (New Brunswick, NJ: Transaction Publishers, 1992; orig. 1899).

[5] See Judith Lichtenberg, "Consuming Because Others Consume," *Social Theory and Practice* 22 (Fall 1996): 273–97.

love to have some of that." The only thing distinctive about the wine mentioned in that sentence is its unusually high price. Yet the high price is sufficient to stimulate a strong interest in consuming it.

This is merely tentative, rather than conclusive, evidence in favor of wine sometimes acting as a Veblen good because price may be considered a proxy for quality. If one thinks that price and quality are correlated, then a preference for Screaming Eagle that develops as a result of learning only of its high price may be a function of assuming that the high price indicates high quality. It would then be the assumed high quality of the wine, not its price, stoking desire for it. Were that true, then it would not be a Veblen good. If the *quality* of the wine is motivating the desire for it, reducing the price of the wine would not reduce the desire for the wine. If desire for the wine did not diminish, this would show that the wine is not a Veblen good, since the desire for a Veblen good decreases with its price.

One might note that Screaming Eagle would continue to sell out in the primary market if we cut its price in half. Does that provide evidence that it is not a Veblen good? No. Two points are important here. First, the definition of a Veblen good refers to the consumer preference for a good, not aggregate demand for it. We cannot infer persons' desires regarding a good from the amount of the good purchased. Noting whether demand for a good has changed is fundamentally a matter of counting. Desire for a good is not as easy to measure. When watching shoppers we can look for the turning of heads, increased salivation, longer lingering gazes, perhaps spikes in galvanic skin response as they see the price tag, but even if this were not impractical, it would still only provide us with material from which to guess what they are thinking. And it is what people are thinking, not merely what they are buying, that we need to know about in order to know whether a good is a Veblen good.

Second, the *Veblen effect* – that is, the degree to which a good's price increase causes an increase in the good's desirability – is subjective. It varies from person to person. For some, the high price of the sports car will make the car more attractive; for others, it will have no effect or make the car less attractive. That some people will not be subject to the Veblen effect of the car does not imply the car is not a Veblen good. For a good to be a Veblen good it need not have a Veblen effect for all consumers. The same is true for wine. That some people are repelled by Screaming Eagle's high

260

price does not indicate that Screaming Eagle is not, for some, a Veblen good.

Taken together, these points provide a plausible explanation for why, even if we think Screaming Eagle will sell out at half-price, the wine may still be a Veblen good. We know that since demand is not equivalent to desire, demand for a good may remain unchanged while desires for the good fluctuate. And, given the subjectivity of the Veblen effect, we can develop a plausible explanation of the lack of actual correlation between demand and desire in this case. As the price of the wine decreases, some people who initially valued it for its expensiveness will no longer do so. They will stop purchasing Screaming Eagle and purchase other wines instead – perhaps 2000 Le Pin ($3,000). Yet there are people of lesser means for whom the wine's Veblen effect will remain strong, and can only afford the wine at its new, lower price. In short, the former group's abstinence is offset by the latter group's newfound purchasing power. Thus, a Veblen good may experience no change in aggregate demand when its price is reduced. In fact, if the former group is smaller than the latter (as it is in our world: the very wealthy are outnumbered by the somewhat wealthy), aggregate demand for a good may *increase* when its price is reduced, and this would not count against the good being a Veblen good.

What does this have to do with us? After all, most of the readers of this book will never spend thousands of dollars on a bottle of wine, so why should we be concerned with the Veblen effect? This question overlooks the subjectivity of the Veblen effect. It is not only the very wealthy who are susceptible to it, or can act on it. Many wine drinkers who are not particularly wealthy may nonetheless long for, say, 1990 Petrus ($3,000) or 1937 Romanée-Conti ($9,000), because of their high price, even though they cannot afford to act on this longing. Yet they also may long for wines that are expensive *for them*. There is the novice who never has spent more than $12 on a bottle and now wants to see how a $32 bottle of, say, Ridge Lytton Springs Zinfandel compares to the Ravenswood Vintner's Blend Zinfandel he has come to like. There is the usually frugal fan of Australian wines whose interest is piqued by the $75 sticker on the bottle of 2001 Glaetzer Amon-Ra Shiraz, a wine he has not heard of before because it is brand new. And there is the dinner party guest looking for a bottle of wine to bring; she declines the clerk's recommendation of the Falesco Vitiano ($10) because it is too cheap and over the clerk's well-informed objections selects a $25 bottle of Barolo. To the extent these wines were desired because of their relative high price – relative to the consumer's budget or to other wines considered by the consumer – they operated as Veblen goods. If Screaming Eagle is a Veblen good, then so are many other, much less expensive wines, and many ordinary persons, not just the wealthy, are swayed by the Veblen effect.

Yet how do we really know that it is the Veblen effect at work in these decisions?

As I noted above, evidence is not easy to obtain. We cannot deduce with certainty what people are thinking. Instead, the case that wines often function as Veblen goods is best made by abductive argument, or inference to the best explanation. If we know that some claim is true, then we have good reason to believe whatever best explains that claim. For example, if you appear at my door with a wet umbrella, I have good reason to believe what would best explain your carrying a wet umbrella, namely, that it is raining.

When it comes to Screaming Eagle, I know that some people spend thousands of dollars on it. What explains this? One plausible answer is that Screaming Eagle is an example of conspicuous consumption, and thus a Veblen good. The rationale is that anyone buying a $2,500 bottle of wine is buying it to show off, and since what one is showing off is how much one can spend on wine, clearly a decrease in the price will decrease the capacity of the good to achieve its goal, and it will thus become less desirable. As I noted earlier, though, showing off may not be the only motivation for desiring a good because of its relatively high price. Other forms of signaling may be at play instead of showing off, for example, keeping up or avoiding shame.[6] Perhaps the Barolo-bearing dinner guest is not trying to appear capable of obtaining expensive goods; she may be trying not to appear incapable of obtaining what are for her wealthier friends rather inexpensive items. Sometimes signaling may not be involved at all, but the good still may be desired because of its high price. If the Ridge Zinfandel were not $20 more than his usual purchase, the novice would desire it less. The Aussie wine fan would not want to try the Amon-Ra were it not so brazenly expensive. Persons in the retail

---

[6] Lichtenberg, "Consuming Because Others Consume."

wine trade inform me that these characters make regular visits to their shops.[7]

Quality, Price, and Pleasure

One alternative explanation for the attraction to high-priced wines is that consumers are taking the high price of a wine as a proxy for quality. As we saw earlier, this would imply that the high-priced wine is not functioning as a Veblen good, since it would be the assumed high quality of the good, not its high price, that is the reason for desiring it. Some people do indeed take price as a proxy for quality. In doing so they avoid the Veblen effect, but only at the expense of making mistakes in their judgments about issues surrounding wine quality, as I will now explain.

Quality. The first problem with considering price as a proxy for quality is that we can say very little about a wine's quality (i.e., how good a wine is). There may be some minimum standards of palatability – a wine with "notes" of balsamic vinegar might be tantalizing, not so much a wine that *tastes* as if it were said vinegar – but in the vast range of possibilities above that minimum there are no agreed-upon standards, nor could there be. This is because different wines serve different uses and engage different persons' palates differently. The strong flavors of a Barossa shiraz may make it the perfect accompaniment to some foods and a dreadful one for others. The translucent brick-red hue of a wine may be exactly what to look for in an older Burgundy, but exactly what to avoid in a younger petite sirah. Some may find the sweetness in a Sauternes glorious, yet others may find it cloying. *Even within narrow categories*, such as classes of wines based on geography or varietal, uniform standards of quality are inapplicable. The merlot-based wines from St. Emilion may differ in their properties in ways that make general assessments of their relative quality impossible. What is better, the powerful Pavie or the more modest Clos de l'Oratoire? You might as well ask: which is a better dog, a mastiff or a miniature greyhound? The answer to both of these questions will change depending on what else you need to make room for.

---

[7] For business considerations, these retailers were reluctant to have their names associated with this claim.

If I were to hold up a suit jacket and a ski jacket and ask you, "which is better?" you would correctly think that I am asking the wrong question. First of all, the jackets serve different purposes. And even for those occasions in which either will do, the better jacket will be different for different persons who have different sartorial tastes.[8] Similarly, the diverse aims we have for wines, as well as variations in our palates, suggest that it makes little sense to ask about the quality of wine. Generally, wines are incommensurable; that is, we cannot mark them as better or worse along a single scale. Yet prices all fall on a single scale, from low to high. Thus, wine prices cannot track wine quality.[9]

Price. Can we learn anything about a wine from its price? The truth is, multiple factors affect the price of a wine. Some of these factors are wholly irrelevant to quality, such as: the need to recoup costs due to weather-caused damage of grapes, the cost of labor, debt owed by winemaker, the strength of the dollar, the ego of the winemaker, gas prices, rarity, and so on. For some wines it is a mystery why they are priced as high as they are.[10]

---

[8] Thanks to Martin Reyes for this analogy.

[9] As an aside, this shows why fine-grained wine ratings – a practice begun by Parker in *Wine Advocate* and picked up by *Wine Spectator*, *Wine Enthusiast*, and others – are problematic. Scoring wines on a 100-point scale mistakenly assumes wines are commensurable. A defender of such rankings might claim that they are not intended to compare incommensurable wines, that the rankings do not imply that a 92-point Châteauneuf-du-Pape is superior to an 88-point sauvignon blanc from New Zealand. Rather, it might be suggested, the model for such rankings is that of a dog show, where individual specimens are judged on how well they approximate the ideal member of their breed. So, to score a Châteauneuf-du-Pape 92 points is only to describe how close it comes to being an ideal Châteauneuf-du-Pape. That is, it is superior to lower-scoring Châteauneuf-du-Papes, not superior to *all* lower-scoring wines, and inferior to higher-scoring Châteauneuf-du-Papes, not inferior to *all* higher-scoring wines. However, this does not solve the problem. As the St. Emilion example above illustrates, the incommensurability is not overcome even within the classifications (e.g., location, varietal) used to categorize wine into narrow breeds of comparable specimens. There is no ideal Châteauneuf-du-Pape. Thus, this defense of fine-grained rankings fails.

[10] One retailer offers Darioush Wines, which came into existence in 1997, as one example (of many). From its inception, the winery priced its reds around $60 per bottle, not exorbitant like Screaming Eagle, but still expensive. Being new, the wines had no track record of quality to justify their prices. The wines have garnered some good but no exceptional critical praise. Yet in the words of this retailer the wines "took off for no apparent reason."

One factor in pricing wine may be the Veblen effect itself. Knowing that some people are attracted to certain wines because of their high prices, a winemaker may seek greater profitability and attention by pricing his or her wine higher rather than lower. While it is hard to determine when this motivation is at work, it may explain the high inaugural prices of some wines, particularly from some newer Australian boutique operations and some of the *garagistes* of Bordeaux.

Pleasure.   Even if it were reasonable to talk about overall wine quality, the question remains as to whether, and if so how, to pay attention to it. It might be more important for your wine expenditures to track the pleasure the wine gives you, rather than the wine's quality, since quality and pleasure can diverge. Suppose that the comments and scores of professional wine critics are correlated to what we can pretend is the quality of a wine. Such critics refer to many things, among them certain characteristics that are very hard for normal wine drinkers to detect, such as "delineation" and "symmetry," and phenomena that are hard for normal wine drinkers to recall, such as what an acacia flower smells like, or the difference in taste between a red plum and a black plum. If these characteristics are beyond one's gustatory grasp, even if their presence in certain formations indicates a higher-quality wine, why should one pay for them? Note that I am not referring to those aspects of a wine that, though unidentifiable by most consumers, actually contribute to their enjoyment of it. That I am unable to identify my sensation as one of, say, "smelling acacia flowers," does not mean I cannot enjoy that sensation. However, if I do not have the sensation – perhaps I do not have the patience, the concentration, the olfactory skill to detect it, etc. – then certainly I should not be interested in paying more for it.

Perhaps at this point someone might interject that I *ought* to develop the capacities that would allow me to identify and appreciate the kinds of qualities usually reserved for expert appraisal. But first, it is not clear that it is in my interest to do so. If, as we are assuming for the moment, price and quality are correlated, unless I am very wealthy it might be in my interest to remain insensitive to quality. Otherwise, I may regularly be disappointed with what is in either my wine glass or my wallet. Second, it is not clear that developing expert-like wine-tasting skills will secure me the ability to actually discern quality wines, for even the experts disagree. Those who follow the wine press may recall that *Wine Spectator*'s raves for the 1997 vintage of Brunello

265

di Montalcino wines were met by Parker's fairly tepid reviews in *Wine Advocate* (most of the wines scored 90 or below). More recently, Parker and well-known wine authority Jancis Robinson disagreed vehemently over the 2003 Pavie, with Parker calling it "a brilliant effort" worth 98 points, and Robinson complaining that it is "completely unappetizing" and scoring it 12 out of 20 points.[11]

Quality and pleasure come apart in ways that do not depend on the taster's lack of knowledge or skill. One can recognize admirable traits in a performance one finds on balance unenjoyable, such as appreciating the agility of dancers and the originality of the choreography, while not enjoying the show they put on. Similarly, we can imagine recognizing aspects of a wine that are usually taken as signs of high quality, like complexity or a long finish, while taking no pleasure in the wine at all. I may be in the mood for an unbalanced "fruit bomb" that will take the edge off of my ravenousness as I wait for dinner, or perhaps I want something very simple and light to sip on the beach. If we were to assume, contrary to fact, that price and quality are correlated, it is not clear why that should motivate us to make the more expensive purchase, since quality and *pleasure* are not correlated.

If we think we should pursue pleasure rather than quality with our wine purchases, some might be tempted to offer another non-Veblen hypothesis for the attraction of high-priced wines, namely, that consuming higher-priced wines will be a more pleasurable experience. This could be interpreted in different ways. If by "more pleasurable" one means that wines that are more expensive will happen to be wines that the consumer thinks taste better, then this explanation will fail for lack of plausibility: there is no reason to think that price and personal taste regularly correlate. Sometimes we find a $25 bottle of wine more enjoyable than a $40 bottle, and there are many people who find "Two Buck Chuck" ($2–$4) more enjoyable than a $25 bottle. If instead "more pleasurable" means that what one enjoys about the experience is not mainly the taste of the wine but the fact that it is the tasting of *a wine that is expensive*, then we have not provided an explanation that avoids the Veblen effect but rather one that confirms it.

---

[11] For a good summary of this dispute, see Roger Voss, "Robinson, Parker, Have a Row Over Bordeaux," *San Francisco Chronicle*, May 27, 2004, p. F2.

Rationality and the Veblen Effect

As we have seen, wines sometimes act as Veblen goods. Some wines are more desired by certain persons as their prices increase, and these persons would find the wines less desirable were they not so expensive. Is it rational to be more desirous of a good *simply because it is more expensive*? I answer: No. I believe common sense is on my side, but as is often the case, it is not so easy explaining why common sense is right. It might help to keep in mind that this "no" answer is compatible with it being rational to desire the more expensive wine because it will yield a greater profit on the secondary market, or because it will impress your boss and get you a promotion, and so on. We might be able to make sense of the rationality of these desires because they are for a good (the wine) the expensive cost of which will be more than offset by benefits of other goods; the price of the wine is worth less than the profit to be made upon its resale or the good favor of your boss. But when these kinds of offsetting considerations are absent, when we want the good simply in virtue of its high price, we are being irrational. We might put the point this way: it is foolish to desire to bear a cost for the sake of bearing a cost.

Let us call a desire for a good simply because it is more expensive a *Veblen desire*. At this point you might expect a theory of rationality to be forthcoming, one that explains the particular irrationality of Veblen desires. I am reluctant to go that route, since I am more confident in the claim that Veblen desires are irrational than I am in any general theory of rationality. However, I will briefly mention two views about rationality and suggest that both of these views give us reasons to think that Veblen desires are irrational.

Desire-based views of rationality hold that what is rational for an agent to do is whatever will best satisfy his or her desires. On a desire-based view, when asking whether having Veblen desires is rational, we are asking whether our desires will be best satisfied if we have among our desires some desires for goods simply because they are more expensive. There is an ambiguity here regarding "whether our desires will be best satisfied." On one interpretation, we could be asking whether we have a desire to desire some goods simply because they are more expensive. If so, it would indeed be satisfied

267

by having Veblen desires. But who says to themselves, "The kind of person I desire to be is one who desires something more simply in virtue of it being more expensive"? To the extent we realize we are motivated by the Veblen effect we view it as an undesirable trait. On another interpretation, we could be asking about our ability to satisfy a set of desires that includes some Veblen desires. But if a person has desires for purchasing goods that are more rather than less expensive, then the price of satisfying the set of her desires increases, and the capacity to actually satisfy them decreases. Thus, on either interpretation, the desire-based view of rationality will tell us that for all but the very shallow or very wealthy, Veblen desires are irrational.

On a different, broader view of rationality, one acts rationally when one does what one justifiably believes one has most reason to do. Could one justifiably believe she has most reason to prefer a good simply because it is costlier? I do not see how. So on this understanding of rationality, being swayed by the Veblen effect is irrational.

But what if our conception of "costly" takes into account non-monetary costs? Perhaps, one might argue, we *could* justifiably believe we have most reason to do something because it is more costly in this broader sense. For example, a person might want to climb one of two mountains *because* it is the taller, more challenging mountain. Climbing this mountain means a greater investment in time and resources and carries a greater risk of injury. It is not an unreasonable use of the term to say that climbing the more challenging mountain is more *costly*. Is it irrational to want the more challenging mountain-climbing experience *because* it is in this way more costly? Do we want to say that this kind of desire is irrational? Recall our complaint against Veblen goods: it is irrational to desire a good simply because it is more costly. The person who wants to condemn as irrational desiring a wine more because it is more costly, but deems as rational desiring to climb one mountain more than another because it is more challenging or risky, has to argue either that we should understand "cost" in strictly monetary terms or that there is some other difference between the cases.

There are not good grounds for restricting "cost" to monetary expenditures. If we substituted "pianos to move" for dollars, we would not think it any less irrational to want a good simply because obtaining it involves moving more pianos. Indeed, it may be even more irrational. So let us look at the second option.

An important difference between the cases is that climbing the more challenging mountain is an achievement, while having consumed the wine one desired because of its high price is itself not an achievement. (It may sometimes indicate achievement, but is not itself an achievement.) Doing something that is more challenging has its own payoff that makes the greater cost – its greater degree of challenge – worthwhile, while consuming something because it is more expensive does not have a similar payoff. Many of us believe that achievement is part of a good life in a way that consuming expensive items because they are expensive is not. If these beliefs are true, it is rational to desire achievement, but it is not rational to desire greater expense. Though they may both involve desiring an encounter with an eagle, screaming or not, the desire for challenging mountain climbing is thus relevantly different from the desire to drink expensive wines because they are expensive.

Now if wine price and quality were correlated and if quality and pleasure were correlated, it might be more rational to desire to drink more expensive wines, despite the fact that they are more expensive, since drinking them would have the side effect of being very pleasurable, and pleasure is part of a good life. However, we have seen that these correlations do not generally hold. As a result we can draw some further conclusions about the rationality of drinking very expensive wines, at least for those who have a finite amount of money.

If you know little about wine, then you should not desire very expensive wines because you will not be in a position to ascertain and appreciate the kinds of details about them that, when present, are sometimes used as part of a justification for their high price. If, on the other hand, you know much about wine, then – unless you want to waste money – you should know better than to want to spend a lot on a wine, for you will know that there are usually lower-priced wines you will enjoy as much as a very expensive one. If you are somewhere in the middle, between novice and expert, it may make the least sense to desire the very expensive wine: if you lack the ability to discern subtle differences between wines, yet you know enough to know that price and quality are not correlated, then you have two reasons to avoid high wine expenditures.

Unless, that is, your behavior is intended to impress others. As we saw earlier, conspicuous consumption provides one explanation for Veblen goods. Some consumers of Veblen goods seek to impress others with their superior economic status. They are, in effect, purchasing the esteem of others, something that may indeed be rational to acquire. And to the extent more esteem can be bought by spending more, these consumers will indeed rationally prefer a good to a greater extent the more expensive it is. So some Veblen desires may indeed be rational.

In response it is fair to ask how effective expensive wine purchases are at securing the esteem of others. After all, compared to high-end cars, luxury homes, and bespoke suits, wines are relatively *inconspicuous* objects of consumption. They are kept tucked away in dark underground closets, usually served to oneself, or to family and friends. Perhaps some neighbors will see the empty bottles in your recycling bin. However, many of these family members, friends, and neighbors do not know enough about wine to be impressed by the labels they see, and if they are not wine enthusiasts, they may think it irresponsible of you to spend even $10 on a bottle of fermented grape juice when you can get over twice as much Black Cherry Vanilla Coke (talk about *complexity*) for one-fifth the price. You may be purchasing not their esteem, but their scorn. Even if it turns out you are improving your status in their eyes through expensive wine buying, it is not clear you have the *most* reason to do it this way. There may be less costly expenditures for more effectively status-projecting objects. It may be more rational to get the car washed so that it shines in your driveway than to purchase another pricey gewürztraminer. In short, if you are in the market for Veblen goods, only in very unusual circumstances will wines be a rational purchase. So, even on the assumption that conspicuous consumption is rational, the conspicuous consumption of wine is probably not. Thus, in general, to be more desirous of a wine because it is more expensive is irrational.

Wine Enthusiast Culture

I have argued that it is a mistake to desire more expensive wines on the presumption that price indicates quality, and that to purchase them because of their Veblen effect is generally irrational. As I noted earlier, wines at all price points are capable of generating a Veblen effect. Insofar as we ought to be rational, we ought not to have Veblen desires. One might wonder, though, to what extent our desires are up to us, and thus, to what extent we can expunge irrational ones. Certainly our desires are subject to external influences. Some of these influences spring from the wine enthusiast culture in which many readers of this book are members. Wine enthusiast culture resists precise definition, but its members are part of a set of persons identified in virtue of their wine-oriented shared interests, practices, and institutions.

Wine enthusiast culture is to a large extent a culture of hype. You thought the 1997 Brunellos were great? Well, the 1999s are even better! 2000 Bordeaux is the vintage of the century! No wait, now 2003 is! Have you tried Gaja's Barbaresco? Guigal's LaLa's? Draper's Monte Bello? Have you read about the new ink-black, purple-edged, truffle-licorice-cassis-nosed, Nicole Kidman-scented, teeth-staining, tongue-coating, mouth-filling, Aztec-barbecue-spiced, espresso-noted, slightly-underripe-passion-fruity, heirloom cherry-laden, graphite-touched, and chocolatey blockbuster-of-a-fully-integrated wine of clearly delineated, seamless harmony, multilayered complexity, and Elvis-like unctuousness, that will evoke the first time you fell in love and has a finish you will predecease?

Critics provide the drool-inducing descriptions. Some do so in glossy magazines that paint an alluring image of wine consumption. Others do so in serious text-only newsletters that impart (intentionally or not) the idea that beneath the glitz and glamour is a precision science of wine assessment that explains and justifies our passionate hobby. Retailers post excerpts and scores in their shops. Even if you have never heard of cassis, or you hate licorice, or you have no idea what it means for a wine to be well delineated, or why anyone would think that "unctuous" is something a wine should be, you recognize this as the language of praise, and you want in. Wine appreciation – being able to identify and enjoy the subtle differences between wines – is a skill that wine marketers tell us projects sophistication and class, and who does not want to be sophisticated or classy? Just as in many other areas of life (e.g., fashion, food, art), here sophistication does not come in a cardboard box; rather, it is routinely identified with expense. So the means by which one becomes sophisticated in wine appreciation generally involves spending a lot of money on wine. Along with the expenditures develop certain attitudes about wine – not merely that wine is worth being interested in, but that it is more than merely a beverage. The extent to which wine is viewed this way varies, but there is the sense that opening a bottle of wine can be special, in a way that opening a can of tuna is not. These attitudes make greater and greater outlays more psychologically acceptable. And such outlays are indeed encouraged by the culture. For not only is there the buying of wine, but also the procurement of wine-related accessories, such as appropriate stemware and decanters. Sometimes the buying of wine becomes the *collecting* of wine. This leads to the storing of wine, perhaps in expensive purpose-built refrigerators or custom-built cellars, in which wines are catalogued, organized, and displayed, and occasionally ogled and fondled.

Because being a wine lover is expensive, it is also exclusive. Part of its attraction lies in having something others do not. This may seem unfair, since one of the pleasures of wine enthusiasm is sharing good wines with others. But these others are part of the club, or potential inductees – rare fellow aesthetes who stand against the hordes of beer- and cola-swilling masses. Instead of writing about wines as Veblen goods I could have written about their similar function as *snob goods*, goods desire for which increases with their rarity. The exclusivity of wine enthusiast culture is obvious at the upper echelons of wine consumption, where the purchase of hundred- and thousand-dollar bottles of wine is routine. But it is no less true at the bottom end of the price range. Even those who purchase only very inexpensive wines, say, around $8 per bottle, could, if they have a few bottles each week, be spending $100 extra each month. For many people this is not a trivial amount of money. So even wine enthusiasts of modest means may be partaking in activities that are prohibitively expensive for their social peers.

The identity of a member of wine enthusiast culture is bound up with caring about wine, with enjoying something that others do not enjoy as much or in the same way, and paying a lot for the privilege. The desire for rarity and exclusiveness motivates one to purchase more expensive wines that, in virtue of their cost, are less available to one's peers. The excitement of a new discovery, the ego boost of telling others about it, the expectation that one's hobby is expensive anyway, the pleasure taken in exercising one's ability to spend, the encouragement of high ratings, all contribute to a propensity to spend a bit more, or a lot more, on wine. Wine enthusiast culture primes us to spend; we become susceptible to the Veblen effect, and many of us end up with at least some Veblen desires.

Rationality or Goodness?

If aspects of wine enthusiast culture encourage forms of irrationality such as Veblen desires, what should we think of it? Irrationalities involve people in some way not being as well off as they could be were they not irrational. So, to the extent that we are interested in how people's lives are going, we might be troubled by these irrationalities. We might also be concerned with the irrationality itself. Many of us believe that thinking clearly is itself important, and a problem with wine enthusiast culture is that it in at least some ways interferes with clear thinking. Still others might be concerned with autonomy, and worry about the ways in which members of wine enthusiast culture are swept up by the culture into patterns of high expenditures.

Of course, we cannot examine just the irrationality-producing part of wine enthusiast culture in our assessment of it. We must look at the whole picture, and once we do we see that wine enthusiast culture seems to do a fairly good job at something very important to wine enthusiasts: stimulating the production of a variety of interesting and enjoyable wines from around the world at varying prices in a manner that is accessible to many people. As a wine lover, it is hard to imagine a time in history when it would have been better to live than now. Furthermore, the counterpart to the reality of wines as Veblen goods is the reality of some wines as bargains. That is, there are some wines that deliver tremendous pleasure for relatively little money, and there are members of wine enthusiast culture who seek out these values. This is exemplary rational behavior in the context of wine consumption.

Is there a way to get the good without the bad? Part of the difficulty of imagining how this might be done stems from the possibility that the bad may be inherent to the features of the culture which bring about the good. That is, Veblen desires are an outgrowth of loving wine. If people did not love wine as much, and did not get caught up in the practices and attitudes of wine enthusiast culture, then yes, fewer people would have Veblen desires for wine. But if that love and enthusiasm receded, then the practices of the culture would be less robust, the demand for wine in general would diminish, and as a result fewer and less interesting wines would be produced. That would be bad.

So, those who care more about rationality than wine could justi-fiably condemn wine enthusiast culture, while those who care more about wine than rationality may sing the culture's praises. To whom should we listen? Any adequate answer to this interesting question is, unfortunately, beyond the scope of this essay. For now, our study of wine enthusiast culture, like much philosophy, leaves us with more questions than answers: we are sometimes in the position of choos-ing between what is rational and what is good, and it is not clear which wins, or why.

19

Shipping across State Lines
Wine and the Law

Drew Massey

Alcohol, especially wine, has always possessed a special place in the cultural realm. Wine holds specific religious connotations for many societies both past and present. From Bacchus, the god of wine, to the particular use of wine made by Christ at the Last Supper, wine is often given significance that more ordinary drinks lack. It should come as no surprise, then, that alcohol has also maintained a singular place in the secular and legal world of humankind.

Alcohol has been alternately blessed and cursed in the history of the United States. However, from an early time it was given special treatment above ordinary articles of commerce. Generally, the law does not distinguish between articles in commerce. Clothes, toys, tools, and medicine all receive the same treatment under the law once these items are put in a box and shipped by truck, train, ship, or plane. Alcohol, on the other hand, possesses a tortuous and complex legal history.

The distinctive status of wine has sparked debate recently with the development of the "wine wars." This term describes the fight between those who hope to ship wine from a winery in one state directly to a consumer in another state and those who assert that a state has the power to stop such direct shipments. The debate can exist around wine, both because of its cultural significance and because particular rules allow ample room to make legal arguments on both sides.

A full understanding of the special rules that Congress enacted for alcohol (whether for good or ill) requires a brief backdrop of the federal system and the rules generally applicable to other goods.

The Federal System and the Commerce Power

The Constitution of the United States sets up both a limited federal government of enumerated powers and many state governments of general powers. The 10th Amendment, the final amendment in the Bill of Rights, states that the "powers not delegated to the United States by the Constitution, nor prohibited by it to the states, are reserved to the states respectively, or to the people."[1] Therefore, the federal government can only do those things specifically enumerated in the Constitution. The states, on the other hand, can do anything not prohibited to them.

The federal government, for example, is given the power to coin money and the states are restricted from doing the same. Alternatively, it is generally left to the states to enact law that deals with the making, interpretation, and enforcement of contracts, for example, because no such power is given to the federal government. However, there are areas where both the state and federal governments have concurrent powers. Examples include the power to collect taxes and the power to make bankruptcy law. These powers are shared by the state and federal government because they are given to the federal government but not denied to the states.

In these concurrent powers, should there be a conflict between state and federal law, the Constitution dictates that the federal laws are to be supreme over state law. While it is generally true that states may legislate in an area when the federal government has not done so, there is a very special exception when it comes to interstate commerce.

The federal government is given the power to "regulate Commerce with foreign nations, and among the several States."[2] This power is given to the federal government without a correlating denial to the states. As such, it should generally give the federal government and the state governments concurrent power over interstate commerce. However, beginning very early, the Supreme Court limited the power of states with respect to interstate commerce.

In 1824, the first birthings of what would eventually be termed the "dormant" Commerce Clause began. In a case called *Gibbons*, then Chief Justice of the Supreme Court John Marshall declared,

---

[1]   US Const. amend. X.
[2]   Id. at art. I, § 8, cl. 3.

276

It has been contended . . . that, as the word "to regulate" implies in its nature, full power over the thing to be regulated, it excludes, necessarily, the action of all others that would perform the same operation on the same thing. . . . There is great force in this argument, and the Court is not satisfied that it has been refuted.[3]

Essentially, Justice Marshall stated that when the Constitution gave the federal government the power "to regulate," that meant the sole power to regulate; thus such a power of regulation should be denied to the states. Later cases expounded along this line of reasoning. Finally, in 1875, the Court embraced the "dormant" Commerce Clause and declared that "[Congress's] inaction on a subject . . . is equivalent to a declaration that inter-State commerce shall be free and untrammeled."[4]

Hence, whenever Congress has not used its power over commerce, the states are precluded from using any commerce power as Congress meant for it to be "free and untrammeled." But if Congress has spoken on the subject, then the Supremacy Clause operates to prevent the state law from taking effect.

Critics of this rationale have pointed to the inherent difficulty in deciphering the intent of Congress through its silence. More to the point, this would seem to enact law (law preventing states from regulating commerce) without passage by both houses and presentment to the president for his signature or veto as required by the Constitution. Despite these criticisms, the dormant Commerce Clause has existed as a judicial construct for over one hundred years and, by sheer inertia, will continue as a viable legal doctrine for the indeterminate future.

The Constitution, as discussed above, creates a limited federal government of enumerated powers. The power enumerated regarding commerce states that Congress has power to regulate commerce "among the several states." Much litigation has occurred over that very phrase to determine whether or not federal laws were valid exercises of power. Generally, "among the several states" is read as giving Congress power over interstate commerce. States, presumably, would then be able to regulate commerce that occurred entirely within the state–intrastate commerce. However, by judicial interpretation, even activities that take place entirely within a state may be deemed

---

[3] *Gibbons v. Ogden*, 22 US (9 Wheat) 1, 209 (1824).
[4] See *Welton v. Missouri*, 91 US 275, 282 (1875).

"interstate" for purposes of the dormant Commerce Clause. The Court asks whether the subject activity, when done in the aggregate, will have an effect on the national market. If the answer is yes, it is deemed "interstate" commerce. Thus, even a wheat farmer who produces wheat solely on his property and solely for his consumption will be subject to the federal commerce power.

In Defense of the Dormant Commerce Clause

As shown above, the dormant Commerce Clause has very little foundation in the text of the Constitution. Further, it would seem to be completely contrary to the requirements that legislation be enacted by two houses of Congress (enactment being the opposite of silence) and then signed into law by the president. However, one of the reasons that the dormant Commerce Clause has existed in American jurisprudence is because of its perceived necessity.

Defenders of the clause have pointed to its ability to eliminate protectionist economic policies. The dormant Commerce Clause prevents a state from enacting, for example, a license that costs an in-state producer one price, and an out-of-state producer a higher price.

In other words, the dormant Commerce Clause ensures the existence and maintains the integrity of a national free-market economy. As one commentator put it,

> Our system, fostered by the Commerce Clause, is that every farmer and every craftsman shall be encouraged to produce by the certainty that he will have free access to every market in the Nation, that no home embargoes will withhold his exports, and no foreign state will by customs duties or regulations exclude them. Likewise, every consumer may look to the free competition from every producing area in the Nation to protect him from exploitation by any. Such was the vision of the Founders; such has been the doctrine of this Court which has given it reality.[5]

This serves a useful purpose, especially in modern society. Today, commercial items can be ordered instantly over the Internet and shipped

---

[5] Jim Rossi, "Transmission Siting in Deregulated Wholesale Power Markets: Re-Imagining the Role of Courts in Resolving Federal-State Siting Impasses," *Duke Environmental Law and Policy Forum* 15 (2005): 315, 323.

278

next-day mail from New York, California, or anywhere else. The complications that could arise if each state adopted its own commercial laws would be staggering. Each state might enact retaliatory commercial legislation against those states that were deemed commercially unfriendly. Reciprocity statutes might abound that would further complicate taxes, duties, and even ability to ship depending on the state in which the consumer happened to reside.

In order to give every consumer in the United States the chance to buy from every market, the dormant Commerce Clause shuts down these discriminatory laws before they can have effect. It prevents a consumer from having to pay more for his products simply because of where he lives, or where the manufacturer of the item does business.

This is especially important in the wine industry. Boutique wineries are becoming increasingly common; these small wineries may produce only five hundred bottles a year of a particular wine. Because they do not produce in large quantities, they do not have the economic wherewithal to navigate the different legal hurdles that crop up in each state. Indeed, it becomes uneconomical to ship wine into other states if it must go through the traditional three-tier system of alcohol distribution (manufacturers to wholesalers, wholesalers to retailers, and retailers to consumers). As such, the dormant Commerce Clause provides a way to cut through the red tape of various state bureaucracies and get boutique wine to consumers.

Unfortunately, the dormant Commerce Clause does not have full effect when applied to wine and to wine shipments. There are unique considerations when alcohol is involved.

The Special Case of Alcohol

At the end of the nineteenth century, the prohibition movement began to gain prominence. Its central tenet was the desire to ban the nefarious consumption of alcohol – a drink blamed by the proponents of the movement for all manner of societal ills. States began to enact legislation that limited the production and sale of alcohol.

In this era, it was often held that certain commercial activities, such as "production" and "mining," were inherently local and thus could be regulated by the states. Thus, the state of Kansas passed a law that prohibited the production of alcohol, for domestic use, entirely.

279

The Supreme Court affirmed the Kansas law. Under this decision, states could prohibit the production of alcohol within their borders. However, states were still powerless to affect interstate commerce. Wine could still be produced in non-prohibition states, and shipped to waiting consumers in a state that had banned production.

Alcohol could be shipped into a prohibition state because the dormant Commerce Clause prevented states from regulating interstate commercial activity with regard to alcohol. Congress had yet to speak on the issue of interstate alcohol importation, and so the area was meant to be "free and untrammeled." As the prohibition movement gained steam, Congress reacted to the desires of its constituents and finally spoke on the issue by passing the Wilson Act.

The Wilson Act, passed in 1890, allowed states to treat imported alcohol the same as if the alcohol had been produced in the state. In other words, a state that banned the sale of alcohol produced in the state could also ban the sale of alcohol produced outside of the state. Therefore, this divested alcohol of its interstate character and abrogated the effectiveness of the dormant Commerce Clause.

Producers of alcohol in "wet" states and consumers in "dry" states soon found a way around the new law. They could simply ship the alcohol directly to the consumer. If they did, then there was no "sale" in the dry state to be prohibited. It never came in contact with state authorities. The Supreme Court affirmed this reasoning and direct shipments of wine flourished.

As the prohibition movement grew stronger, and the Anti-Saloon League came to prominence, Congress decided to "fix" the direct shipment loophole. To do so, they passed the Webb-Kenyon Act. The act prohibited "the shipment or transportation . . . of any [alcoholic beverage] from one State . . . into any other State . . . to be received, possessed, sold, or in any manner used . . . in violation of any law of such State." Therefore, if the shipping of alcohol directly to consumers violated the law of the recipient state, then it also violated a law of Congress. Hence, the dormant Commerce Clause could have no bearing on state law regarding liquor importation because Congress had spoken on the issue.

This law, like the Wilson Act before it, was quickly tested in the Supreme Court when a West Virginia law banned all shipments directly to consumers. Undaunted, an out-of-state producer of wine shipped directly to a Virginian consumer as it had previously done. The Supreme

Court held that Webb-Kenyon allowed West Virginia to regulate alcohol despite the effect it had on interstate commerce. Significantly, that law in that case did not discriminate between in-state producers and out-of-state producers. West Virginian wineries, as well as the wineries of Maryland, were prohibited from shipping alcohol directly to consumers.

Getting Serious about Alcohol

Unfortunately, Webb-Kenyon did not receive further testing in the courts of this nation. Just two years after its passage, the nation ratified the 18th Amendment to the Constitution and enacted the "noble experiment" of Prohibition. As prohibition movements gained strength and an increasing number of states became "dry," the citizens of the United States decided to amend the Constitution to make all sale, manufacture, or transportation of alcohol "for beverage purposes" illegal.

Prohibition, however, ultimately failed. The freedom to imbibe alcoholic drinks for "beverage purposes" was again restored with the repeal of the 18th Amendment by the ratification of the 21st Amendment. The 21st Amendment did not simply repeal Prohibition and return alcohol to a "free and untrammeled" economic system. Instead, it also incorporated language that has since been the subject of much debate and litigation. The 21st Amendment declares, "[t]he transportation or importation into any State, Territory, or Possession of the United States for delivery or use therein of intoxicating liquors, in violation of the laws thereof, is hereby prohibited."[6]

The Rise and Fall of the 21st Amendment

Read by itself, the 21st Amendment[7] seems to completely abrogate the dormant Commerce Clause. Just as Webb-Kenyon made violations

---

[6] US CONST. amend. XXI § 2.

[7] For an in-depth analysis of the history of the 21st Amendment and the many judicial decisions that have considered it, see generally Drew D. Massey, "Dueling Provisions: The 21st Amendment's Subjugation to the Dormant Commerce Clause Doctrine," *Transactions: The Tennessee Journal of Business Law* 7 (2005): 71–121.

of state law also violations of federal law, the 21st Amendment makes violations of state law violations of the Constitution. In addition, the very specific language of the 21st Amendment would seem to override the older and more general effect of the dormant Commerce Clause.

Initially, this is the exact approach taken by the Supreme Court just three years after the passage of the Amendment. In the *Young's Market* case, California required all wholesale distributors of beer to be licensed. In addition, they charged an extra fee if the distributor was importing beer from out-of-state. The Court recognized the plain language of the 21st Amendment and held that the discriminatory law was valid. Even though this was the exact sort of economic protectionism that the dormant Commerce Clause halted, the Court held that the 21st Amendment abrogated the power of the Commerce Clause.

However, even in those early days, the Court recognized some limits to the 21st Amendment: the Amendment protected *state* laws, and nothing more. When California tried to use the Amendment to justify a new law that would exercise control over liquor sold in Yosemite National Park, the Supreme Court struck down the California legislation. Because a state law cannot validly extend onto federal lands, the 21st Amendment could not shield such a law that reached beyond the state's borders.

The 21st Amendment allowed economic protectionism. It allowed states to prevent willing sellers to meet willing consumers because of tariffs or other licensing fees laid on out-of-state producers of alcohol. As an increasing number of states set up protectionist legislation and mandated that wine go through the standard three-tier system, it became exceedingly difficult for small wineries to make a profit anywhere but on a very local scale. As the national economy became more robust, and as producers and consumers became better able to trade, even over long distances, the Court became increasingly hostile to the 21st Amendment.

In 1964, the Supreme Court decided the *Hostetter* case. What is most significant about this case is that after more than two decades of settled law (law that stated the 21st Amendment dominated the dormant Commerce Clause), the Supreme Court reinvigorated the debate. The Supreme Court immediately took the offensive against the 21st Amendment. In *Hostetter*, they framed the issue so one-sidedly that they could not help but limit the plain language of the Amendment.

The Court asked, "whether the Twenty-first Amendment so far obliterates the Commerce Clause as to empower New York to prohibit absolutely the passage of liquor through its territory . . . for delivery to consumers in foreign commerce."[8] Rather than look to the language of the Amendment or analyze its purpose in connection with the Wilson and Webb-Kenyon Acts that came before it, the Court phrased the issue so as to revive the dormant Commerce Clause as the adversary to the 21st Amendment. Refusing to stop there, the Court went on to say that any holding that the 21st Amendment operated to "repeal" the dormant Commerce Clause was an "absurd oversimplification." The Court found that the dormant Commerce Clause prevented New York from enforcing its state regulation.

Continuing to free alcohol and wine from state regulation, the Supreme Court decided the case of *Bacchus Imports*. In that case, the state of Hawaii placed a tax on all liquor with two exceptions: Okolehao (a native alcoholic drink) and pineapple wine. The stated purpose of this tax was to encourage the locally produced alcoholic beverages. Importers of other wine brought suit to challenge the law because of its discriminatory nature. The law absolutely discriminated because only the locally produced beverages were exempt. Thus, this is exactly the kind of economic protectionism that the dormant Commerce Clause would prevent. Recognizing this, the Court struck down the Hawaii law and noted that such economic protectionism could not stand under the dormant Commerce Clause.

Bacchus Imports shows a basic shift in the priorities of the Court. The Supreme Court, in *Young's Market*, had already faced the issue of a discriminatory tax. That case involved an outright fee hike on wholesaler licenses for out-of-state applicants, and there, the Court had upheld the law. This shift represents, among other things, a dedication to a nationwide economy. It became more important to let a national economy in wine grow than to hold to the text of an Amendment that had been enacted nearly a half-century before.

In succeeding cases, the Supreme Court continued to whittle away the power granted by the 21st Amendment. Foreshadowing its eventual irrelevance, Justice Scalia remarked at one point that the "immunity" provided by the 21st Amendment would evaporate if

---

[8] *Hostetter v. Idlewild Bon Voyage Liquor Corp.*, 377 US 324, 329 (1964).

a law was discriminatory.[9] Interestingly, that opinion, though held by only one Justice, rendered the 21st Amendment a virtual nullity. The Amendment was meant to allow states to discriminate. But, by Scalia's reasoning, if the law was discriminatory, and thus the 21st Amendment would be implicated, its protection would disappear. By that logic, the effect of the 21st Amendment is ephemeral at best.

Once again, this reading of the 21st Amendment completely obliterates its power to prevent a nationwide economy in wine. Each state would have to treat its consumers, as well as consumers in other states, the same. In essence, the direct shipment "loophole" was beginning to breathe again. However, the final blow to the Amendment came in 2005 in the case of *Granholm v. Heald*.

The state of Michigan enacted a set of laws that allowed a Michigan producer of wine to directly ship that wine to any consumer within the state. However, the laws prohibited any out-of-state producer of wine from shipping directly to a Michigan consumer. This resulted in great benefits to domestic, that is to say, in-state wineries. A winery could sell its wine without first having to sell to a wholesaler who then sold to a retailer who then sold to a consumer. Because they were able to bypass the middlemen, their wine could be sold cheaply. By contrast, out-of-state wine had to go through the wholesaler and retailer. As such, it was much less competitive and gave Michigan wines a decided edge in cost.

Wineries in other states, notably in California, took offense at this discriminatory practice. They brought suit alleging that the dormant Commerce Clause prevented this kind of legislation notwithstanding the enactment of the 21st Amendment. The case traveled the road of appellate review until it finally came to the Supreme Court. Many sound arguments were made on both sides, and the Justices were jokingly invited by the winery's counsel to visit their California site for a free tour. The case was decided five to four against the discriminatory Michigan law.

Justice Kennedy began the opinion broadly, speaking about the economic implications of the decision rather than by restating dry legal principles. He pointed out that "small wineries do not produce enough wine or have sufficient consumer demand for their wine to

---

[9] *Healy v. The Beer Institute*, 491 US 324, 344 (1989) (Scalia, J., concurring).

make it economical for wholesalers to carry their products."[10] With this economic reality in mind, Kennedy brought low the 21st Amendment and found in favor of the out-of-state wineries. He rejected the state's arguments that such discrimination was necessary to ensure the collection of taxes. Justice Thomas included a vigorous dissenting opinion, but with only three additional Justices in support, the 21st Amendment gave way to economic necessity.

Although this development would, at first, seem to be a boon for the wine industry, it may be a wolf in sheep's clothing. Firstly, the reasoning in *Granholm* applies equally well to reciprocal shipping states. States like California allow direct shipping to consumers within the state, but only if that shipment comes from a state that will allow direct shipping to its consumers from California wineries. Because those laws discriminate based on the source of the wine just as surely as did the Michigan law, they will also be struck down.

This turn of events leaves states only two options. Either they can allow all direct shipments from every state, or they can prohibit direct shipments entirely – from wineries within as well as without. Looking at the alternatives, the second may prove more attractive for a state that would rather ensure its collection of fees from wholesalers. This would be particularly true if the state does not have a vigorous wine industry that would be harmed by such a move. Thus, this could lead reciprocity states, states that were once open to at least some direct shipment, to entirely prohibit such shipments, thereby harming consumers as well as the winery industry as a whole.

New Trends and Current Developments

The impact of the *Granholm* case has already been felt in the state of Washington. There, the state had essentially the same direct-shipping regulations that existed in Michigan: in-state producers could sell directly to a retailer, skipping the distributor, but out-of-state wineries had to sell to a distributor who could then sell to a retailer. Costco, a large warehouse-style bulk retailer, brought a court action. They alleged that this system prevented them from making large purchases of wines and negotiating discounted prices. They wanted the

---

[10] *Granholm v. Heald*, 544 US 460, 467 (2005).

285

same ability to skip the middleman (and the price markup) that was allowed when they bought in-state wine.

Initially, some small wineries in Washington were concerned about the litigation. They feared that Washington might end its discrimination by prohibiting any producer from skipping the distributor and force all small wineries to trudge through the economically untenable three-tier system. On December 21, 2005, the federal district court ruled that the Washington law was unconstitutional after *Granholm*. However, the court felt that the legislature should be the one to address the question and gave them until April 14, 2006, to do so. The legislature quickly passed a law that eliminated the out-of-state restriction and allowed all retailers in Washington to bypass the distributors. The Attorney General for the state of Washington as well as the Washington Beer and Wine Wholesalers Association have filed an appeal.

The initial fears of Washington wineries were well founded. In Indiana, the Alcohol and Tobacco Commission sent a directive warning to all in-state wineries that direct shipments were a misdemeanor. This warning came just days after the *Granholm* decision. Essentially, the state hoped to avoid the discriminatory aspects of the Michigan law by preventing any direct shipments – either from within or without the state.

The directive was challenged by nine wineries within the state. Importantly, their arguments centered around the way in which the directive was made, and how it abruptly changed policy without any input from the public rather than arguments under *Granholm*. This is because without discrimination, *Granholm* would not support the law's demise.

Fortunately, the state legislature reached a compromise position. If an Indiana resident actually visited a winery, and had his identification checked, he would be allowed to receive some direct shipments from that winery. This law applies to both in-state and out-of-state wineries. Therefore, if an Indiana resident wants a direct shipment from the winery down the street, he has to visit it first. And if he wants a vintage produced in Napa Valley, then he has to book a plane trip to California and visit the site. While this does allow consumers some access to direct shipments, it is hardly ideal. Consumers have to jump through an extra hoop and, in the case of a connoisseur whose favorite wines are grown in many different

286

locations around the world, it makes those wines very expensive, at least initially. Though consumers have won great victories in *Granholm* and similar discriminatory cases, they should be wary of where they make their challenges lest the state decide that the more favorable course is to restrict all direct shipments entirely, as a number of states do.

Reflections on the Special Case of Wine

As stated previously, alcohol in general, and wine in particular, holds a special place in the cultural identity of many Americans. As such, it is not surprising that particular rules are adopted when the government regulates wine through the passage of statute, Amendment, or judicial decision. What is interesting, however, is how the different branches of government react to questions regarding alcohol.

The Congress passed legislation intended to exempt alcohol from the concerns of the dormant Commerce Clause. It did so in order to create a unique exception for alcohol. Some thirty years later, the judicial branch set forth a different policy in regards to alcohol. That branch slowly but surely created a new set of rules for the purpose of "repealing" Congressional action. Congress was motivated by the prohibition movement, and the Court by the plight of boutique wineries and a national economy. However, each adopted a novel approach to deal with what they perceived as a problem with the current laws surrounding alcohol.

Though most of the litigation to date has centered around wine and wineries, the law generally applies to all alcohol. Today's movement to open up direct wine shipments will lead to similar movements among producers and consumers of beer and other spirits. Because of the boutique, hard to obtain yet high in demand wines, it has been wine that has led the charge to open the national economy and strike down protectionist legislation. However, the law applies with equal force to shipments of other alcoholic beverages as well.

As the jurisprudence surrounding alcohol continues to progress, the only thing that can be said for certain is that increasingly irrelevant legal paradigms based on older belief structures will give way to newer models based on more current attitudes toward alcohol.

287

Notes on Contributors

Fritz Allhoff, PhD. Fritz Allhoff is an assistant professor of philosophy at Western Michigan University. He has held fellowships at the American Medical Association's Institute for Ethics, the Australian National University's Centre for Applied Philosophy and Public Ethics, and the University of Pittsburgh's Center for Philosophy of Science. His research areas are in ethical theory, applied ethics, and philosophy of biology/science. In addition to editing this book, Fritz is also the co-editor, with Dave Monroe, of *Food & Philosophy* (Blackwell, 2008). He enjoys, especially, Napa and Russian River wines as well as wine travel around the world.

Jonathon Alsop. Jonathon Alsop has been writing about wine, food, and travel since 1989. He is author of the wine column "In Vino Veritas" as well as articles for *Frequent Flyer*, *La Vie Claire*, *Cultured Living*, *Beverage Magazine*, the Associated Press, and many others. In 2000, Jonathon founded the Boston Wine School. In addition to writing, he lectures on wine, conducts wine-tasting classes, and hosts wine events around the country.

Orley Ashenfelter, PhD. When he is not writing about wine, Orley Ashenfelter is the Joseph Douglas Green 1895 Professor of Economics at Princeton University. In the wine world he is known for the controversial newsletter/journal *Liquid Assets: The International Guide to Fine Wines*, which he started in 1985. He now also acts as a co-editor of the newly formed *Journal of Wine Economics*, and he is the first President of the American Association of Wine Economists, which publishes the journal.

Kent Bach, PhD. Kent Bach is a professor emeritus of philosophy at San Francisco State University. He received his PhD in philosophy at the University of California, Berkeley. He has written extensively in philosophy of language, theory of knowledge, and philosophy of mind. Kent's books include *Thought and Reference* and, with Robert M. Harnish, *Linguistic Communication and Speech Acts*. He is an associate editor of *Linguistics and Philosophy*. In 1996 Kent morphed from a wine heathen into a wine zealot; he has since learned not to accumulate wine at a faster rate than he consumes it. He spoke at the first-ever wine and philosophy conference, held in London in December 2004.

John W. Bender, PhD. John W. Bender received his PhD in philosophy at Harvard University and is a professor of philosophy at Ohio University. He previously taught at Dartmouth College and has written for the *Quarterly Review of Wines*. John has published numerous articles in aesthetics and epistemology, and is especially interested in the intersection of these two areas. He has been a judge in many wine competitions, with his love of wine dating back to the early 1970s. He is also a painter specializing in abstract expressionism.

Douglas Burnham, PhD. Douglas Burnham is a philosopher working at Staffordshire University (United Kingdom). He is the author of two books on Kant (*An Introduction to Kant's Critique of Judgment* and *Kant's Philosophies of Judgment*) and a forthcoming book on Nietzsche (*Reading Nietzsche*). Other research interests include the relationship between philosophy and literature. He is co-authoring *The Universal Nose: Wine and Aesthetics* with Ole Martin Skilleås. Although displaying geek-like properties in other fields, he is not a wine geek; he just enjoys a thoughtful tipple.

Steve Charters, MW, PhD. Steve Charters originally qualified as a lawyer in the UK but was seduced by the allure of wine; he went on to work in retail and wine education in London and Sydney. He became a Master of Wine in and then worked for nearly a decade at Edith Cowan University (Perth, Australia) before going to Reims Management School in France to become Chair of Champagne Management. Steve's areas of research interest focus on the consumer's engagement with wine, including the nature of quality, wine tourism, and the social and cultural context of wine, as well as the way producers operate.

John Dilworth, PhD. When not drinking wine and musing about consciousness, John Dilworth is a professor of philosophy at Western Michigan University, where he specializes in the philosophy of art, philosophy of mind, and cognitive science. He is the author of a recent book, *The Double Content of Art*. His current work includes further developments of the self-prompting theory of consciousness outlined in his wine essay here.

Kirsten Ditterich-Shilakes. Kirsten Ditterich-Shilakes is a fusion of art historian, multimedia producer, author, and an ambassador to the arts. Between San Francisco's Asian Art Museum and Fine Arts Museum, she has garnered over ten years of intensive training in art history; she is schooled in art ranging from Chinese, European, and African to Contemporary American. She holds a degree in political economy of industrialized societies from the University of California, Berkeley and has authored *Services: Exports of the 21st Century* and *Pop Mandarin: A Postmodern Phrasebook from Fengshui to Wall Street*. She lives under the redwood trees in Mill Valley, California, smack-dab between her two favorite locations: the Napa Valley and the museums of San Francisco.

George Gale, PhD. George Gale is University of California at Davis' first PhD . . . in philosophy, although some of his best friends were in the wine school. He is Professor of Philosophy and Physical Science at the University of Missouri-Kansas City, and Executive Secretary of the Philosophy of Science Association. During the 1970s and 1980s, Gale was partner and winemaker of an estate winery outside Kansas City. His research mostly concerns philosophy of physics, although he recently has published several articles on the phylloxera disaster in France. His small vineyard produces around 25 gallons of pretty decent red every year.

Jamie Goode, PhD. Jamie Goode studied biological sciences at the University of London, specializing in plant biology. After working for ten years as a science editor, he turned to wine. As well as establishing www.wineanorak.com, he has written regularly for several wine magazines and is a weekly columnist for UK tabloid newspaper the *Sunday Express*. His first book, *Wine Science*, won the 2006 Glenfiddich Award for best drink book. Jamie's current obsessions are viticulture and the perception of flavor.

Randall Grahm. Randall Grahm attended the University of California at Santa Cruz, where he was a permanent liberal arts major. Some time later, he found himself working at the Wine Merchant in Beverly Hills sweeping floors. Through exceptional fortune, he was given the opportunity to taste a goodly number of great French wines; this singular experience turned him into a complete and insufferable wine fanatic. He returned to the University of California at Davis to complete a degree in viticulture, and he then went on to found Bonny Doon Vineyards. Randall lives in Santa Cruz with his muse Chinshu, their daughter Amelie, and his thesaurus.

Matt Kramer. Matt Kramer has been a full-time, independent wine writer for thirty years. He is the author of the acclaimed *Making Sense* series of wine books: *Making Sense of Wine*; *Making Sense of Burgundy*; *Making Sense of California Wine*; *Matt Kramer's New California Wine*; and *Matt Kramer's Making Sense of Italian Wine*, as well as *A Passion for Piedmont: Italy's Most Glorious Regional Table*. Kramer is a longtime columnist for *Wine Spectator* magazine, where he appears in every issue. He is also the wine critic for *The Oregonian* and *New York Sun* newspapers.

Adrienne Lehrer, PhD. Adrienne Lehrer taught linguistics at the University of Rochester and then the University of Arizona from 1974 until her retirement in 1998. She has written two books: *Semantic Fields and Lexical Structure* and *Wine and Conversation*. More recently, she has published research on the semantics of derivational morphemes and on neologisms, especially blends and combining forms. She is currently working on a new, greatly updated and revised version of *Wine and Conversation*.

Keith Lehrer, PhD. Keith Lehrer works in the areas of epistemology, free will, rational consensus, Thomas Reid, and, most recently, aesthetics. He has received many distinguished fellowships and awards, including Doctor of Philosophy from Karl-Franzens University

291

of Graz, Austria, and is a Fellow of the American Academy of Arts and Sciences. He is the author of seven books and the editor of ten others as well as numerous articles in scholarly journals. He teaches regularly at the University of Arizona, University of Miami, and University of Graz. Major exhibits of his art occurred in Miami, Florida; Santa Clara, California; and Graz, Austria.

Drew Massey, JD. Drew Massey graduated magna cum laude from Pepperdine Law School in 2006. He currently works in southern California practicing special education law and representing students and families. He has written a scholarly article on the subject of the 21st Amendment entitled "Dueling Provisions: The 21st Amendment's Subjugation to the Dormant Commerce Clause Doctrine," in *Transactions: The Tennessee Journal of Business Law*.

Frederick Adolf Paola, MD, JD. Frederick Paola is a graduate of Stony Brook University, Yale University School of Medicine, and New York University School of Law. He is medical director of the Nova Southeastern University Physician Assistant Program, Naples Branch, and associate professor in the NSU Health Professions Division. Frederick is affiliate associate professor of medicine at the University of South Florida College of Medicine in Tampa, and a member of their Division of Medical Ethics and Humanities. He is board certified in internal medicine, and practices internal medicine and medical acupuncture in Naples, Florida. He is the author of *The Wine Doctor*. He is an avid home winemaker, having learned the art from his father, and has a weakness, too, for wines from Oenotria.

Richard E. Quandt, PhD. Richard Quandt is an economist, now retired from Princeton University, whose contributions mostly span econometrics and microeconomic theory. Since his retirement, he has directed the East European Program of the Andrew W. Mellon Foundation and has produced two books dealing with Eastern Europe: *The Changing Landscape in Eastern Europe* and *Union Catalogs at the Crossroad*. He has always enjoyed wine, and has been interested in devising tests to see whether judges can identify wines in blind tastings significantly better than by chance.

292

Ole Martin Skilleås, PhD. Ole Martin Skilleås teaches philosophy at Bergen University (Norway), where he previously also taught English. He is the author of *Literature and the Value of Interpretation* and *Philosophy and Literature*, as well as several articles in journals such as the *British Journal of Aesthetics*, *English Studies*, and *Metaphilosophy*. His main research interests include philosophy and literature, aesthetics, and moral philosophy. He is co-authoring *The Universal Nose: Wine and Aesthetics* with Douglas Burnham. He is a certified wine geek and a father of two young children.

Kevin W. Sweeney, PhD. Kevin Sweeney received his PhD in philosophy from the University of Wisconsin-Madison. He currently teaches philosophy at the University of Tampa. His research interests include topics in modern philosophy, ethics, and aesthetics. Recently, he has written on philosophy and literature, film theory, the nature of film horror, and film comedy, especially the silent films of Buster Keaton. He is fond of cabernet franc wines from France's central Loire and artisanal wines from California's Central Coast and northeastern Italy.

George M. Taber. George Taber writes about wine, and his most recent book is *Judgment of Paris: California vs. France and the Historic 1976 Paris Tasting that Revolutionized Wine*. He is currently working on a new book about the great debate over the future of wine-bottle closures. Taber was a reporter and editor for twenty-one years for *Time* magazine, working for many years in Europe. He founded the weekly business newspaper *NJBIZ* in 1988, which he sold in 2005 to pursue a career writing wine books. Taber is a graduate of Georgetown University and has a master's degree from the College of Europe in Bruges, Belgium.

Harold Tarrant, PhD. Harold Tarrant studied in the United Kingdom at Cambridge and Durham universities, and received his PhD in Classics from the latter. He has taught principally in Australia, first at the University of Sydney, and then at the University of Newcastle, where he is professor of classics. He has served on the Committee of the International Plato Society, and on the editorial boards of three journals devoted to the history of philosophy. He is a fellow of the Australian Academy of the Humanities, and has published several books on Platonism in antiquity.

Justin Weinberg, PhD. For several years Justin Weinberg attempted to amass a collection of bottles that would live up to his last name, which, in German, means "mountain of wine." He is now content with merely a molehill of wine, but refuses to change his name to Justin Weinmaulwurfshügel. He has taught philosophy at Georgetown University and the College of William and Mary, and is now an assistant professor in the philosophy department at the University of South Carolina. He writes on topics in political philosophy and ethics.

Warren Winiarski. Warren Winiarski is the owner, president, and founding winemaker of Stag's Leap Wine Cellars. Warren earned his BA from St. John's College and his MA from the University of Chicago, where he also served as a lecturer in liberal arts. Warren then moved to California with his wife, Barbara, and their children; there he worked as a cellarman for Souverain Cellars and then as assistant winemaker for Robert Mondavi Winery. His experience working for his two mentors at these wineries and his passion for crafting fine wines led him to found Stag's Leap Wine Cellars. Warren has also published several articles for *Decanter* and *Wines and Vines*.

Index

Index

301

Index

Madsen, Virginia 37, 38
malic acid 177n, 212, 215
malolactic fermentation 212,
    215
Marino, Italy 64
Martini 35
Massey, Drew 10–11, 275–87
materialism 46
mathematics and beauty 48, 50
Mayacamas Vineyards 237, 247
Meades, Jonathan 145–6
meaning, filling in 113, 115,
    116–19
meaningful wines 8, 219–24
media portrayal of wine and wine
    lovers 37–8
Meilgaard, Morton 115
memory, and wine tasting 100,
    101, 102, 108, 143
merit-quality 130
merlot 38, 112, 222, 223, 263
Merwin, W. S. 232, 233
metaphor, wine as 51, 53
metaphorical descriptors 108–9,
    114, 120, 125, 128–9, 146,
    149, 150, 153
metaphysics of wine 8, 205–24
    metaphysical perspective on wine
        tasting 205–18
    soul of a wine 8, 219–24
    terroir 9, 60, 86, 175, 178–9,
        181, 183, 220, 221, 222, 223,
        225–34
methoxypyrazines 211
metonymy 149
Meursault 231, 233
micro-oxygenation 38
Missouri 182–3
moderation in wine drinking *see*
    temperance
Mona Lisa 113
Mondavi 35, 38, 39

Mondovino (documentary) 38–9
Monticello 31
Montrachet 226, 234
moon waffles 258
Mosel 132, 160, 162
mouseion 44
mouthfeel 150
multimodal sensory experience
    143, 152
Muscadet 218
music 87, 88, 89, 91, 94, 129,
    131, 157, 194–5, 201
myricetin 71

Nader, Ralph 168
nanny state philosophy 27
Napa Valley 41, 205, 238, 257
NASCAR 41, 259
Nation, Carry A. 32–4
naturalism 173, 174
nebbiolo 213
Neolithic period 1
nephrolithiasis 75–6
New World wines 139, 222, 223
    European grapes 32
    Old and New World wines,
        distinctions between 10,
        248–56
Noah 72, 251
Noble, Ann 126
non-alcoholic wines 90, 92
North Carolina 40, 41
Nossiter, Jonathan 38
novelty, appreciation of 101
Nuits-Saint-Georges 214, 231

oak 211, 212, 233, 234
Odysseus 15, 16
Oh, Sandra 37
Ohio wine industry 34
Old World wines 139, 179,
    222